☐ AMERICAN COMMERCIAL BANKING

A History

TWAYNE'S
EVOLUTION
OF
AMERICAN
BUSINESS
SERIES

———

Industries,
Institutions,
and
Entrepreneurs

———

Edwin J. Perkins,
SERIES EDITOR
UNIVERSITY OF
SOUTHERN CALIFORNIA

OTHER TITLES

The American Automobile
Industry
  John B. Rae

DuPont and the International
Chemical Industry
  Graham D. Taylor and
  Patricia E. Sudnik

E.H. Harriman: Master
Railroader
  Lloyd J. Mercer

The Credit Card Industry
  Lewis Mandell

The U.S. Tire Industry
  Michael J. French

The American Amusement Park
Industry
  Judith A. Adams

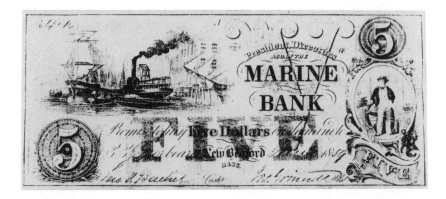

Antebellum state bank notes.
Courtesy of the Public Services Department, Federal Reserve Bank of Boston.

☐AMERICAN
COMMERCIAL
BANKING
A History

Benjamin J. Klebaner

TWAYNE PUBLISHERS ☐ BOSTON
A Division of G. K. Hall & Co.

American Commercial Banking: A History
Benjamin J. Klebaner

Twayne's Evolution of American Business Series:
Industries, Institutions and Entrepreneurs No. 5

Copyediting supervised by Barbara Sutton
Book design and production by Gabrielle B. McDonald.
Typeset in Aldus with Optima display type
by Huron Valley Graphics Inc., of Ann Arbor, Michigan.

The paper used in this publication meets the minimum requirements
of American National Standard for Information Sciences—Permanence
of Paper for Printed Library Materials, ANSI Z39.48-1984. ⊚™

Printed and bound in the United States of America.

Library of Congress Cataloging-in-Publication Data

Klebaner, Benjamin Joseph, 1926–
    American commercial banking : a history / Benjamin J. Klebaner.
        p.   cm.—(Twayne's evolution of American business series ;
    no. 5)
    Includes bibliographical references.
    1. Banks and banking—United States—History—20th century.
    I. Title.   II. Series.
    HG2481.K6   1990
    332.1'2'0973—dc20   90-4405
                                                                             CIP

0-8057-9804-8 (alk. paper). 10 9 8 7 6 5 4 3 2 1
0-8057-9815-3 (pbk.: alk. paper). 10 9 8 7 6 5 4 3 2 1
First published 1990.

To Ruth, my helpmeet
Strong and courageous

CONTENTS

PREFACE

THIS VOLUME TRACES THE EVOLUTION OF commercial banking in the United States. The reader who gains a historical perspective can better understand the contemporary scene and policy issues. No special background in finance or economics is assumed.

Horace White's *Money and Banking* of 1895 was "illustrated by American history" (as the subtitle stated). It went through ten editions by 1936. Others followed White's example by including extensive discussions of American banking history, but recent texts on banking rarely devote more than a few pages to the subject. *American Commercial Banking: A History* is intended to fill the gap.

Research was made possible by grants from the Schwager fund, established by the generous bequest of Harry Schwager, City College of New York 1911. Edwin J. Perkins of the University of Southern California and Irving Stone of Baruch College of the City University of New York offered valuable suggestions.

Benjamin J. Klebaner

City College of the City University
of New York

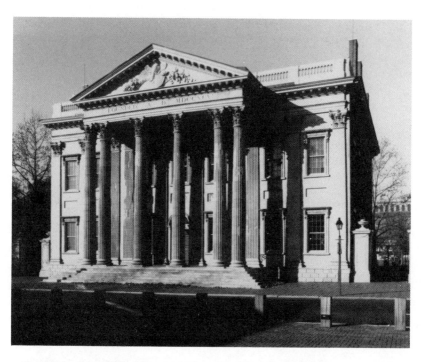

First Bank of the United States headquarters, 116 South Third Street, Philadelphia. The bank's designer, New Hampshire-born Samuel Blodget, used the Exchange in Dublin as a model. The building, the oldest extant bank building in the United States, was used for banking purposes until 1926. It is now part of Independence National Historic Park. *Courtesy of the National Park Service, Independence National Historic Park Collection.*

Part I.

Banking before 1863

1

The Rise and Spread of Banking

COMMERCIAL BANKS MAKE LOANS, INvest in securities, offer a variety of deposit arrangements, and provide means of payment—checking account services and, in earlier eras, bank notes. Nowadays about 75 percent of the net funds supplied each year in the United States are channeled through financial intermediaries. From their beginnings in the late eighteenth century, commercial banks have been America's main category of financial intermediary. Even after the development of many rival types, banks have as great a share of U.S. financial assets as all the other intermediaries combined.

☐ Banking without Banks in the Colonial Era

There were no commercial banks in the British North American colonies. Arrangements for clearing business transactions and providing short-term credit were underdeveloped, just as they were in the provinces of eighteenth-century England. Much of the specie (silver and gold) obtained from trade with the Spanish and Portuguese empires left the Atlantic seaboard to pay for imports. Small-denomination coins were in short supply. Beaver skins, wampum, and tobacco were widely used for money in the seventeenth century.

To finance a military expedition to French Canada, Massachusetts issued the very first bills of credit in 1690. New York, New Jersey, the

Carolinas, and the rest of New England followed by 1712. The other colonies also found issuing bills of credit an attractive means of financing government expenditures, although Virginia waited to do so until 1755.

Public land banks were another source of paper money. Starting with South Carolina in 1712, all colonial governments except Virginia's sponsored these arrangements for issuing bills of credit to borrowers offering real estate as collateral.[1] In addition, there were some private note issues (such as the Massachusetts Land Bank Company). In 1741 London ordered an end to these private schemes.

In 1751 the New England colonies were forbidden to make further issues of legal tender bills of credit. The ban was extended to the other American colonies in 1764. After several years of controversy, Parliament allowed note issues for taxes and other public dues in 1773.

In the colonial era most banking functions in the modern sense were performed by merchants with access to London and Glasgow. In the nineteenth century, even in so economically advanced a state as Massachusetts, tradesmen extended long credits on their books, transferred debits and credits between customers, and lent their own and neighbors' capital. "Crackerbarrel" bankers served many communities before incorporated banks appeared.[2]

☐ The Earliest Banks

In 1781, when Alexander Hamilton argued that banks had proved to be the happiest engines ever invented for advancing trade, he had no American examples to cite. Already in the early 1600s London goldsmiths were discounting inland bills and circulating their own notes. On the Continent the main function of banks continued to be money-changing, as in the Middle Ages. Seventeenth- and eighteenth-century business manuals defined a banker as one who dealt in bills of exchange, operated with foreign correspondents, and speculated on exchange rates.

The first incorporated commercial bank in the New World—and one of the oldest anywhere—opened in Philadelphia on 7 January 1782, just one week after the Continental Congress had granted a perpetual charter to the Bank of North America. Congress's superintendent of finance, Robert Morris, intended it as "a principal pillar of American credit" that would "facilitate the management of the finances of the United States."[3] The hard-pressed Confederation received over $1.25 million in loans during the bank's first three years. Even more significant was its role in reviving credit and confidence. The bank's bills were the first paper convertible into specie issued in the country.

Unlike its European antecedents (including the Bank of England), the Philadelphia bank's sole aim was profit for its shareholders. The Bank of North America's success inspired imitators. The February 1784 petition of Boston merchants for the incorporation of the Massachusetts Bank was promptly granted, but in New York political opposition delayed a charter until 1791. Meanwhile, the Bank of New York opened as a private company in June 1784.

Proponents of a Bank of Maryland argued in 1784 that the state needed "an institution which naturally increases the medium of trade, promotes punctuality in the performances of contracts, facilitates the payment of public dues [taxes], furnishes a safe deposit for cash, aids the anticipation of funds on paying common interest, advances the value of the country produce, and facilitates the negotiations of the foreigner, while it provides an advantage to the stockholder."[4] The Baltimore bank was made to wait until 1790 for a charter.

Three commercial banks were active when the Constitutional Convention assembled in March 1787, the oldest located a short walk from the meeting place. Though the majority of delegates were friendly to banks, the Constitution does not mention them. Unnecessary controversy was thus avoided, as the public at large was not so well disposed to banks.

By the time the federally chartered First Bank of the United States opened in December 1791, Philadelphia, New York, Boston, Baltimore, and Providence each had a state-incorporated bank in operation. In 1794, a century after the founding of the Bank of England, there were only five chartered banks in the British Isles; while the United States had eighteen just thirteen years after the incorporation of the Bank of North America.

The Bank of New York is the oldest American bank retaining its original name, while the First National Bank of Boston proudly points to an earlier charter. First Pennsylvania Bank's claim to be the oldest commercial bank is based on its being the successor to the Pennsylvania Company for Insurance on Lives and Granting Annuities (chartered 1812), into which company the Bank of North America was absorbed in July 1929. A reproduction of the original 1782 bank office is in the lobby of First Pennsylvania's headquarters.

Banks were preeminent among eighteenth-century American business corporations. By 1800 states had chartered twenty-eight; five of the first eight, and seven of the next twenty, are still active (see Table 1). Sixteen of the twenty-eight were in New England. Among towns with at least 5,000 inhabitants, only Norwalk, Connecticut, and Marblehead and Bridgewater in Massachusetts had no bank by 1800. Indeed, six

New England communities with populations *below* 5,000 had their own banks. Two of the thirteen banks in the rest of the nation were in places with under 5,000 in population, while four localities with over 5,000 inhabitants had no bank in 1800: Schenectady, New York, Norfolk (served by a branch of the Bank of the United States), Richmond, Virginia, and Savannah, Georgia. Boston led the nation in 1800 with three banks, while New York, Philadelphia, and Baltimore each had two; all four cities also had offices of the Bank of the United States. Six of the sixteen states in 1800 had no incorporated bank. Kentucky's first bank was established in 1802, North Carolina's and New Jersey's in 1804, Vermont's in 1806, Tennessee's in 1807, and Georgia's in 1810.

Table 1.　　State Banks Chartered before 1802.

State and Original Name	Year Opened	Year Chartered	Dates of Operations as National Bank (including charter number)	Later History
New Hampshire				
New Hampshire Bank (Portsmouth)	1792	1792		Charter expired 1842
Massachusetts				
Massachusetts Bank (Boston)	1784	1784	1865– (#974)	Renamed First National Bank of Boston
Union Bank (Boston)	1792	1792	1865–1925 (#985)	Merged into State Street Bank & Trust Company 1925
Essex Bank (Boston)	1792	1799	—	Charter expired 1819
Merrimack Bank (Newburyport)	1795	1795	1865–1979 (#1047)	Renamed the Merchants National Bank of Newburyport; merged into Naumkeag Trust Company 1979; part of Eastern Savings Bank since 1983

Bank of Nantucket	1795	1795	—	Charter expired 1816; no new business after 1812
Gloucester Bank	1796	1800	1865–1985 (#1162)	Renamed Gloucester National Bank of Gloucester; part of US Trust, N.A. since 1985
Portland Bank (Maine)	1799	1799	—	Failed 1815

Rhode Island

Providence Bank (Providence)	1791	1791	1865–1954 (#1302)	Merged with Union Trust Company in 1951 to become Providence Union National Bank, which in 1954 merged into Industrial Trust Company, which is now Fleet National Bank
Washington Bank (Westerly)	1800	1800	1865–1904 (#952)	Renamed Washington Trust Company
Bank of Rhode Island (Newport)	1795	1795	1865–1900 (#1532)	Voluntarily liquidated 1900
Exchange Bank (Providence)	1801	1801	1865–1926 (#1339)	Merged in 1926 into Industrial Trust Company which is now Fleet National Bank
Bank of Bristol (Bristol)	1800	1800	—	Liquidated 1865

Connecticut

Union Bank (New London)	1792	1792	1865–1882 (#1175)	Merged into Connecticut Bank & Trust Company, N.A. 1963
Hartford Bank (Hartford)	1792	1792	1865– (#1338)	Renamed Hartford National Bank & Trust Company, which is now Connecticut National Bank

New Haven Bank (New Haven)	1796	1792	1865–1957 (#1243); 1957–1977 (#2)	Consolidated into First National Bank & Trust Company 1957, later First New Haven National Bank; part of Connecticut National Bank since 1984
Bank of Norwich (Norwich)	1796	1796	1865–1889 (#1358)	Voluntarily liquidated 1889
Middletown Bank (Middletown)	1801	1795	1865–1955 (#1216)	Merged in 1955 into Hartford National Bank & Trust Company, which is now Connecticut National Bank

New York
_____

Bank of New York (New York City)	1784	1791	1865–1922 (#1393)	
Manhattan Company Bank (New York City)	1799	1799	1965– (#2370) (revived)	Merged in 1955 with Chase National Bank, which is now Chase Manhattan Bank, N.A.
Bank of Albany (Albany)	1792	1792	—	Suspended 1861
Bank of Columbia (Hudson)	1793	1793	—	Suspended 1829
Farmers' Bank (Lansingburgh)	1801	1801	1865–1926 (#940)	Consolidated in 1930 with National City Bank of Troy (#7612), which merged into State Bank of Albany 1959; now Norstar Bank of Upstate New York

Pennsylvania
_____

Bank of North America (Philadelphia)	1782	1781 (31 Dec.)	1864–1923 (#602); 1974– (#1) (revived)	Now part of First Pennsylvania Bank, N.A.

Bank of
  Pennsylvania
  (Philadelphia)
	1793	1793	—	Failed in panic of
				1857

Maryland				

Bank of
  Maryland
  (Baltimore)
	1791	1790	—	Failed 1834

Bank of
  Baltimore
  (Baltimore)
	1797	1795	1865–1930
			(#1432)
				Merged in 1930 into
				Union Trust Company
				of Maryland, which is
				now Signet Bank,
				Maryland

Bank of
  Columbia
  (Georgetown, D.C.)
	1794	1793	—	Failed 1823

Delaware				

Bank of
  Delaware
  (Wilmington)
	1795	1796	1865–1930
			(#1420)
				Merged into Security
				Trust Company in
				1930, called Bank of
				Delaware since 1958

Virginia				

Bank of
  Alexandria
  (Alexandria)
	1793	1792	—	Failed 1836

South Carolina				

Bank of
  South Carolina
  (Charleston)
	1792	1801	—	Gone by 1865, victim
				of Civil War

Source: Benjamin J. Klebaner, "State Chartered American Commercial Banks, 1781–1801,"
Business History Review 53 (1979): 530–533, updated.

Commercial rivalry between towns prompted the early organization of banks. Providence needed a bank, wrote a leading merchant
named John Brown in the fall of 1791, to avoid the transfer of wealth
acquired in Rhode Island to other states that "by their banks promote all
the valuable arts of mankind."[5] In 1792 Hartford merchants were eager
for a bank, which they thought could put a stop to the diversion of
Connecticut River trade from "its natural place, into other channels, out

of the State." In the same year Alexandria merchants alerted the Virginia legislature that

> Establishment of a Bank in the Town of Alexandria, has become the most necessary, not only to increase the commerce of this place, and of course of this State, but to preserve that share of it which it at present possesses. In consequence of Banks being Established at Baltimore and Philadelphia, through the medium of which the commerce of these Towns are so much facilitated as to enable the Merchants that to draw to them almost all the Trade of the fertile and extensive back Country of this State, and also of the states of Maryland and Pennsylvania, and of all the Western Country, which Nature seems to have intended should be carried on, through the channels of the Potomack and James rivers, and to purchase the produce brought to this market with their Bank paper. And by this means the wealth which ought to center in this State, is diverted from its natural course, and enriches the neighboring States.[6]

The earliest banks aspired to a position of exclusivity in their states, or at least in their localities. The Bank of North America squelched an effort to establish a second rival bank by selling stock to its subscribers at a bargain price. In Boston, the Bank of Massachusetts, the state's sole bank for eight years, apparently gave rivals "a doubtful welcome and hard terms."[7] Providence Bank candidly protested that a rival "would materially damage the interests of the stockholders . . . who first ran the hazard of the experiment,"[8] but Rhode Island's legislature was not convinced that its monopoly should last beyond a decade; the state chartered the Exchange Bank in February 1801. The directors of Providence Bank then proposed a merger on 26 March 1801; but in vain. Few of the original banks were as fortunate as Hartford's, which had no local rival for twenty-two years.

Dissatisfaction with existing banks generated pressures for additional services. From the beginning, the Bank of North America catered mainly to merchants in foreign trade; the Bank of Pennsylvania opened eleven years later (1793) chiefly to serve retailers. The Philadelphia Bank was launched in 1803 by merchants who resented their treatment by the city's existing banks. Baltimore's two banks limited loans to a small circle of favorites, or so advocates of a third bank claimed. Richmond merchants were frustrated by the limited lending capabilities of the Bank of Virginia: "Men of the first characters and responsibility have been often disappointed, not only in obtaining accommodations, but even in discounting the best paper, given in *bona fide* transactions, and coming within the rule of the Bank. So numerous, so notorious, and so great, in the aggregate, have been these disappointments, that it would be disingenuous to ascribe them to any other motive or course than the poverty of the active Bank-capital."[9] Accordingly, the Virginia legislature responded to their petition by chartering the Farmers Bank in February 1812.

Established banks feared that newcomers would deplete specie reserves and necessarily reduce profits. Nevertheless, by 1818 New York, Philadelphia, Boston, and Baltimore had thirty-two banks between them. Yet as late as 1837 historian Richard Hildreth could write of "the rabid and desperate fury with which all old banks have ever opposed and calumniated all new ones."

In commercial centers, banks were founded on a specie base and made short-term loans to merchants. In agricultural localities, the main or sole capital was often the state's credit. Yet another arrangement combined banking with an unrelated, promising activity. Aaron Burr's Bank of the Manhattan Company (formed in 1799) was derived from part of the capital raised to provide New York City with wholesome water. The Miami Exporting Company, chartered to ship farm produce from Cincinnati to New Orleans, went into banking as soon as it opened its doors in 1803.

Already in 1811 Secretary of the Treasury Albert Gallatin could report that "the banking system is now firmly established; and in its ramifications, extends to every part of the United States." An unhappy contemporary, Jesse Atwater, reported in 1810 that "the states are overwhelmed by banks; we live in a paper world."

☐ The Mushrooming of Banks

By 1816, when the Second Bank of the United States opened, there were 246 banks in the country. By 1840 there were three times as many banks as there had been in 1820, and between 1840 and 1860 the number doubled, to over 1,500. After 1820 the increase was not much quicker than the growth of national income or population. Even in the pre-1820 period, banking growth was not "inordinately rapid in comparison with other aspects of economic development."[10]

In 1815 "villages without trade or importance of any kind must have their two or three banks," it was alleged.[11] Seven banks were established in Jefferson County, Ohio, in 1814; a clergyman reported that "a money mania like an epidemic seized the people."[12] Between

1790 and 1830 authorized capital stock of all state-chartered banks rose from $3 million to $168 million.

Meanwhile, between 1811 and 1830 around 165 banks closed. One reason was "too great a multiplication of banks, in places not adapted to the proper and regular banking business."[13] In October 1816 publisher Hezekiah Niles remarked that "wherever there is a 'church, a black-smith's shop and a tavern' seems a proper scite for one of them." A French observer in the 1830s, economist Michel Chevalier, was surprised to see a bank in a Pennsylvania locale of thirty houses, with stumps still standing in the streets.

The number of banks doubled between 1832 and 1837, in anticipation of the expiration of the federal charter of the Second Bank; many hoped to attract federal deposits. Rashness, derived from the characteristically American "ardor of enterprise," had been most markedly manifested in banking, according to the 1839 evaluation of the Virginia economist George Tucker.[14]

For some years after the panic of 1837, that ardor cooled. In 1851, however, new banks were opening at the rate of one a month in New York City, with another fifteen opening in the next two years. During the summer of 1857 charter applications were filled for five banks in Philadelphia, and for thirty-three elsewhere in Pennsylvania.

A contemporary New York banker reported that "not a few" of his colleagues in the city lacked training in business and could not even "conduct the simplest commercial correspondence." Country bankers commonly held all the jobs, from president to janitor. Their customers expected "some inquiries about their families, and remarks upon the news of the day, the weather, and other matters of personal or local interest."[15]

As late as 1836 some villages in western New York State resorted to barter because of the difficulty of obtaining "current money." Chicago, with over 4,000 inhabitants in 1840, opened its canals and first rail connection in 1846, yet in the 1840s over half of its transactions with surrounding territories were without the convenience of money. Mark Twain describes the great impression made by a cash payment to a Hannibal, Missouri, printer's shop in 1847: "No such mass of actual money as sixteen dollars, in one bunch, had ever entered that office on any previous occasion. People didn't pay for their paper and for their advertising in money; they paid in dry-goods, sugar, coffee, hickory wood, oak wood, turnips, pumpkins, onions, watermelons—and it was very seldom indeed that a man paid in money, and when that happened we thought there was something the matter with him."[16] Barter declined as the proliferation of banks brought ever more Americans into the orbit of the money economy.

□ Free Banking

Andrew Jackson's secretary of the treasury, Roger Taney, argued in 1834 for opening "to the most free competition" the "certain and liberal" profits of banking, so that "all classes of society" could share its advantages. In the quarter of a century after Jackson left the White House, a majority of states did so.

For many decades bank incorporation had required a special act of state legislatures. A transplanted Georgian was dismayed by the Albany scene; "base bargaining, intrigue and corruption" marked the occasion of chartering banks.[17] It had become "so shameless and corrupt that it could be endured no longer," future President Millard Fillmore recalled in 1848. Governor William Marcy called upon New York's legislature "to open . . . banking to a full and free competition, under such general restrictions and regulations as are necessary to insure to the public at large a sound currency." The Free Banking Act of April 1838 invited investors fulfilling the specifications of the law to associate themselves for banking purposes. Minimum capital was set at $100,000. A contemporary hailed the act "as equal to a second declaration of independence."[18]

The bill was still before the New York Assembly when Michigan passed the first free banking act in March 1837. Michigan's governor hailed it as "destroying the odious features of a bank monopoly and giving equal rights to all classes." Within a year some forty banks opened in Michigan, all of which were in receivership before another year had elapsed. In April 1839 "an Act to more effectively protect the public against various frauds" repealed Michigan's law.

The New York law was "the most important event in American banking history," Bray Hammond claimed; it established "a distinctively American system of banking."[19] Only Georgia followed New York in legislating free banking, in December 1838. After stalling for a dozen years, the movement brought free banking to Alabama and New Jersey in 1850; to Massachusetts, Vermont, Ohio, and Illinois in 1851; to Connecticut, Wisconsin, Indiana, and Tennessee in 1852; to Louisiana and Florida in 1853; to Iowa and Minnesota in 1858; to Pennsylvania in 1860; and to Kansas in 1861. Michigan voters approved a return to free banking in 1858.

Most free banking states did not follow the policy of prohibiting any special bank charters, as New York did in its 1846 constitution. Thus, Vermont, Connecticut, Massachusetts, and Iowa did not charter a single free bank in the 1850s. In Alabama only two of the ten chartered between 1850 and 1861 were free banks. Special enactments embodying fewer restrictions proved more attractive.

☐ Bank Capital

The lure of banking was the anticipation (generally unrealized) of great profit. Though highly regarded as an investment, bank stock did not usually yield exceptional earnings. Pennsylvania bank dividends averaged 7 percent in 1835 and 1859.

Even in the nineteenth century, when banks were no longer a novelty, investors were eager to subscribe to stock of new banks. In order to avoid trouble, the Pennsylvania legislature had specified a maximum to be allocated each day, yet scandal and riot accompanied the awarding of stock for the Girard Bank in 1832. The next year William Gouge noted that the opening of bank stock subscription books was marked by "the most disgraceful riots that occur in Philadelphia."[20] In South Carolina, subscribers sought 894,000 shares of the Bank of Charleston, chartered in December 1834 with only 20,000.

Subscribers' enthusiasm was not necessarily accompanied by the inclination or capacity to pay up in specie or equivalents. Starting with the 1795 charter for the Nantucket Bank, Massachusetts usually forbade shareholders to borrow from their bank if any installment on their shares remained unpaid. By 1830 the New England states began to insist that capital be paid in cash when a bank was being organized. Inadequate paid-in capital characterized so-called wildcat banking.[21]

All (or most) shareholders were often required to be residents of the state in which a bank was incorporated. Less developed areas in the South and West, however, welcomed outside capital. In December 1837 nonresidents owned $1.65 million in Ohio banks, while residents owned $1.38 million. In 1838, thirty-three banks in Ohio, Kentucky, Tennessee, and Mississippi were owned mainly by capitalists in New York, Philadelphia, and Boston. Throughout the period 1815–1840, Easterners owned Tennessee bank stock.

Some states held shareholders liable beyond the par value of the bank stock. New York bank shareholders were responsible for twice their investment. This "double liability" provision became popular after 1837, and it was applied to national bank shares in 1863.

☐ Private Banks

Individuals and partnerships conducting a banking business with their own capital resources were known as "private banks"; these banks were especially significant in the antebellum economy. Pressured by incorporated banks and wanting to regulate firms that issued currency, nineteen of the twenty-four states that made up the Union in 1820 passed restraining acts, beginning with Virginia in 1785. Another three enacted similar laws: Tennessee in 1827, Connecticut in 1830, and Mississippi in 1840. The 1837 Louisiana law and the 1838 Albama law merely banned unincorporated firms from issuing bank notes. New York's law forbidding note issues and other activities reserved for incorporated banks was applied to unincorporated firms in 1804 and extended to individuals in 1818. In 1837, however, New York granted individuals the right to receive deposits and make discounts. Elsewhere, private banks generally avoided issuing bank notes.

Stephen Girard owned the outstanding antebellum private bank. When the First Bank of the United States closed, the millionaire French immigrant bought the magnificent Philadelphia headquarters and succeeded to most of its business in May 1812. Alexander Baring, a leading British banker, welcomed the development: "Such an establishment was wanted in America and could not fail of success. . . . People cannot transact business confidentially with 24 Directors . . . and are besides exposed to the jealousy and observation of their neighbors."[22] The Bank of Stephen Girard wound up its affairs soon after his death at the end of 1831. The incorporated Girard Bank (chartered in 1832) occupied the historic building until it was merged into the Philadelphia National Bank in 1926.

Another leading private bank, Alex. Brown & Sons, began in Baltimore in 1800 as a linen import firm. The business became more and more involved in foreign exchange dealings and credit extensions to importers. Branches were opened in Liverpool and London as well as New York, Philadelphia, and Boston. Baltimore remains the headquarters of Alex. Brown & Sons, which claims to be America's oldest investment bank. The banking activities of the New York partnership today known as Brown Brothers, Harriman & Company, date from 1818.

During the period from 1830 to 1844 private banks may have been more numerous than chartered institutions. By 1860 deposits in 437 private banks in Ohio, Indiana, Illinois, Michigan, and Wisconsin exceeded the combined deposit and note liabilities of those states' chartered banks. In the entire United States there were 1,108 private banks in 1860—constituting 40 percent of all banks, but holding only 8 percent of total bank capital.[23]

The collapse of numerous incorporated banks after 1837 stimulated the growth of private banking. Reputable private banks had concentrated "mercantile banking" in their hands "because of the superior facility they afford over associations of irresponsible men doing business in palaces at enormous expense," explained *Hunt's Merchants Magazine* in 1843.

☐ States without Incorporated Banks

Five states reflected the hard-money sentiments of their inhabitants by refusing to incorporate note-issuing banks: Texas (1845–69 and 1876–1904), Iowa (1846–57), Arkansas (1846–64), California (1849–79), and Oregon (1857–80). In 1852 there were also no active incorporated banks in Florida, Illinois, Wisconsin, and Minnesota. The policies of nine of the thirty-three states and organized territories reflected agrarian hostility to the instability that banking corporations were thought to create, as evidenced in the aftermath of the panic of 1837.

Indiana, Missouri, and Iowa limited the bank note privilege to state-regulated institutions. Borrowers from Iowa's State Bank were limited to a four-month maturity. Those needing longer term credit resorted to private banks. In 1860 Missouri had twenty-eight private banks outside St. Louis; a decade later the state had ninety-one. Many towns continued to depend on them long after the Civil War.

Private banks were found most commonly in states that refused to incorporate banks. Thus, in Iowa land agents bought federal lands that they sold to settlers on credit. They also received deposits, sold drafts on domestic and foreign commercial centers, and exchanged bank notes. Soon after the Fort Dodge land office opened in 1855, seven private banks were in operation, one in a tent. Iowa bankers wishing to issue bank notes (which was illegal) would acquire an out-of-state bank (Nebraska was favored) and circulate its notes. This was one flaw in the argument of those who believed, like Gouge in 1835, that by getting rid of paper money and money corporations, "we shall get rid of very efficient instruments of evil."[24]

☐ Branch Banking

The Philadelphia-based First Bank of the United States opened in 1791 with branches in Boston, New York, Baltimore, and Charleston, later adding offices in Norfolk (1800), Washington, D.C. 1802, Savannah (1802), and New Orleans (1805). In addition to these eight locations, the Second Bank of the United States had seventeen branches in other important towns at its peak in 1831, reaching from Portland, Maine, to St. Louis and Natchez, Mississippi.

Incomplete information submitted to the secretary of the Treasury reported around 100 branches in the United States in 1834, and 174 in 1861. Few Northern banks had branches, but they were important in the South and West—especially in Virginia—where they proved convenient for river towns with insufficient capital for independent banking facilities.

The State Bank of Indiana was described by Hugh McCulloch as "a bank of branches." All ten branches had assets that belonged exclusively to their shareholders, but all were liable for all the debts of every other branch. The parent bank in Indianapolis served as supervisor. The successor Bank of the State of Indiana, with twenty branches, continued the arrangement of mutual control and inspection.

The State Bank of Ohio had thirty-six branches by 1860. Each had to contribute an amount equal to 10 percent of its note circulation to a safety fund. The State Bank of Iowa had a 12.5 percent safety fund levy for bank notes and, like Indiana and Ohio, supervised the fifteen branches through a central board of directors.

Fifteen New Orleans banks chartered by Louisiana between 1818 and 1836 also had a total of thirty-six branches. By pooling illiquid rural loans with more diversified loans in the great southern port, these institutions acquired safer portfolios. Altogether, there were eighty-three branches in the nine Confederate states on the eve of the Civil War—led by Virginia with forty, Tennessee with nineteen, and North Carolina with seventeen.

Whether operating as part of a branch network or (as was far more common) out of a single office, whether chartered or unincorporated, banks were used increasingly by the business community. At first confined to the major seaports on the Atlantic coast, commercial banking spread rapidly to all settled parts of the young nation.

2

Bank Notes and Deposits

☐ Bank Note Usage

Commercial banks issued the only paper money regularly circulating in the United States before 1862. The dollar total of bank notes in circulation exceeded coins shortly after the earliest banks opened. Already in 1800 bank notes amounted to some $3.50 per capita, while specie averaged $3–4. The United States had carried "the system of a paper currency . . . to a greater extent than anywhere else in the world," Alexander Baring noted in 1819.[1] State-chartered institutions had issued over 30,000 varieties of bank notes—differing in size, design, and denomination—by 1865.

Notes of solvent banks fetched varying amounts, depending on the distance to the place where they were redeemable. Counterfeits abounded, including spurious notes of nonexistent banks and genuine notes with forged signatures or raised denominations. Notes of failed banks—or sometimes of older banks that had simply closed—were altered to correspond with those of solvent ones. As early as 1805 a sheet describing counterfeits appeared in the *Boston Centinel*. In 1819 Hezekiah Niles estimated that some 10,000 were "wholly or in part engaged in swindling the honest." A worn, dirty note was considered more likely to be genuine than a clean one. Pinholes (made by banks as they filed the notes) further attested to a note's authenticity.

A business receiving substantial amounts of diverse notes would have to consult the counterfeit detector six days a week. *Bicknall's*

Counterfeit Detector and Bank-Note List for 1839 carried 1,395 descriptions of bad notes in denominations from $1 to $500. By 1859 the *Nicholas Bank-Note Reporter* had 5,400 separate descriptions of spurious notes, and the 1859 edition of *Monroe's Descriptive List of Genuine Bank Notes* itemized 1,323 authentic ones. An 1862 publication estimated that only 100 out of 1,300 U.S. banks had notes that had not been counterfeited.

John Thompson's prospectus of "a new Bank Note Reporter" promised a weekly committed to accuracy and integrity "regardless alike of the favor or ill will of the great financiers."[2] Not for him the $1,900 bribe a bogus Ohio bank paid a publisher in 1859 to "quote the money right." Thompson was sued for denouncing fraudulent issues, but won each time.

☐ Small Notes

Around 1830 bank notes constituted the circulating money stock. Except for change-making purposes, gold and silver did not circulate. The U.S. mint coined less than $3.3 million in silver from its opening in 1792 through 1862. Gold dollars first appeared in 1849; the total reached $17.7 million by 1863. The largest coin in general circulation was the Spanish dollar (the "pieces-of-eight" in *Treasure Island*). All foreign coins were legal tender until 1857.

During the War of 1812, the U.S. Treasury issued $3 million in non–interest bearing notes of less than $20, some for as little as $3. Neither the First nor the Second Bank of the United States issued any notes for less than $5.

Notes under $5 were already prohibited by 1792 in Massachusetts and Virginia, but such bans were not always enforced or even enforceable. By 1832 they were also banned in nine other states, including Pennsylvania and Louisiana. An 1835 New York law forbade notes under $10.

Such laws aimed to provide a more balanced medium of exchange, consisting of a mix of coin and paper. Reformers wanted to avoid further victimization of laborers by counterfeits in an era when many day laborers earned $1 a day. As the secretary of the Treasury argued in 1839, these laws would "enlarge the quantity of specie within the country, increase the use of it . . . and thus protect . . . the laboring classes from losses." As secretary of the Treasury James Guthrie repeatedly reminded Congress, continued use of small notes was an "evil and danger to our currency." Estimating that one-quarter of the $200 million in bank notes circulating in 1856 was in notes of $5 and under, he urged a constitutional amendment that would enable the federal government to regulate small notes. Nine states banned notes under $5 on the eve of the Civil War.

Although former secretary of the Treasury Albert Gallatin decried notes under $10 as a "public nuisance," and some states prohibited small notes, the public demanded them. Governor William Seward, who earned the nickname "Little Bill" not only for his height but also for his advocacy, led the movement to repeal the New York ban. In February 1839 notes for less than $5 were legalized. In 1837 Missouri's State Bank could not issue notes for less than $10, but illegal issues of private banks and out-of-state banks circulated widely. Finally, in 1857, the State Bank was allowed to issue $5 notes. Florida prohibited notes less than $5, but local railroads resorted to small promissory notes to transact their business. (The Tallahassee Railroad Company was still using them in 1870.) Richard Hildreth was impelled to publish *An Apology for One-Dollar Notes* in 1840. He believed that a majority of New England's country banks would have to close if notes under $20 could not be issued.

Notes for a fraction of a dollar also had a long history. Massachusetts banks issued 25¢ notes in 1805. Even sums as low as 5¢, 6.25¢, 10¢, 12.5¢, and 20¢ were widespread during the post-1815 depression. By 1830 many states restricted denominations to a round-dollar minimum, but laws against fractional notes were hardly ever enforced. It was not unusual to find cut-up parts of $1 notes circulating as fractional amounts.

Coins became particularly scarce when banks suspended specie payment. British traveler Captain Frederick Marryat observed in New York City in May 1837 that "every man is now his own banker." Hotels and theaters gave IOUs. He received as change for one glass of brandy fifteen tickets, each good for an additional glass.

Fractional notes were almost entirely driven out after 1840—thanks to the improved coinage situation—only to reappear a decade later when the market value of the silver in a quarter-dollar coin exceeded 25¢. When Congress reduced the silver content of fractional coins in 1853, the problem disappeared until the Civil War.

☐ Bank of the United States and Quality of Bank Notes

Both the First Bank of the United States (1791–1811) and the Second Bank (1816–36), afforded the public reliable note issues. The federal institutions held in check the tendency of state banks to overissue notes. Resumption of specie payments in the aftermath of the War of 1812 and the panic of 1819 diminished the discount on state banks' note issues in the 1820s. Gallatin considered that the Second Bank's control kept state bank issues "within reasonable bounds."[3] Increasingly, notes were held in lieu of specie and were less frequently returned to the issuing banks. Complaints by many state banks that they were checked and controlled offered the best evidence to former Secretary of the Treasury Gallatin (1833) that the Second Bank was operating as Congress had intended.

Around 1830 the Second Bank had about one-fifth of the nation's total bank note circulation and the same percentage of bank loans, while its share of specie reserves was about one-third. As with the First Bank, the Second Bank's notes carried the special privilege of being receivable for public dues, reflecting the bank's distinctive fiscal agent relationship to the federal government. Such was the reputation of its notes that the $19 million outstanding in 1831 circulated as far away as Montreal and Mexico City. The country went from "a state of currency approaching as near to perfection as could be desired" in 1830 (the finding of the Senate Finance Committee), to a situation "worse than that of any other country" (Gallatin)[4] following the expiration of the federal charter in 1836 and the demise of the Second Bank in 1841.

Acting alone, individual states could accomplish little, as Pennsylvania's governor recognized in 1858. Cooperation was needed especially between adjoining states, but was not forthcoming. Iowa, without any local banks in the mid-1850s, was flooded with "some of the worst money in the Union" issued by free banks in Illinois, Indiana, and Wisconsin.[5] In Iowa City in 1856, notes of over 300 banks circulated, most below par; bank notes from eastern Pennsylvania, New York, and New England, "choice par funds, rating next to gold," were shipped to New York in return for domestic exchange. "Bankable funds" (some of the best notes) came from Ohio, Indiana, Missouri, Virginia, Maryland, and Kentucky. The Illinois and Wisconsin compartment in the currency tray was mainly for Chicago and Milwaukee banks. "Western mixed" bank notes were the most troublesome: "stump-tail" from Illinois and Wisconsin and "red-horse," "wildcat," "bridle-pup," and "red-dog" from Indiana and Nebraska.[6]

The British economist John R. McCulloch described American paper money as "the most gigantic abuse by which an intelligent people ever permitted themselves to be disgraced and oppressed."[7] About 7,000 different kinds of bank notes, in addition to over 5,500 varieties of fraudulent ones, circulated in the loyal states by 1862.

☐   Redemption of Bank Notes

States usually required banks to redeem their notes on demand in specie or its equivalent. As this often proved difficult, banks developed a variety of evasive stratagems.

Loans would be made with the understanding that the borrower would see to it that the bank notes would not be returned for redemption before a minimum interval had elapsed. For instance, in 1825 a borrower from the Union Bank in Portsmouth, New Hampshire, agreed to keep $12,000 of its marked bills in circulation for one year, by redeeming them "weekly or as often as may be requested, in such manner as shall be satisfactory to the Bank." The borrower would then put these notes into circulation again. Connecticut legislated against the practice in 1837, only to find some banks lending to out-of-state borrowers willing to offer this guarantee. This "protected circulation," specially marked for the purpose, amounted to over $1.3 million in 1853. Connecticut prohibited the practice again in 1854.

Banks naturally preferred borrowers who were slow to redeem the notes given them. Those who had directly or indirectly taken specie from the bank in connection with a previous loan were ineligible to borrow from the Cheshire Bank in Keene, New Hampshire, according to its 1804 rules. In the old Southwest notes payable at some place other than the bank itself became customary. Tennessee's Union Bank had over $1.5 million payable in New Orleans in 1837, and another larger amount payable in Philadelphia. Commonly, notes were put into circulation in a place distant from the bank of issue, sometimes by a mutual exchange between two banks. Richmond banks paid out notes of distant branches rather than their own, the governor of Virginia complained in 1846. The Bank of Southern Illinois was established to circulate notes in more populous places; it counted on the fact that few would take the trouble to redeem its notes in Bolton, a remote locale with one family. An 1857 Illinois law required that there be at least 200 residents where a bank was located. Bolton-type banks were the exception, however. Most Western banks were in recognized places "as accessible as travel conditions of the day permitted."[8]

Yet another tactic that the Illinois legislature attempted to eliminate in 1857 involved banks trying to exhaust the redeemers' patience by requiring the notes to be presented one at a time, and by paying out small change. Well might the Philadelphia free-trade journalist Condy Raguet declaim in 1840 against "those miserable and discreditable expedients so frequently resorted to by banks on the eve of insolvency.[9]

By omitting the prudential provisions of the New York law, some free banking states made it possible for nonresidents to open banks that did little (if any) business at the place of issue. Organizers transmuted depreciated state bonds into bank notes. If any significant amount of these notes was presented for redemption, the state authority would have to draw on the insufficient proceeds from the bond sales.

An engraving plate to print $50,000 in bank notes cost about $1,500. In Indiana, when the state auditor countersigned the bills, the Indiana banker had funds to pay for the security bonds as well as leftover notes. Some restraint was provided by the Adams Express Company, which established a special squad in the early 1850s to redeem Indiana issues for their own as well as their clients' accounts.

The hospitality for which Southerners and Westerners were famous did not extend to strangers coming to redeem local bank notes. In 1818 Georgia authorized the Bank of Darien to require a written oath that the redeemed notes did not belong to any other bank or corporation. Between 1855 and 1859 persons who presented notes for redemption in Ohio, Indiana, and Missouri were threatened with lynching, or at least a coat of tar and feathers. Residents of Versailles, Kentucky, passed a formal resolution early in 1855 denouncing an agent from Lexington, Kentucky, who had been appearing to redeem notes of the local bank. Hanged in effigy, he was promised an early demise if he ever again molested their bank's specie.

Hailing the new banks in New London and Hartford, the *Connecticut Gazette* for 6 September 1792 instructed readers that it was the duty of "every well-wisher to the prosperity of the community, to give credit to the notes of the bank." The long forbearance of Americans who did not exercise their right to claim specie from banks astonished David Ricardo, an outstanding London financier and a major economist. His Philadelphia correspondent Condy Raguet explained in 1821 that anyone seeking to redeem bank notes "would have been persecuted as an enemy to society." Public sentiment opposed specie redemption because it diminished a bank's lending capacity and contracted the money supply. Americans' "firm faith in paper [was] founded in reason," Michel Chevalier thought.[10]

During periods of general suspension of specie payments, banks remained open but ceased to redeem their notes in specie. Such episodes occurred in 1814, 1837, 1839–41, and 1857. The general suspension that began late in 1861 lasted for eighteen years. In addition to geographically widespread general suspensions, there were numerous partial suspensions associated with bank failures in various locales.

☐ Noteholder Protection

Beginning with Connecticut in 1831, a number of states gave note-holders of failed banks the status of preferred creditors. After all, they "were mostly of that class which is least able to bear losses," as Indiana banker Hugh McCulloch remarked[11] in connection wth the 1857 collapse. Legislatures might wish to avoid the scene that occurred when a northern Pennsylvania bank's Philadelphia agent ceased to redeem its notes: "Hundreds of poor laborers were . . . running in every direction with their hands full of the trash and not able to induce a broker to give a six-pence in the dollar for them. We passed in the market a woman who makes her living by selling butter, eggs, and vegetables, who had almost all she was worth, about $17, in Towanda Bank notes. When apprized that it was worthless, she sank down in agony upon her stool and wept like a child. This is but one of a hundred similar cases."[12]

Banks chartered under New York's Safety Fund law (1829) had to pay an amount equal to 0.5 percent of their capital yearly for six years. Failed banks' obligations were paid out of the fund, which had a $10,000 balance on its termination in 1866. The pioneering safety fund idea spread to Vermont (1831), Indiana (1834), Michigan (1836), Ohio (1845), and Iowa (1858). New York, Vermont, and Michigan compelled all banks chartered after the passage of their safety fund acts to join the system. Michigan, the only one of the six also requiring its free banks to join, exhausted its safety fund by around 1842, effectively terminating the system there. Vermont's fund closed in 1859, with losses of $17,000 to creditors. In the four remaining states the scheme ended when the 1866 federal tax eliminated state bank notes.[13]

Notes issued by free banks were secured by collateral representing obligations of the United States, various states, and mortgages, which were valued at par or market, depending on state law. Losses in Michigan were $1 million because the 1837 law based bank notes entirely on inflated mortgages and personal bonds. In Minnesota free bank notes could be secured by that state's 7 percent railroad bonds, with a market value substantially below par. Five opened between November 1858 and May 1859; all failed in the summer of 1859. Notes of these banks were redeemed for around 20¢ on the dollar.

☐ The Suffolk System

New England bank notes circulated at par throughout that region thanks to the Suffolk system. Boston merchants, unlike businessmen of other major commercial centers, did not have to contend with varying discounts on notes of banks in their immediate trade area. In part, the success of the system derived from the greater conservatism of Boston's entrepreneurs: Lowells, Lawrences, and Appletons were among the Suffolk Bank's directors. What had originated as a measure to restrain the flood of country bank notes (thought to deprive Boston banks of an opportunity for issuing additional notes themselves) developed by 1824 into the first successful regional clearing system in the United States.

Daily redemption averaged $400,000 in 1834, and $750,000 by 1850. In 1857, $400 million—some ten times the average circulation of New England's banks—was sorted and counted annually. In 1858 country banks that felt themselves unduly restrained under Suffolk's autocratic attitude organized the Bank of Mutual Redemption, which paid interest on deposits. Even so, Suffolk retained the loyalty of about half of all the country banks.

☐ Domestic Exchange

The Second Bank of the United States began to buy and sell domestic bills of exchange in 1817 in all the cities where it had branches and came to dominate the market for domestic exchange. When its federal charter expired in 1836, state banks succeeded to this business. Complaints of excessive charges became commonplace.

As with international currency movements, the cost of shipping precious metals set limits on domestic exchange rates. The 1834 increase in the Treasury price of gold served to reduce the spread. Between New York and Boston, for example, gold would be transported when the rate approached a 0.25 percent premium; in the pre-1834 silver era, the differential might climb to 1 percent before a shipment of silver would be undertaken.

In 1809 notes of the First Bank of the United States were accepted all over the continent, but one could not be sure that any other bank's paper money would pay for a dinner even fifty mile's from the issuing bank's locality. Foreign visitors were cautioned that a given bank note would be worth progressively less as they proceeded further from the place of issue. A South Carolinian detailed his experience in 1840:

> At Wheeling exchanged $50 note Kentucky money, for notes of the Northwestern Bank of Virginia; reached Fredericktown; there neither Virginia nor Kentucky money current; paid a $5 Wheeling note for breakfast and dinner; received in change two $1 notes of some Pennsylvania bank, $1 Baltimore and Ohio Railroad, and

> balance in Good Intent shinplasters; 100 yards from the tavern
> door all notes refused except the Baltimore and Ohio Railroad;
> reached Harper's Ferry; notes of Northwestern Bank in worse
> repute there than in Maryland; deposited $10 in hands of agent;
> in this way reached Winchester; detained there two days in get-
> ting shaved. Kentucky money at 12 per cent, and Northwestern
> Bank at 10.[14]

Travelers often participated in the transfer of funds from one place to
another. If sent by mail, bank notes were often torn in half, and one part
held until the other arrived safely.

A number of states tried to limit or eliminate the discount on their
banks' notes. In 1851 New York required redemption in New York City,
Albany, or Troy at a 0.25 percent discount, instead of the 0.5 percent
discount permitted since 1840. The superintendent of banks claimed
that the measure "literally closed the door to illegitimate banking."
Pennsylvania's attempt in 1850 to require par redemption at Philadelphia or Pittsburgh was unsuccessful. The Farmers and Mechanics Bank
of Philadelphia then agreed to maintain at par locally the notes of
country banks east of the Alleghenies and to send them for redemption
for a fee of 0.25 percent.

Outside New England, par bank notes were found only in the state
banks of Illinois and Indiana and in branch banks in Louisiana. Henry
Clay's campaign in 1844 for "uniform bank currency" was realized in
1863 with the adoption of national bank notes.

In addition to bank notes legally payable on demand, a number of
other types of bank liabilities circulated between 1812 and 1840. "Facility
notes," inconvertible into specie, were received for payments owed the
issuing bank. "Post notes" were payable (with or without interest) at
some future date. Illegal in New York after 1828, their issuance was made
a misdemeanor in 1840. Post notes were forbidden to national banks.

□ Deposits as Money

The Massachusetts Bank began by charging for keeping money on deposit but soon did away with the fee and enjoyed rapid growth in
deposits. At first, checks were used in local payments and for withdraw-
ing cash from a deposit account. Already in the 1780s a busy merchant
might write forty-five checks a month on an account at the Bank of
North America. In the first decade of the nineteenth century, checks
came to be used for more than local settlement, and in the next decade
for more than local exchange.

A popular 1838 business manual explained the modern usage of checks to pay debts or obtain currency. In 1840, except for small retail transactions, almost all payments in the cities were by check. Depositors, not small noteholders, were responsible for bank runs in the late 1830s. Bank accounts multiplied twentyfold in the 1850s.[15] By 1860 most Massachusetts shopkeepers, substantial mechanics, and professionals had joined the large merchants who kept bank accounts. Total deposits exceeded bank notes outstanding by the mid-1850s.

Already in 1790 Hamilton pointed out that borrowers often transferred the proceeds of a loan through the vehicle of a check. Putting deposits on a par with bank notes, Gallatin in March 1809 described them as "the circulating medium substituted by the banking operations to money; for payments from one individual to another are equally made by drafts on the bank, or by the delivery of bank notes."[16] Samuel Hooper wrote in 1860 that "the great mass of deposits in the banks of the large commercial cities originates in discounts made by banks, and is therefore the creation of the banks."[17] Antebellum writers came to recognize the monetary nature of demand deposits, but the general public continued to hold the literal (and erroneous) view that these deposits were mainly money brought to the bank for safekeeping.

Failure to comprehend that bank lending involved deposit creation explains the well-nigh universal distinction drawn between banks of deposit and discount and banks of note issue. In 1839 Daniel Webster affirmed that without note issue an institution was not a bank. "Banking in America always implies the right and the practice of issuing paper money as a substitute for a specie currency," Gallatin observed in 1841.[18] Yet deposits may have equaled notes outstanding as early as 1811. Certainly this was the case from 1834, when the (incomplete) statistical series began to be published by the secretary of the Treasury. Not until 1856, however, did deposits *excluding* balances due other banks *consistently* exceed bank notes.

The rising volume of checks led to the October 1853 opening of the New York Clearing House Association (nineteen years before Paris and Vienna, but eighty years after London) for daily settlement of net balances arising among the city's fifty-two banks. Boston's clearinghouse began to operate in March 1856. Philadelphia's was conceived prior to the crisis of 1857 but began in February 1858. Baltimore's banks, as an outgrowth of the crisis, selected the Union Bank of Maryland as their clearing agent in 1858. Cleveland's Clearing House Association (1858) had as its purpose, "to effect at one place, and in the most economical and safe manner, the daily exchange between the several associated banks and bankers; the maintenance of uniform rates for eastern exchange and the regulation of what descriptions of funds shall be paid and received in the settlement of business."[19] The only other locality to establish a clearinghouse arrangement before the coming of the national banking system was Worcester, Massachusetts, in 1861.

Interbank deposits reflected bank relationships beyond the locality. By 1812 Massachusetts country banks kept Boston deposits. In 1813 the Massachusetts Bank had deposits in the Bank of New York and the Bank of North America. The Union Bank of Boston kept accounts with the Mechanics Bank and the Bank of the Manhattan Company and with the Farmers and Mechanics Bank of Philadelphia. In the 1830s important correspondent bank balances were also held in Baltimore, New Orleans, and Troy, New York. Such deposits were useful for note redemption and check collection.

Large banks paid interest on interbank deposits. In New York City this competitive device was used more often by private banks and trust companies than by incorporated banks. In 1858 the Philadelphia Clearing House Association members resolved "not to allow interest on deposits or balances of any kind."

☐ New York City's Rise to Dominance

Philadelphia, headquarters to both federally chartered banks of the United States and the first commercial bank, was the nation's leading financial center until around the mid-1830s. New York's location, enhanced by the Erie Canal, enabled the Empire City to overtake Philadelphia in foreign commerce by 1797, in population by 1805, and in the number of banks by 1812. In 1860 New York City's bank capital was almost $70 million, compared with $38 million for Boston and $12 million for Philadelphia. The fifty-five banks in New York—about 4 percent of the total in the country—had 32 percent of all deposits. By 1860 some 1,600 incorporated banks and 900 private banks from all over the country held $25 million of bankers' balances, mostly in a few Wall Street banks.

As the Boston entrepreneur Nathan Appleton noted, "New York is the great central banking power," but power was fragmented. Each of the fifty-five banks acted "its own separate part" during the panic that struck in October 1857. Appleton deplored the 30 percent contraction of the circulation medium despite a strong specie position in New York. This would be a recurring problem, which the Federal Reserve System was supposed to solve.

☐ Compensating Balances

Well before the Civil War era a compensating balance requirement for would-be borrowers took hold. Beginning in April 1782, the Bank of North America gave preference "to those who keep their cash at the Bank."[20] Girard insisted that "the scale of deposits ought to be the ratio of the loans."[21] Men secured the favor of the banks "by leaving a considerable amount *constantly on deposit*." the economist Amasa Walker noted in 1857. The practice had become a "sort of" general rule, "to which men are expected to conform themselves, if they wish liberal assistance from the bank," he added.[22]

☐ Banks and the Payments Mechanism

Banks eventually provided the greater part of the means of payment as the American economy developed and became increasingly market-oriented. In January 1860 almost 70 percent of the American money stock was in the form of bank deposits and bank notes.[23] Quality ranged from excellent to scandalous, depending on the period and the state in question; the quality of the money stock tended to improve in former frontier communities. Uniformly high standards would not prevail until the coming of the national banking system in 1863.

3

Bank Loans

LENDERS IN THE COLONIAL ERA MIGHT BE neighbors or acquaintances. In more populous communities by the second half of the eighteenth century, newspapers were the main vehicle for bringing together borrowers and lenders. But banks soon assumed a critical intermediary role. By 1853 Connecticut's bank commissioner remarked (with considerable exaggeration), "Every businessman is at the present time compelled to borrow of banks."

☐ Loans to Merchants

In Philadelphia, New York, Boston, and Baltimore the earliest banks specialized in commercial credit at short term. Banks had "a close connection with the whole mercantile interest," the Philadelphia merchant Pelatiah Webster explained in 1791. Half a century later Albert Gallatin recalled that "in their origin the banks were instituted for the purpose of affording accommodations to the commercial interest."[1] Inevitably, urban banks have financed wholesale and retail trade, down to the present day.

☐ Agricultural Loans

Agrarian hostility derived from the feeling that banks would not be of direct assistance to farmers, that they would only channel loanable funds away from agriculture. In 1811 Richmond-area merchants sought to allay rustic suspicions with the argument that an additional bank in Virginia would mean 10 percent higher prices realized by growers of wheat and tobacco: "The substantial benefit will be enjoyed by the owner of the soil."

After striving in vain to block the chartering of banks to serve merchants, agricultural interests turned to the establishment of their own institutions. The Washington Bank in Westerly, a Rhode Island village with 400 inhabitants was established "to remedy the embarrassments into which the farmer is frequently drove for the want of the means of stocking his farm at those seasons of the year when money is obtained with the greatest difficulty."[2] As early as 1816 most petitions for banks in Virginia came from small towns and rural areas. In July 1817 Marylanders were called upon to establish a bank that would afford landholders "the same facilities of obtaining money for the cultivation and improvement of their estates, which persons engaged in commerce obtain from the commercial banks . . . for the carrying on of trade."[3] Yet as late as the 1830s in northern and western New York, farmers often preferred private lenders to banks.

The policy of compelling some lending to agriculture began when Massachusetts required the Union Bank of Boston to make one-fifth of its loans to agricultural parties outside Boston in amounts ranging from $100 to $1,000 for at least one year on the security of real estate. All but one of the fourteen Massachusetts banks chartered in the 1802–03 period had to make one-eighth of their loans to agriculture on the same terms. Starting with the 1811 charters of the Merchants Bank and the State Bank, one-tenth of the loanable funds had to go to agricultural as well as manufacturing interests. Thirty of the thirty-four Massachusetts banks chartered between 1812 and 1815 were similarly restricted, but only six of the twenty-eight chartered between 1815 and 1826 were. Each of the forty-one banks chartered by Pennsylvania in 1814 had to lend up to one-fifth of its capital to farmers, mechanics, and manufacturers of their respective districts for one year at 6 percent, with "sufficient security being given," a provision continued in the general banking law of 1824.

In 1843 the Bank of Indiana adopted the policy of financing not only the flow of farm products to market but also the increase of cattle and hogs by "judicious loan to farmers." This policy "greatly stimulated and increased production," Hugh McCulloch, then manager of the Fort Wayne branch, reported.[4]

Southern banks lent on the security of the great staples, usually through the cotton factors and commission merchants. Augusta, Geor-

gia, banks required notes of country merchants and planters to be endorsed by two local residents. These merchants and planters would
exchange endorsements either reciprocally or upon receipt of a 2.5 percent commission.

☐ Real Estate Loans

Loans on real estate were made throughout the nation. Some banks in
the North came to dislike the long term of such loans because of the
difficulty in receiving prompt payment at maturity. Yet in Charleston
the Bank of South Carolina, with extensive real estate loans, paid its
notes in specie, while five of the six banks that did not lend on real estate
and bonds suspended in 1839. In the 1830s Cincinnati banks preferred
real estate loans to trade bills. On two occasions when speculators could
not meet their obligations, almost the entire city was foreclosed and sold
by the Second Bank of the United States. The Bank of the State of
Indiana began refusing loans for the purchase or improvement of land
after 1843 because they were "sluggish and unreliable."[5]

During the colonial era provincial and private loan offices made a
limited number of loans on mortgage security. The earliest public land
bank, Charleston's Land and Loan Bank of the Carolinas, had £52,000 to
lend. Any landowner was eligible to borrow; while agriculture was
obviously favored, merchants and other nonagriculturalists also took
advantage of these loan offices, which could be found in all the colonies
except Virginia. These colonial enterprises probably served as the inspi-
ration for the Southern antebellum real estate banks and the twentieth-
century federal farm loan banks.

Property banks aimed to attract foreign capital through the sale of
bonds secured by real estate mortgages. Louisiana incorporated the very
first one in 1827, the Consolidated Association of Planters, and later
chartered two others. Louisiana's property banks also made loans on
urban real estate. These property banks had the note issue privilege and
performed commercial banking functions. Subscribers to land banks in
Mississippi, Louisiana, Arkansas, and Alabama gave a mortgage on their
property in payment for the stock. When the state's bond issue was
sold, the 10 percent cash down payment would be returned with interest. The Real Estate Bank was founded in 1836 in conformity with the
Arkansas constitution's provision for a "banking institution calculated
to aid and promote the agricultural interests." The hope of increasing
land values by "coining the wild lands of Arkansas into money"
prompted the chartering of its first commercial banks in 1838.

□ Loans to Manufacturers

Bankers were generally dubious about the prospects of manufacturing and insisted on collateral security. Organizers of the Bank of Pittsburgh surely exaggerated when they affirmed in 1810 that "individuals of genius and enterprise" had received "important aid" from banks "by which they have enriched our country with the establishment of various valuable manufactures."[6] In 1792 the Bank of New York advanced $45,000 to the Society for Establishing Useful Manufactures to permit completion of the society's Paterson, New Jersey factories. Baltimore's Mechanics Bank, chartered in 1806 "to give aid especially to practical mechanics and manufacturers," was authorized to lend up to $80,000 (representing one-eighth of its capital) in amounts no greater than $3,000 secured by property.

Massachusetts banks would not lend to manufacturing firms in the 1820s, when the Lowell textile mills were erected. An 1859 study of the Philadelphia manufacturing scene complained that its banks had "not yet exercised a wise discrimination" in favor of manufacturers.[7] Yet in nearby Lancaster, the Farmers Bank advanced $20,000 for ten years to enable the Conestoga Steam Cotton Mills to be built in the 1850s.

□ Internal Improvements

Projects of internal improvements were financed in part by banks—over one-fifth of some $40 million spent in Ohio, Illinois, Indiana, and Wisconsin. This took the form in part of short-term loans in anticipation of proceeds from the sale of long-term securities. Maryland banks were active in road and bridge projects. Banks in Baltimore, Washington, and Allegheny counties contributed in 1813 to the construction of the historic Cumberland Turnpike. The Girard Bank lent $266,000 to the Schuylkill Navigation Company in 1827, $30,000 to the Mt. Carbon Railroad in 1830, and $20,000 to the Danville & Pottsville Railroad in (1831). New Orleans banks assisted large railroad projects in the 1850s. The Philadelphia Bank's holdings of railway and canal securities soared from $46,000 in 1861 to $600,000 by 1863, mostly for issues of the Pennsylvania, Reading, and Lehigh lines. Portland's Canal Bank, chartered in 1825, was authorized to invest one-fourth of its capital in the Cumberland and Oxford Canal. The Maine canal succumbed to railroad competition, but the bank continues to do business as the Key Bank of Maine.

Sometimes transportation companies were granted banking privileges in the hope of accelerating construction. The Georgia Railroad and Banking Company (in business since 1833) built a line from Augusta to Athens, and the Central Railroad and Banking Company connected Savannah with Macon. Georgia gave banking authority to three additional corporations that also undertook to build trunk lines.

Between 1835 and 1837, South Carolina, Georgia, Mississippi, and Louisiana chartered sixteen banking and railroad companies and authorized them to issue $33 million in bank stock. Note issues of its banking subsidiary made possible the early completion of the Erie and Kalamazoo Railroad in Michigan. Maryland chartered the Susquehanna Bridge and Bank Corporation in 1814, with banking privileges. Louisiana's first improvement bank, the Canal Bank, was required to devote one-fourth of its $4 million capital to construction of a canal connecting New Orleans and Lake Pontchartrain. New Jersey's legislature attached a banking privilege to the 1831 charter of the Morris Canal and Banking Company "for the encouragement of so great an undertaking as the erection of said canal, and in some measure to induce capitalists and others to subscribe." The right to engage in banking for thirty-five years was made contingent on completion of the canal between Newark and Phillipsburg. Within a decade the corporation was in receivership. On reorganizing in 1844, it became exclusively a canal company.

Not always did the bank–transportation company linkage produce the desired outcome. Mississippi, for example, from 1831 to the panic in 1837, "was gridironed with imaginary railroads and beridden with railroad banks. There was more watered stock sold than there were crossties laid."[8] South Carolina's eminent Senator Robert Hayne headed a project to link Charleston with the Ohio River. In 1839 the South Western Railroad opened a bank, which lasted until 1868 when its charter expired. The railroad project got as far as Columbia, South Carolina, before it was abandoned.

☐   Joint Nonbank Enterprises

Banks were sometimes linked with organizations other than transportation firms, as the 1799 Manhattan Company illustrates. In 1824 the charter of the Chemical Manufacturing Company (today the giant Chemical Bank) was amended to include banking. An early Kentucky bank (1818) was part of Sanders Manufacturing Company. In 1822 New Jersey chartered the Salem Banking and Steam Mill Company, which disposed of the flour mill in 1826, remaining an independent bank until 1967.

New Orleans had several unusual arrangements. The New Orleans Gas Light and Banking Company financed in 1829 the erection of reputedly the best street lighting system in America, and the Commercial Bank operated the Crescent City's waterworks from 1833 to 1843. To meet the terms of its 1835 charter, the Exchange Bank constructed the St. Charles Hotel in the American quarter of New Orleans.

Most banks established to provide capital funds for nonbanking enterprises collapsed in 1837; after that, improvement banks were no longer created.

☐ State Government Borrowers

State governments often required a loan as a condition for granting or renewing a charter. During the War of 1812, Massachusetts, Pennsylvania, Maryland, Virginia, and South Carolina borrowed over $5 million for defense outlays. In 1840 Pennsylvania called on its banks to lend the state up to 5 percent of their capital. By the end of 1841 Louisiana owed its banks over $1 million.

☐ Securities Activities

Bank underwriting of and trading in newly issued bonds provided industry and government with capital funds. In the period following the War of 1812 banks also bought stocks and resold them in small lots or acted as agents selling on commission. Ohio banks took up over half of the canal bonds sold by the state between 1836 and 1840, to cite one example.

Investment banking activities were especially notable among commercial banks in New York, Albany, and Philadelphia. The United States Bank of Pennsylvania, successor to the Second Bank of the United States in February 1836, acquired shares in over twenty banks from New York to New Orleans, as well as in numerous internal improvement companies. After an unsuccessful effort to sustain cotton prices, the bank closed for the last time in February 1841. This marked the end of significant involvement in corporate stock and bond dealings by incorporated commercial banks until the 1920s. Most investment banking business, except for purely local issues, was handled by private bankers by the 1850s.

Securities also served as collateral for bank loans. An 1837 New York legislative committee report criticized banks for thereby facilitating speculation. Widespread use of bank loans extended on security collateral, as the practice had evolved by the 1850s, was "a distinctly

American development."[9] Interbank balances, which could be withdrawn at any time, had become an important source of call money by
1850. Virtually all speculative trades came to depend on call loans after
1857; New York Stock Exchange settlements occurred more quickly and
stock brokers' credit extension to their customers increased. The city's
antebellum banks kept their secondary reserves almost exclusively in
the form of call loans. Agitation to eliminate call loans as secondary
reserves began in the aftermath of the panic of 1857 and continued into
the 1930s.

□ Out-of-Town Loans

Interbank deposits led to direct interbank loans through correspondent
banks. Upstate New York banks were able to extend credit locally by
rediscounting paper with the New York City banks. The Philadelphia
Bank lent $150,000 to the Bank of Georgia in 1821, and the same
amount to the Bank of New Orleans in 1831. Local borrowers usually
came first. On 6 January 1857, however, the board of directors authorized the president of the Farmers Trust Company of Lancaster, "when-
ever this Bank shall have more money to loan than is required by the
local demand, to apply the surplus in taking the paper of well-known
and substantial firms or corporations doing business in Philadelphia."[10]

□ Loan Maturities

Even the earliest banks broke their own rules by granting loans for
other than short-term business purposes. In 1786 the Bank of North
America discounted commercial paper based on the sale of goods, with
no more than forty-five days to maturity (earlier, it had been only
thirty days), and no renewals. Twenty years later it was lending for
longer terms and renewing frequently. Early in the 1800s Philadelphia
banks generally confined discounts to sixty days; within thirty years
competition had raised the customary limit to four to six months. Following the example of the First Bank of the United States, the Second
Bank placed a sixty-day limit on its discounts, but the rule was abandoned soon after it opened. By 1827 the limit was six months, and by
1830, with ample funds to reinvest as a result of the repayment of the
federal debt, the Second Bank bought mortgage-secured paper payable
in New Orleans in twelve to thirty-six months.

Banks introduced punctuality in commercial payments. Indeed,
this was a main reason for the unpopularity of banks in the early days.

Already in 1816, however, the average American bank based over half its loans on its legal right to demand payment, "but it is understood . . . that it would not be called for many months—some part of it for several years," a committee of the Virginia legislature reported. By the 1820s and 1830s banks were discounting at longer terms than in earlier times. In the century after 1830 maturities did not change much: one to six months, with renewals, was the norm. Some renewals continued for years, making the sixty- or ninety- day limit set by a bank's bylaws inapplicable in practice.

Accepted theory followed Adam Smith in confining banks to the discount of short-term, strictly business paper. Actual practice, as various legislative committees discovered after the 1837 crisis, diverged sharply. The Charleston economist Jacob Cardozo criticized the promoter of the Bank of South Carolina for holding to the view that loans to planters were the safest: "They are the most insecure, for the essential principle of all safe and sound banking consists of advances to merchants, on short dated paper, not renewable." He claimed that this principle "is now [1866] universally admitted," but bankers did deviate from it.[11] The British principle of lending on "real bills of exchange," based on goods moving from merchants and manufacturers to consumers, was the exception in American practice. Here, renewable accommodation paper based on promissory notes was popular. The borrower on accommodation paper anticipated it would be renewed; with business paper, payment at maturity was expected.

Importers sold to country storekeepers on nominal six-month credits that actually lasted for a year or longer. The storekeepers in turn sold on book credit to people who did not expect to make a settlement in less than a year. Banks in the large cities moved away from accommodation paper, so that by 1850 such loans were rare. Among country banks, however, accommodation paper continued to be popular. In the West, agricultural and business loans were "nominally on comparatively short term, but really with the understanding that indefinite renewals would be granted." Thus, H. Parker Willis regretfully noted, "American banking very early found itself compelled to compromise sharply with its principles."[12]

Three-month accommodation paper, with the borrower confident of renewal, financed the construction of vessels and factories. Textile manufacturers customarily received eight-, ten-, and twelve-month credits from Rhode Island banks, although for a time after the panic of 1857 a six-month term was the limit. A comprehensive study of 2,385 loans extended by commercial banks to eight Waltham-Lowell textile firms from 1840 to 1860 shows 63 percent outstanding for a 6–12-

month period. Banks provided 58 percent of the local loans borrowed by these Massachusetts companies.

Edmond Forstall, president of the Citizens Bank of New Orleans, convinced Louisiana in 1842 to require banks to hold short-term, self-liquidating assets along the lines of the British "real bills" principle. Banks had to offset demand liabilities by one-third specie and two-thirds paper due in ninety days. In the earlier years of the Forstall system, any renewal of ninety-day paper was regarded as equivalent to protest; its maker was publicly dishonored. A bank could not make any further discounts when specie holdings fell below one-third. Except for the prohibition of renewals, these principles prevailed at least until the late 1850s. New Orleans businessmen considered themselves at a disadvantage in competition with New York, Philadelphia, Charleston, and other rival ports, where loans could be had (or renewed) for six months or a year at 6 percent.

Short-term lending was the law only in New Orleans. Typically, antebellum banks extended both short- and long-term credit. Agrarian and frontier pressures for long-term credit affected rural banking practices and led to the establishment of public banks for long-term loans, as occurred in Georgia. Indeed, part of the attractiveness of free banking was its lack of "inhibitions as to long-term credit."[13]

☐ Lending Biases

Political loyalties influenced bank directors who passed on loan applications, particularly in the early decades. Jeffersonian Republicans who thought the Federalist-dominated Bank of New York had acted illiberally toward them formed the Bank of the Manhattan Company, which in turn lent to politically important individuals. Elkanah Watson, a Republican who disagreed with Federalist colleagues in the Bank of Albany (which he had also helped found), organized the Albany State Bank.

Politics inevitably showed up in state-owned banks. Legislators would select directors who promised to lend to constituents. Of the $15.3 million owed to the Bank of the State of Alabama (founded in 1823) when it was placed in liquidation in 1844, over half was bad or doubtful. In contrast, during the twenty-five-year history of the State Bank of Indiana (in which the state had a half interest), bad debts totaled less than $50,000. Even small sums were loaned only after careful investigation of a borrower's standing, habits, and character.

Loans secured by bank stock were sometimes used to evade laws governing the amount of paid-in capital. Such loans might also tend to favor the bank's owners or directors. Stockholders were the principal and preferred borrowers in the early years of the Bank of North America. In 1819 the City Bank of Baltimore loaned out over $400,000 to every official save the porter and one clerk, prompting Hezekiah Niles to denounce banking as "a cheat . . . a machine for the exclusive benefit of a few scheming men." In Virginia in the early 1840s directors had borrowed an amount equal to almost one-fourth of the capital of the reporting banks. A hostile critic claimed that "most directors serve, and value their places, merely to borrow as much money as possible."[14] A formal resolution in July 1840 by directors of the Bank of Illinois stated that stockholders "have the preferences." It was commonly believed that directors and friends received special consideration, and that others offering superior security were refused loans. As president of the City Bank around 1815, Colonel William Few "was disgusted with the cupidity and partiality of the Directors" and remonstrated with them.[15] Of course, his New York City associates did not reappoint the former Georgian. Vermont's moral climate must have been more wholesome than New York's. In 1837 bank commissioners found in all but two Vermont banks the proportion of loans to directors was "extremely small," and the two in question had loaned no more than the directors would have received if they had not been on the board. Directors of early nineteenth-century New England banks often lent to their own firms. These banks afforded "extended kinship groups . . . a stable institutional base from which to raise the capital consumed by their diverse . . . enterprises."[16] When eleven banks in or near Boston (whose capital had never been paid in) failed in 1837–38, a local paper denounced "the manufacture of banks by those who sought to borrow all the fictitious capital they could create."

In capital-hungry communities it is not surprising that the organizers of a new bank were often aspiring borrowers. "Banks never originate with those who have money to lend, but with those who wish to borrow," Amasa Walker noted in 1857. To deal with abuses in loans on bank stock, legislatures set maximum limits or prohibited such loans outright. Some tried to prevent favoritism and spread the benefits of banks more widely by limiting the amount that could be loaned to any one borrower—$50,000, for instance, in Pennsylvania and Maryland.

Banks were accused of channeling loans in undesirable directions by not helping farmers, by encouraging speculation, and by discriminating in their loan decisions. Such indictments frequently reflected borrower disappointment. Nevertheless, a recent scholarly investigation concluded that antebellum Louisiana banks did show "some preferences" to large planters over small farmers, to merchants over planters, and to public works.[17]

Banks in major cities often emphasized the financing of specific business activities, which would be reflected in their names. Capital for the four St. Louis banks established in 1857 derived from distinct groups: the Bank of St. Louis—steamboat men and manufacturers; the Merchants Bank—dry goods and grocers; the Southern Bank—boots, shoes and the mechanical trades; and the Exchange Bank—lumber. In 1860 there were over sixty farmers' banks, fifty mechanics', forty-five merchants', thirty with commerce (or commercial) in their title, twenty traders', and fifteen manufacturers' banks.

4

Government–Bank Relations

☐ State as Shareholder

By 1812 a majority of states owned at least some bank stock; New Jersey and several small New England states were the exceptions. Massachusetts, which made its first subscription in 1793, owned one-eighth of all the bank stock in the state by 1812. Pennsylvania in 1793 held one-third of the Bank of Pennsylvania's stock. The par value of that state's various bank stock investments reached $2.1 million in 1815; in 1843 the shares were liquidated. North Carolina's investment in three of its banks generated $1 million when the shares were later sold. Delaware owned one-fifth of the Farmers Bank chartered in February 1807 "to promote the agriculture, commerce and manufactures." The state had increased its holdings to 49 percent by January 1982, when it was sold to become the Girard Bank of Delaware.

Half of the State Bank of Indiana (1832–57) was privately owned. When this outstanding institution was liquidated and its business taken over by the entirely privately owned Bank of the State of Indiana (1855–65), the state received a handsome profit. Most other states, however, did not fare too well with their bank investments.

☐ States as Bank Owners or Sponsors

Eight states organized wholly owned banks. Vermont's was first in 1806. By the time it closed in 1812, it had sustained losses of $200,000.

The only other wholly owned public bank in a Northern state was the State Bank of Illinois (1821–31). The successful Bank of the State of South Carolina survived the Civil War but went into receivership in 1870, a victim of Reconstruction politics. The South also had the Bank of the Commonwealth of Kentucky (1820–34), the Bank of the State of Tennessee (1820–31), the Bank of the State of Alabama (1823–45), the Central Bank in Georgia (1828–42), and the Bank of the State of Arkansas (1837–43). The Illinois and Kentucky banks aimed to relieve agrarian distress in response to the heavy borrowing that preceded the depression of 1819. Alabama's bank "was supposedly to have promoted growth, whereas in fact it directly stifled growth by destabilizing the money supply, stifling credit, and directing the credit supply to areas where demand existed and denying it to areas that were starved for it."[1] The Bank of Tennessee, a second effort by the state, was established in 1838 "to raise a fund for the internal improvements and to aid in the establishment of a system of education." It redeemed its notes when it wound up operations in 1866, but not its deposits and other debts: early in the war, its assets had been removed to the deep South.

Political strife followed the establishment of these banks. Longtime South Carolina legislator John M. Felder wrote in October 1846 of "the vile concubinage of banks and state. Wherever . . . such cohabitation exists, the bank runs into politics and politicians run into the bank and foul disease and corruption ensue. . . . Bank master, state slave."[2]

To promote the production and marketing of cotton and sugar, Georgia, Alabama, Mississippi, Louisiana, Florida and Arkansas established one or more banks, beginning with Louisiana in 1824.[3] To provide banking capital, states in the South and West incurred over $65 million of bonded debt by 1840. All but 5 percent of bond proceeds went for banking, especially property banks. As of 1838 the bonds had provided almost half of the banking capital in Louisiana. The state was not ordinarily an actual stockholder in the real estate and property banks, but its credit provided the bank with a guarantee. In return, the state usually received a portion of the profits.

☐ Bank Taxation

At first the dividends from stock ownership promised to diminish—or even eliminate—the need for regular taxes. Charter bonuses also generated revenues. South Carolina received $15,000 from the Bank of South Carolina when it was chartered in 1801, and another $22,000 upon its renewal in 1822. The Bank of North America had to give Pennsylvania

$12,000 for a charter renewal in 1814. The Philadelphia Bank paid a bonus of 1 percent of its capital on the occasion of the renewal of its charter in 1859.

The first state to tax bank stock as property was Georgia in 1805, followed by New Jersey (1810) and Massachusetts (1812). Pennsylvania led the way in 1814 with a tax on bank stock dividends, followed by Ohio (1815) and Virginia (1846).

Taxation of dividends and capital stock became more prevalent than bonuses after 1820. From about 1800 to 1860, all states east of the Appalachians, except for New York, Vermont, and Virginia, derived at least one-fifth of their public revenues from banks for extended periods. Massachusetts, Rhode Island, Connecticut, Pennsylvania, Delaware, the Carolinas, and Georgia relied on bank taxes for one-third or more of ordinary revenues. By converting to national bank status in 1864, a dozen Philadelphia banks aimed to reduce their taxes by about half.

□ Government Supervision

Ten states with significant shareholdings appointed directors in one or more banks. Stock ownership was not a prerequisite, however, for state control. Charters contained explicit bank regulation of a sort. On incorporating the Commercial Bank of Albany in 1825, New York specified for the first time that the bank was authorized to "have and possess all incidental and necessary powers to carry on the business of banking—by discounting bills, notes, and other evidence of debt; by receiving deposits; by buying gold and selling bills of exchange, and by issuing bills, notes and other evidence of debt." This definition, carried over in New York's Free Banking Act of 1838 and the 1863 National Currency Act, became basic in state and federal banking legislation.

The charter also specified for the first time that "the said company shall have and possess no other powers whatever, except such as are expressly granted by this act." Instead of this broad restriction, earlier incorporation acts had enumerated various restraints. Of ninety-seven New York charters still in effect in 1839, ninety-two forbade dealings in real estate (except mortgages and the banking house), while eighty-eight prohibited dealing in any merchandise, or in bonds of the states or the United States (except in liquidating loan collateral).

The American discovery of "giving publicity" to the "actual condition" of banks was the most effective check "to the imprudence of banks," economist George Tucker claimed in 1839. States began to demand regular reporting in the early 1800s, but banks often disregarded the requirement, or submitted inaccurate or misleading statements. Even accurate reports could not reveal developments in the intervening period, as Pennsylvania's governor noted in 1846. Massachusetts's insistence on frequent, regular reports "perpetuated a hypothetical, not an actual control that permitted transgressors to 'cover real delinquency by a show of correctness' and to 'mislead the public' by an appearance of supervision which really did not exist."[4] In Illinois from 1817 to 1863, private banks had a "very much more creditable" record than the "elaborately safeguarded state institutions."[5]

New York set up the earliest special bank supervisory authority under its Safety Fund Act of 1829. Three commissioners made on-the-spot investigations of every bank's affairs at least four times a year. The bank commission was "an innovation of prime importance [that] . . . effectively initiated the independent regulatory agencies," according to Lee Benson.[6] Goaded by the 1837 panic, New York's example had been copied within a decade by all of New England except New Hampshire, as well as by Mississippi and Michigan. New Hampshire opted for an annual, unannounced inspection in 1843.

New York abolished the commissioners in 1843, however. The legislature reasoned that they were superfluous when bankers were honest, and of no avail when bankers were dishonest. Pennsylvania's governor remarked in 1846 that inspections in states with bank commissioners "are apt to induce a dangerous reliance on the vigilance of such officers."

Nevertheless in 1851 New York reestablished a banking department on a permanent basis. Massachusetts followed a parallel course, reestablishing in 1851 the bank commissioners' office that had been in existence from 1838 to 1843; it had been abolished on the pretext of an economy drive, but actually was closed because of country bank hostility. The basic official check on New York's banks remained the mandatory quarterly report of condition. The superintendent could examine a bank only if an irregularity was suspected. He might well hesitate, since even rumors of a planned examination could start a run on the bank. Because he did not want to further "delude the unwary public," the superintendent asked (in vain) for the elimination of his examining powers in 1858. Until 1884 his examination authority remained confined to cases in which he suspected illegal or unsound activities. Most other states did not provide for the continuous regulation of banks. Thus, when Pennsylvania recognized the need in 1860, banking was merely added to the responsibilities of the auditor general.

There was universal agreement that every phase of banking save the note issue function "not only must be open to all, but requires no more restrictions than any other species of commerce," Gallatin, then an eminent conservative New York banker, wrote in 1841. Deposit and discount operations "open to all" were also distinguished from bank notes issue, which was "confined to the few" and subject to state restraint by Millard Fillmore when he was New York State comptroller in 1848. California's first constitution in 1849 allowed banks to accept deposits but made the issuance of paper money a crime. Oregon did the same in 1857. State policy as described by the highest court in New York in 1857 was to set down strict requirements for bank notes but "to leave banking, in all its other operations, with the fewest possible restraints, and to permit it to be carried on like other branches of business."[7] "Take away from the banks of the United States the power of issuing paper money, and the whole difficulty of banking vanishes," it was argued in *Hunt's Merchants Magazine* (1858). Impressed with the benefits of free competition in all economic activities, Richard Hildreth in 1840 advocated "as much liberty for capitalists to invest their money in a bank as in a cotton mill." The head of the Massachusetts Bank was distressed, however, that Boston had "twenty-six machines [his rivals] running a race in the manufacture of money, with no flywheel or regulator to control their movements."[8] In the absence of an effective supervisory mechanism, statutory constraints were largely meaningless.

☐ Legal Reserve Requirements

To prevent the overissue of bank notes, a dozen states had established reserve requirements by 1861, ranging from 5 percent in Maine to one-third in Louisiana, Ohio, and Missouri. Early charters that limited liabilities to some multiple of the bank's (supposedly specie) capital in effect specified legal reserves. In 1837 Virginia was the first to express the requirement directly in terms of a percentage of note liabilities. New York followed in 1838, but country bank opposition led to the repeal in 1840 of the 12.5 percent specie reserve requirement for redemption of notes outstanding. Georgia (1838), Ohio (1839), Mississippi (1840), Connecticut (1848), Indiana (1853), and Missouri (1857) also instituted reserve requirements.

The most important precedent for the reserve provision included in the 1863 federal law was Louisiana's 1842 statute, which specified for the first time a specie reserve of one-third for both bank notes and deposits. Three months before the panic of 1837, Edmond Forstall explained to fellow Louisiana legislators that deposits were a threat no less than bank notes. The legal requirement he advocated was enacted five years later, but already in 1839 the associated banks of New Orleans had agreed among themselves to follow the practice. Under Louisiana's 1853 free banking act, reserves had to be held for bank deposits but not for bank notes.

Early in 1858 New York's governor pointed with envy to "the chief banks of New Orleans, [which] above all banks of the country, were enabled to resist the pressure of universal suspension elsewhere and maintain their integrity." His proposed 25 percent requirement for deposits was not enacted. Nevertheless, all but four of the forty-six New York City clearinghouse members voluntarily agreed in March 1858 to keep a 20 percent cash reserve, increased to 25 percent in 1860.

With the experience of the 1857 suspension of specie payments in view, a few states acted. After years of opposition on the part of bankers who viewed the proposed measure as unnecessary meddling, in 1858 Massachusetts passed a law that established a 15 percent legal reserve for deposits as well as notes. Iowa's law covered both deposits and notes. Maine (1858) and Pennsylvania (1860) legislated a reserve requirement only for bank notes.

□ Usury and Banks

Colonial legislatures—beginning with Massachusetts in 1661 and ending with Delaware and Georgia in 1759—and state legislatures—starting with New Hampshire in 1791—enacted usury laws. Congress limited the two banks of the United States to interest rates of 6 percent. The Second Bank was accused of charging a loan discount that, when combined with the fee for domestic bills, exceeded the legal limit. The practice was common among banks as a way of evading the usury law. To guard against such stratagems, a May 1835 law required New York's bank commissioners to examine the officers of safety fund banks on compliance. In 1820 Alabama, which authorized an 8 percent limit, permanently disqualified persons who violated the limit from serving as bank directors. A prospective director had to take a solemn oath that he had not violated the usury law "directly or indirectly."

Connecticut's bank commissioners reported widespread violations in 1856. That usury laws were not a dead letter, however, is evidenced by petitions for their repeal. Only Massachusetts did so by 1860. *Bankers Magazine* regularly reported court cases and changes in various state usury laws. The laws represented "occasional inconveniences" that "may at times have hampered the banks."[9] The legal limit in the various states averaged 8.1 percent in 1840, ranging from 6 percent in New

England to 15 percent in the West North Central states. In 1860 the usury ceiling averaged 7.8 percent, with a spread from 6 percent to 13 percent.

☐ The First and Second Banks of the United States and the Federal Government

The federal role in banking was not inconsiderable even before 1863. Both the First and the Second Bank of the United States were chartered to serve the Treasury's needs for a federal depository and a fiscal agent to transfer funds and make payments. Possessing a branch network, the First Bank had transmitted public funds more easily, more widely, and with greater security against possible loss than the existing state institutions. In vain, the Bank of New York pleaded for renewal of the First Bank's charter as highly useful to the state banks. "From the extent of its capital, its numerous branches, and above all from the protection of the Government, it is enabled to facilitate remittances to every part of the United States, to equalize the balance of specie capital among the different cities, and in cases of any sudden pressure upon the merchants to step forward to their aid in a degree which the state banks are unable to do. It is also able to assist any state institution which from peculiar circumstances may require it."[10] Most state banks, however, were pleased when the charter expired in February 1811.

During the War of 1812 the Treasury keenly felt its absence. As bank notes depreciated to varying degrees, tariff collections were de facto at variable rates from 1812 through 1816. To eliminate this inequity, Congress chartered the Second Bank of the United States in 1816. The Second Bank was to help state banks to resume specie payments, thereby restoring bank notes to par or near par. As with the First Bank, the federal government subscribed to one-fifth of its capital. Opponents denounced it as "a political engine . . . identified with the aristocracy."[11]

Even in the heyday of the federal banks' role as government depository and paying agent, the Treasury used state banks where there was no nearby branch. As part of Jackson's war on the Second Bank, the Treasury began to draw down its balances in the fall of 1833. The eighty-eight state bank depositories were purportedly safe, but all except four joined the general suspension of specie payments in May 1837. The Treasury lost perhaps $500,000 in unrecovered deposits and unredeemable bank notes. Altogether, from 1789 to 1841, Treasury losses amounted to some $5 million from bad bank notes and another $900,000 from uncollectable deposits in state banks.

☐ The Independent Treasury

Soon after the start of the panic of 1837, William Gouge urged the separation of government finances from the bank. The Treasury could easily and safely conduct its affairs without relying on any bank or using any kind of bank paper, he insisted.[12] The Independent Treasury Act signed by President Martin Van Buren on 4 July 1840 was hailed by advocates as the "Second Declaration of Independence." Whigs repealed the law the following year. The Democratic platform of 1840 insisted that "separation of the moneys of the government from banking institutions is indispensable for the safety of the funds of the government and the rights of the people." The identical language appeared again in their platforms of 1844, 1848, and 1856. In 1852 they affirmed that the Constitution and sound policy dictated separation.

Reestablished in 1846, the Independent Treasury did not go out of official existence until 1920. From 1789 to 1846 the U.S. Treasury used a federally chartered institution for thirty-seven years, and state-chartered banks for all but one year. After 1846 the government was to be its own banker. Subtreasuries were opened in major cities (See Appendix). Treasury receipts and payments were to be in gold, silver, and Treasury notes. Secretary of the Treasury Robert Walker hoped the measure he had sponsored would increase the amount of specie in circulation as well as restrain banks from excessive issues of bank notes.

On 7 December 1847 President James Polk reported success at the end of the first year of operations. In December 1857 President James Buchanan could boast that in the aftermath of the recent panic, "the government has not suspended [specie] payments, as it was compelled to do . . . by the failure of the banks in 1837."

From 1846 to the Civil War the Independent Treasury had "behaved creditably. It deliberately prevented pressures from developing in the money markets."[13] With federal spending about $1 million a week in its early years, the Independent Treasury had a minimal impact on the economy. But later in the century the ideal of separation proved to be increasingly unrealistic.

5

Antebellum Banking: An Assessment

☐ Banks and Business Fluctuations

Reviewing the monetary history of the United States from 1800 to 1875, Amasa Walker saw panics and suspensions as the consequence of allowing banks to manufacture the circulating medium.[1] Presidents Van Buren and Buchanan, like most of their contemporaries, blamed the operations of banks for the major financial crises and ensuing depressions that occurred during their administrations. Van Buren informed Congress in September 1837 that suspension of specie payments in May "was solely due to the unwise issue of too many notes by the State banks and the wild spirit of speculation engendered thereby." As president during the panic of 1857, Buchanan echoed his predecessor: "Our existing misfortunes have proceeded solely from our extravagant and vicious system of paper currency and bank credits, exciting the people to wild speculations and gambling in stocks." Buchanan warned that crises would recur

> so long as the amount of the paper currency and bank loans and discounts of the country shall be left to the discretion of 1,400 irresponsible banking institutions, which . . . will consult the interest of their stockholders rather than the public welfare. If experience shall prove it to be impossible to enjoy the facilities which well-regulated banks might afford without at the same time suffer-

ing the calamities which the excesses of the banks have hitherto
inflicted upon the country, it would then be far the lesser evil to
deprive them altogether of the power to issue paper currency and
confine them to the functions of banks of deposit and discount.[2]

Variations in aggregate specie supplies—which were related to the
ebb and flow of merchandise and capital movements in the nation's
balance of international payments position—were mainly responsible
for fluctuations in bank-created money. By the mid-nineteenth century
this fact came to be understood by bankers and legislators. The tendency
of specie imports to increase bank notes "by enlarging the means of the
banks to extend their issues" was remarked by Pennsylvania's governor
in 1848.

Public holdings of specie relative to total money in the early 1830s
was at its lowest since banking had first appeared. Over the period
1823–37 specie was no more than 15 percent of the public's aggregate
monetary holdings. After 1838, however, the public never held less than
23 percent. For the years 1815 to 1840 the banks did not originate
fluctuations, but they did transmit and magnify impulses leading to
expansion or contraction.[3] After each crisis, banks became more cautious about loan quality and maturity, only to relax standards as business recovered.

☐ Losses from Failure

The first American bank to fail was the Farmers Exchange Bank in
Gloucester, Rhode Island, in 1809. During its five-year existence the
bank had issued up to $600,000 in bank notes, but it had less than $87 in
specie when it closed. Yet from 1782 to 1837, as the American economist
Henry C. Carey boasted, the total number of failures was about one-
fourth less than in England over a three-year period from 1814 to 1816.[4]
However, in the six years following the panic of 1837, about one-fourth
of American banks went out of business.

From beginning to end, the U.S. banking system had been "a
compound of quackery and imposture" without a single redeeming quality, wrote John R. McCulloch in 1839.[5] Almost forty years later Francis
A. Walker commented that conditions then had "almost justified" the
British economist's severe language. Walker characterized "the greater
part of" American banking history down to 1840 as ranging "from
recklessness . . . to downright swindling."[6] The cumulative deprecia-

tion of the currency during periods of bank suspension aggregated $95 million by 1841, $72 million of which had occurred from 1837 to 1841, according to Secretary of the Treasury Levi Woodbury.

Almost two-fifths of the 2,500 incorporated banks organized between 1781 and 1861 closed within a decade of their opening. No reliable estimate of direct financial loss to creditors is available. John Sherman told his fellow senators in 1863 that bank note holders lost about 5 percent each year. The amount of worthless bank notes to 1861 was placed at $100 million.[7] The distinguished Committee on the Currency, set up in New York City after the panic of 1857, estimated total losses, including shareholders, depositors, and bank note holders, at over $200 million in the previous fifty years.

Losses were not uniformly distributed. Ohio bank note holders lost $1.4 million when forty-seven banks failed from 1831 to 1844. In New Orleans ten of the sixteen banks in business in 1837 had gone into liquidation by 1844. The ten bank failures in Massachusetts from 1784 to 1836 brought losses to shareholders and the public of a mere $333,000. When thirty-seven of 134 banks organized under an 1829 law collapsed in the panic of 1837, however, shareholders lost $2.5 million and the public was out $750,000. Under the Suffolk system, losses in New England were under one-eight of 1 percent, for an average circulation of $33 million from 1840 to 1860. Virginia's banks had an unblemished record before the Civil War. In South Carolina only two of the twenty banks chartered in the antebellum period failed, both in 1826. In New York under the Safety Fund Law (1829–66), losses averaged less than one-eighth of 1 percent.

The importance of wildcat banks has been exaggerated.[8] Banks in the Michigan territory around 1836 were the first to carry the label. Of sixty-seven banks chartered between 1835 and 1846, only one had "an untarnished credit record." "Michigan never achieved a balance between a reliable currency for its farmers and enough local bank credit for its businessmen."[9]

Of the 709 free banks operating between 1838 and 1863 in New York, Indiana, Wisconsin, and Minnesota, 104 failed. Note holders suffered losses from inadequate collateral. Wildcatting was responsible for perhaps seven of the nine Minnesota failures, nine of the twenty-four in Indiana, and six of the thirty-four in New York. Not one of the thirty-seven failures in Wisconsin reflected wildcat banking. Most of the free bank failures, Rolnick and Weber insist, reflected a deteriorating economic climate and shrinkage in the value of bank portfolios, not speculative forays by wildcatters.[10]

☐ Hostility toward Banks

In 1811 John Adams at seventy-six mentioned his lifelong abhorrence of "our whole banking system." His friend Thomas Jefferson characterized banks with the note privilege as "more dangerous than standing armies" in 1816.[11] Niles regularly included reports of bank antics in his *Weekly Register.*

On 12 January 1845 Andrew Jackson wrote to Sam Houston urging that the Texas constitution ban note-issuing banks "to protect your morals and . . . the labor of your country."[12] Jackson did not live long enough to hear that the Texas convention voted on 6 August 1845 in favor of the ban. The very next year Iowa and Arkansas followed Texas's example.

Those who advocated the abolition of banks altogether reveled in the final collapse of the Second Bank of the United States (1841). Other Jacksonians—especially in the East—wished to reform banking: to eliminate small notes, increase stockholder and director liability, and set specie reserves for notes. The relative stability and "more responsible conduct" of banks from the early 1840s on have been credited to reforms sponsored by Democrats at the state level.[13]

Specie averaged about 55 percent of currency in circulation from 1843 to 1863. In order to place the United States on a specie footing, Secretary of the Treasury James Guthrie proposed a prohibitive tax on all state bank notes in the mid-1850s. The tax enacted during the Civil War took effect in 1866 but did not bring the country to an all-specie currency. Instead, new national bank notes replaced state bank notes.

☐ Banks and Economic Development

Traveling in the United States in the 1830s, the French economist Michel Chevalier observed that banks had "served the Americans as a lever to transfer to their soil . . . the agriculture and manufactures of Europe, and to cover their country with roads, canals, factories . . . with everything that goes to make up civilization."[14] The system of bank credit was the usual explanation Americans gave a German visitor in 1839 for the impressive material progress achieved in a short span of years.[15] "Is there any instance in any of the United States, where any town or city has increased to any considerable extent without the aid of banking institutions," a delegate to the Pennsylvania constitutional convention of 1837 asked rhetorically.[16]

Albert Gallatin, then serving as president of the National Bank in the City of New York, wished for slower economic progress, but recognized in 1836 that "this does not accord with the extraordinary and irresistible energy of this nation." The Geneva-born aristocrat perceived the banking system as having adapted "to our democratic institutions and habits,"[17] In contrast to the 8,000 bank stockholders in New York City, London and Paris had a small number of very wealthy capitalists who were private bankers.

In December 1837 Ohio's governor reminded the legislature that bank "credit has given us one of the most enterprising and active set of businessmen that have lived in any age or any country. . . . Credit has bought our land, made our canals, improved our rivers, opened our roads, built our cities, cleared our fields, founded our churches, erected our colleges and schools."[18] Reviewing the record in 1838, Henry C. Carey praised American banks for having "brought the owner of capital into direct communication with the active, the industrious, and the enterprising who desired to use it."[19] Carter H. Golembe credits the state banks for "the rapidity and character of western growth" from 1830 to 1844.[20]

Banks participated in the process of economic development by increasing the productivity of existing capital and facilitating the transfer of resources to those activities that promised greater profit. In Louisiana, the shift was from subsistence farming to cotton or sugar. It is estimated that in the 1830s as much as $20 million of development capital was attracted from outside the state (including foreign investors) by the sale of both bank stocks and Louisiana's bonds to finance banking activities.[21] "Southern financial growth occurred at a rate and with enough soundness to have supported any activities that entrepreneurs wished to pursue," Larry Schweikart concluded.[22] That antebellum banking had "contributed to the development of capital resources" was conceded by as unsympathetic a modern historian as Fritz Redlich.[23]

Rondo Cameron has argued that "the rapidity of American economic growth and industrialization owes much to the restless spirits who did not shrink from devising radical and untried instruments to cope with what they regarded as an intolerable shortage of money."[24] Residents of Orford, New Hampshire, petitioning the state legislature for a bank charter in 1807, pointed to "the great scarcity of money" and expressed the conviction that "a competent supply of a circulating medium is highly beneficial to the commercial, agricultural and manufacturing interest of this State and of our common Country."[25] In 1843 Calvin Colton noted that "it is to this system of a sound credit currency, that, as a nation, we owe our unrivalled march to prosperity and wealth."[26]

By 1850 gold and silver amounted to $150 million, or 3.5 percent, of reproducible tangible wealth in the United States, a peak for the century. Even so, Jackson's 1834 objective of a "metallic currency throughout the Union sufficient for the laboring class," was not to be attained. Specie was under $6.50 per capita.

Bank notes and deposits made possible the economizing of specie, which was a more costly form of money. Indeed, the specie basis of antebellum banking seemed "almost insanely small" to Francis A. Walker, a hard-money economist.[27] Stanley Engerman estimated the social saving to the economy from bank notes at 0.46 percent of GNP from 1825 to 1834, when the Second Bank was in its prime. Subsequently, as the public's desire for specie increased, the saving declined to 0.35 percent of GNP from 1839 to 1848, and to 0.43 percent of GNP in the following decade.[28]

On the eve of the Civil War the greater part of the American circulating medium derived from incorporated commercial banks whose expanding numbers were bringing former frontier areas into the money economy. State bank notes were accepted everywhere except on the Pacific coast between Acapulco (Mexico) and Sitka (Alaska), where gold was king.[29]

Per capita bank money increased from $3.72 in 1820 to $6.57 in 1860. Total specie in 1860 was about ten times what it was in the 1790s, while bank notes were sixty times as great. Deposits soared from a negligible amount to over $220 million in these seventy years. In a bank's home territory most bank notes circulated at par; in distant places they might trade at a discount that did not exceed costs of shipment. Private banks, legally excluded from issuing bank notes, offered other financial services. There were over 1,100 by 1860, compared with almost 1,600 state-chartered banks.

Banks had become inextricably "interwoven with the commercial operations of society," remarked a House committee in 1830. "Banks are now regarded as necessary establishments," New York's governor told the legislature in 1834. President Buchanan recognized in 1857 that "the existence of banks and the circulation of bank paper . . . [are] so identified with the habits of our people that they can not at this day be suddenly abolished without much immediate injury to the country." For every 100,000 citizens, there were 3.2 banks in 1820, and almost five by 1860. Bank capital (par value) doubled between 1834 and 1860.

The multiplication of banks demonstrated that the public considered them to be "an advantage if not a necessity." During the 1850s the number of state-chartered banks increased by 79 percent. Most Americans came to look upon banks with favor after some eighty years of experience with them. To remedy the problems associated with existing banks, there was usually a call for creating more banks rather than eliminating existing ones.

Oldest banking house in the South, 16 Broad Street, Charleston, South Carolina. Erected in 1817 as a branch of the Second Bank of the United States, it was acquired in 1835 by the Bank of Charleston, which became South Carolina National Bank in 1926. *Courtesy of the South Carolina National Bank.*

Part II.

Banking from 1863 to 1913

6

Banks in the Civil War

WHEN THE AMERICAN REVOLUTION BE-
gan there were no commercial banks in the former colonies; near the
end of the war, one was chartered. By the time of the War of 1812 all
states east of the Appalachian Mountains had one or more chartered
banks. When the Civil War broke out, both North and South had well-
developed banking systems.

☐ Specie Payments Suspended

Banks in the loyal states had some $250 million in specie in April 1861.
Secretary of the Treasury Salmon P. Chase insisted that banks pay in
specie for U.S. bonds. By 30 December 1861 the New York banks
(whose reserves had been shrinking rapidly) suspended; banks in other
cities soon followed. Early in 1862 the U.S. Treasury also suspended.
Resumption of specie payments came only in 1879. Until then, gold
coins were accepted by banks as "special deposits."

Banks in the Confederate states held some $25 million in specie. In
the weeks after Lincoln's election on 6 November 1860, Southern banks
suspended specie payments, except in New Orleans and Mobile. Mobile
banks waited until August 1861, and on 16 September 1861 New Orleans banks gave in to the governor's request that they suspend specie
payments. When the great port fell to Union forces in April 1862, New

Orleans banks shipped about $4 million of gold out of the reach of the federal invaders.

□ Greenbacks

With the suspension of specie payments, paper money consisted of inconvertible bank notes. Soon both sides printed government-issued paper to finance the war.

On 17 July 1861 the federal Congress authorized demand notes in denominations of $5, $10, and $20, and on 25 February 1862, the first issues with legal tender power. This was a revolutionary action from the standpoint of both the Constitution and monetary practices since 1789.[1] U.S. notes first appeared on 10 March 1862; they reached a peak amount of $450 million by the end of the war. At the urging of New York banks, they were made legal tender from the start. On 17 March 1862 the previously issued demand notes were retroactively made legal tender as well. The new paper currency was thus available to settle claims expressed in U.S. dollars.

"Greenbacks" (as the public called the federal issues) exceeded the total of outstanding state bank notes by 1863. As the value of the metal rose above the nominal amount stamped on the coin, some $25 million in silver coins disappeared; by July 1862 only pennies were still in circulation. Bank notes were cut up, and fractional bank notes were issued. These notes wore out so rapidly that most banks found that the cost of reissue exceeded the interest income to the bank. Finally in July 1862 the issuance of bank notes in denominations of less than $1 was made a federal offense. Ordinary postage stamps served for a while. Then in August 1862 unglued paper was issued— "postage currency." In March 1863 Congress authorized $15 million in fractional notes; in October, paper in 5¢, 10¢, 25¢, and 50¢ denominations began to appear. The need for small change also brought forth unofficial private issues from many nonbank sources ("shinplasters").

□ Confederate Notes

The Confederacy resorted to paper money issues to a greater extent than the Union, $1.55 billion in all. Already in November 1861, with the war seven months old, Treasury notes constituted two-thirds of Confederate debts. Treasury notes, like greenbacks, did not bear interest, but unlike the federal issues, were never made legal tender. Individual Southern states also issued their own currency. The Constitution prohibited Northern states from doing so.

After the first year of war, Southern bank notes were at a premium in Confederate notes. A gold dollar fetched $20 in Confederate notes, but only $3.25 in Southern bank notes by the end of 1863. For small change, the South also used shinplasters, including 5¢ omnibus tickets in New Orleans.

In the Confederacy government-issued notes and bank notes "shaded off imperceptibly into unauthorized issues, these shading off again into counterfeits."[2] Greenbacks also circulated, and they gained in acceptability as Southern currency declined in value. Between January 1861 and February 1864, 91 percent of the $1 billion increase in the Southern money stock was represented by Confederate currency: 3 percent was state-issued currency; 2 percent, bank notes; and 4 percent, bank deposits.

□ Confederate Banks Decimated

At the start of 1861 nine Confederate states had 121 chartered banks; Texas and Alabama had none. The banks had about one-fifth of all U.S. banking capital and assets, corresponding approximately to the ratio of free Confederate state residents to the entire nonslave population of the United States. The Confederate secretary of the treasury praised the "loyal and patriotic" conduct of the banks, which had "contributed their means most liberally in aid of the government" (October 1864).[3] As the U.S. Supreme Court later noted, "The banks of the insurgent states . . . were used extensively in furtherance of the rebellion, and . . . nearly all their available funds were converted in one way or another into Confederate securities."[4]

In November 1860 South Carolina's comptroller-general predicted that the northern credit system was "doomed inevitably to topple to earth" as soon as the southern prop was removed. The South's banking system, he boasted, was "based on a much more stable foundation."[5] However, a year after Appomatox, the former Confederacy was "almost entirely destitute of currency and banking facilities," the secretary of the treasury reported. No banks remained in North Carolina, Mississippi, or Florida. Georgia and South Carolina had forty-nine state-chartered banks in 1860. Only one survived in South Carolina, and three in Georgia. In 1870 Charleston's banking capital was under $2 million, contrasted with $13 million before the firing on Fort Sumter. On the other hand, Richmond, with 45,000 inhabitants, had eleven banks two years after the guns were stilled.

☐ National Banks

Greenbacks, a wartime expedient, were supposed to be retired with budget surpluses in peacetime. In the end, $347 million were left in circulation to satisfy agrarian clamor.

Secretary of the Treasury Salmon P. Chase (like his predecessor, Alexander Hamilton) preferred that privately owned banks rather than the government issue paper money. The bill providing for a "national currency" under private auspices was signed on 25 February 1863; it realized Lincoln's goal of "a safe and uniform currency." It also provided a "steady market demand" for government bonds: each national bank had to subscribe an amount equal to one-third of its capital, with a $30,000 minimum. Establishment of the national banking system "at once inspired faith in the securities of the government and more than any one cause, enabled the Secretary [of the Treasury] to provide for the prompt payment of the soldiers and the public creditors," Chase reported at the end of 1863. By the end of the war national banks held $128 million of federal bonds, one-twentieth of the increase in the preceding four years.

Fewer than 500 national banks were chartered between February 1863 and June 1864, when an amended act enhanced their attractiveness. Around one thousand were doing business by the war's end. National bank notes exceeded $146 million in mid-1865, an increase of $115 million in one year. State bank circulation peaked at $239 million in 1863, declining to $126 million in mid-1864.

☐ The Independent Treasury in Wartime

Wartime exigencies dictated departures from the principle of separation of banks and Treasury. Banks served as depositories for federal bond subscriptions; national banks also served as Treasury revenue depositories. The only significant role of the Independent Treasury was specie collection of custom duties and specie disbursement of interest payments on public debt.

☐ Paying for the War

The cataclysmic war was enormously expensive in lives and treasure. Government outlays came to $3.2 billion on the Union side, and $2 billion on the Confederate side. In the North, taxes covered 22 percent, and in the South, 5 percent. Bond issues financed 65 percent in the North, and 21 percent in the Confederacy.

Union banks provided some 75 percent of wartime money expansion; Southern banks provided only 6 percent. Most of the balance consisted of greenbacks and Confederate Treasury notes. The latter became worthless in April 1865, while U.S. notes amounting to more than one-third of a billion dollars remain outstanding to this day.

7

The Heyday of
Unit Banks

□ Early Years of the National Banking System

The war that strengthened Washington's power over the nation marked
the beginning of a new era in banking and an end to a quarter of a
century of unchallenged control of banking policy by the states. After
February 1863 federal regulation and chartering came to the fore. As
amended in 1864, the essentials of the national banking system remained unchanged until December 1913.

The National-Bank Act (as it was renamed in 1874) drew on the
antebellum experience and the statutes of several states. New York's
Free Banking Act provided the idea of a bond-secured currency. A national bank would receive notes of uniform design carrying its name
when eligible U.S. government bonds were placed in the hands of the
comptroller of currency, the Washington official in charge. An 1858
Massachusetts law based on an 1842 Louisiana law provided the concept
of required reserves against both deposits and bank notes; the reserve
requirement for bank notes was eliminated in 1874.

Federal guarantee of bank notes was the major new element. The
Treasury would redeem at par the national bank notes issued by a failed
bank, canceling the bonds deposited as collateral. The bank note holder
also had a legal claim on shareholders, who were liable to creditors for
an additional amount equal to the par value of the stock. This "double
liability" feature (eliminated in 1935) was also in the New York law.

64

For the first time, the nation had a uniform bank currency, without creating "a moneyed power in a few hands over the politics and business of the country," as Hugh McCulloch, first comptroller of the currency, pointed out in 1864.[1] Jay Cooke, the great war bond salesman, thought the new system combined the finest aspects of American banking experience: "the unity of action and general control, and the uniformity of currency—which were the best features of the United States Bank—with the diffusion of issue and freedom in local management which characterize the State system."[2]

Expectations that all state banks would soon be absorbed into the national system were disappointed. Of the 456 charters issued during the life of the original act (25 February 1863 to 3 June 1864), only twenty-four represented the conversion of a state bank. Charter #1, dated 20 June 1863, was issued to the First National Bank of Philadelphia, newly organized by Cooke. Chicago's First National was #8; New York's First National (#29) was founded by John Thompson, whose widely used *Bank Note Reporter* soon became obsolete. Cleveland's First National Bank was charter #7; Cincinnati's, #24; Washington, D.C.'s (also a Cooke bank), #26; Pittsburgh's, #48; Newark's, #52; and St. Louis's, #89. Boston's, which was #200, represented a state bank conversion. Baltimore's new First National was #204. Under the original act, ten national banks were chartered in New York, seven in Philadelphia, five in Chicago, and four each in St. Louis and Cincinnati. The first banks to open, on 29 June 1863, were the First National of Davenport, Iowa (#15) and the Second National of Dayton, Ohio (#10).

New York, Ohio, and Pennsylvania accounted for 242 charters; Massachusetts, Indiana, and Illinois, for another ninety-one. By June 1864 only Delaware of the twenty-two Union states had not one national bank charter.

At first, the proud members of the New York Clearing House (whose bank notes commanded a premium over greenbacks and other states' bank notes) refused to convert. Nor would they admit the newly opened national banks to membership, considering them dangerous institutions doomed to repeat the dismal record of the free banks chartered by Western states in the 1850s.

In rebuttal, McCulloch pointed to the significant statutory safeguards. Capital had to be paid up in full, and bank notes were secured by U.S. bonds valued at no more than 90 percent of par value. The Treasury stood ready to redeem instantly the notes of all failed national banks. Moreover, Treasury appointees would make frequent examinations of national banks. Some bankers were concerned that Congress might enact hostile legislation or meddle in banks' affairs for political reasons. The first comptroller of the currency was confident, however, that "there was as little to fear from Congressional as from State legislation." If anything, trouble could arise from "the control which the banks might have over Congress, rather than in annoying interference by Congress with their legitimate business," McCulloch argued.[3]

Long-established banks also balked at Secretary of the Treasury Chase's insistence that time-honored names be dropped and replaced with a numerical designation. This requirement was soon abandoned; in March 1864 the National Currency Bank in New York City became the first national bank without a number. Newly established banks, however, often preferred a number in their name. The prestige attached to being "First National" led to many bitter contests well into the twentieth century. "Tenth National" was the highest numeral used—in New York by 1864, and in Philadelphia in 1885.

Conversion of state banks proceeded too slowly for Senator Sherman of Ohio, whose aim was to have national banks "supersede the state banks." There were 855 national banks on 4 March 1865, the day after the prospective tax on state bank notes was signed into law, and 1,601 at the end of 1865, 922 of which were conversions of state banks. The tax took effect on 1 July 1866; only national banks could now profit from issuing notes.

Fewer than 300 state banks remained. These had previously emphasized deposit banking and now retired all their notes. Many larger state banks were less concerned about the tax than about the prospective loss of correspondent balances, as only deposits with national banks satisfied the legal reserve requirement.

McCulloch wrote to the head of the largest state bank in New York within a month after Lincoln signed the 1864 act:

> Our National Banks in the country and in other Cities, are now selecting their correspondents in New York, and the longer the conversion of the Bank of Commerce is deferred, the fewer valuable accounts will it secure at the start, and the more difficult will it be for it to take that controlling position in the National System of Banking, which with its large capital and the ability of its managers, it ought to assume.[4]

Non-national banks—both state and private—had 40 percent of all commercial bank deposits held by the public in 1867, and 50 percent by 1871. By around 1880, however, their share dropped to less than half.

The $300 million statutory maximum on the amount of national bank notes restrained the formation of national banks. By November 1866 all $300 million had been allocated by state, half on the basis of population, and the rest in relation to "existing banking capital, resources and business." Only thirty-nine charters were granted in 1866, and only thirty-one more over the next three years.

The first three comptrollers of the currency exercised some discretion in granting charters. Before sending the necessary forms, McCulloch asked about the local economy, already existing banks, and the background of the organizers. Not uncommonly, he sought to discourage applicants. In states with adequate banking capital, the comptroller was anxious to secure the conversion of existing state banks rather than the formation of new national banks.

The greater part of the note issue went to national banks east of the Appalachians and north of the Mason-Dixon line. In 1870 the former Confederacy had just sixty-nine out of 1,614 national banks. Illinois, Wisconsin, and Missouri complained that their bank note circulation was smaller than in 1860. In Indiana, Iowa, and Minnesota the increase was not commensurate with growth in their trade during the 1860s. In July 1870 the note ceiling was raised $54 million.

In the wake of the major depression of 1873, Senator Sherman (who had insisted on the original maximum) sponsored a bill eliminating the ceiling on 14 January 1875. "Banking shall be free," he proclaimed. Thereafter, every application conforming to legal requirements was granted, Comptroller John Jay Knox reported. With the 1875 amendment, Silas Stilwell, one of the authors of the 1863 act, could accurately speak of the "National Free Banking Law of the United States."

☐ The Dual Banking System Takes Root

National bank charters had a twenty-year life. For some time the system's abandonment loomed as a distinct possibility. Starting in 1876 the Greenback party demanded abundant paper currency issued exclusively by the federal government. Other enemies of national banks sought repeal of the 10 percent tax on state bank notes (a plank in the Democratic platform as late as 1892) so that state banks might flourish, especially in less developed sections of the country. The 1882 law extending the charter of existing national banks for an additional twenty years marked the defeat of these hostile forces, permanently as it turned out.

Meanwhile, state-chartered banks grew in strength, assuring perpetuation of the dual banking system—concurrent state and federal chartering and regulation—as a powerful political and economic force down to the present. There were 2,239 national banks, and 704 with state charters, in 1882. Within a decade, however, national banks were outnumbered. By 1900 there were 5,000 state banks, but only 3,731 national banks. Of total commercial bank deposits held by the public (excluding interbank and federal government deposits), 51 percent were in national banks in 1882; that percentage was reduced to 45 percent in 1900, and to 42 percent by 1913.

Federal policy encourged free banking, and so did most states. In 1863, eighteen states had free banking. Beginning with Nevada in 1864, the principle was embodied in the constitutions of all new states west of the Mississippi. Texas chartered 311 banks in its first twenty-six months of state banking (1905–1907). In the East a special legislative charter for a new bank was still an option in North Carolina and Maryland in 1913; this was the exclusive method of chartering in Delaware.

Minimum capital requirements for national banks before 1900 ranged from $50,000 in places with fewer than 6,000 inhabitants up to $200,000 where over 50,000 people resided. States commonly demanded less than $10,000 in starting capital. As a result, almost 80 percent of Wisconsin localities with banks in 1898 were state-chartered institutions. National banks were found mainly in larger cities. To encourage an increase of banks serving farmers, the Dakotas, Nebraska, Kansas, Oklahoma, and Wisconsin authorized banks with as little as $5,000 in capital. Other farming states set a $10,000 or $15,000 minimum.

The stock savings bank (which did a commercial bank business, despite its name) became very popular in Iowa because only $10,000 in capital was needed in towns with a population under 10,000. By 1913 Iowa had 759 out of a U.S. total of 1,355 stock savings banks, and in 1935 (the last year they were reported separately), 306 of the 341.

In 1900 capital requirements for national banks in towns under 3,000 in population were cut in half. Even the new $25,000 minimum was higher than that required by many states. From 1900 to 1913, 2,858 small-town national banks were added. Almost three-fifths of national banks with less than $50,000 capital were located in predominantly agricultural regions in Southern and Midwest states. Although as many national banks were chartered from 1900 through 1913 as from 1863 through 1899, they managed to earn a rate of return on total capital averaging 8 percent a year.

Cass County, Iowa, typical of better agricultural sections, boasted seventeen banks in 1912. The largest of its eight towns (population 4,560) had five; places with a population ranging from 490 to 1,118 had two banks each. By 1910 there was hardly a hamlet in the nation with over 200 people that did not have one (and sometimes two) banks.

By the end of 1913 there were over twice as many state as national banks. A state charter usually demanded less capital and lower reserves, while authorizing a greater variety of promising activities, including real estate lending and trusts. Such considerations sometimes more than compensated for the generally greater prestige enjoyed by national banks, as well as for whatever earnings the note issue privilege brought.

State banks were mostly locally owned. A federal charter was more attractive to distant investors. Nonresidents owned about one-third of the stock of all national banks in the prairie and Rocky Mountain states in 1889. Foreigners invested in national bank shares to a slight extent— under 0.4 percent in the 1880s.

Unlike his predecessors since 1875, Comptroller Lawrence Murray, who took office six months after the panic of 1907, considered charters subject to a test of need, paying special attention to small town applications. He also initiated a policy in 1908 of examining every new national bank before it could open, a practice previously adopted by states concerned with verifying the payment in full of capital subscriptions and compliance with the law. From 1908 to 1913 Murray authorized only 650 new national banks while the states issued over 4,000 charters.

□ Private Banks

There were 3,412 private banks holding 15 percent of all deposits, in November 1882 (the last time official data were collected). The number of banks operating without any governmental charter reached some 5,200 by 1900. Until 1905 private banks were more numerous than national banks. Frequently, they combined banking with mercantile, commission, real estate, and brokerage operations. Typically, they were located in small communities; in 1900, 83 percent of Wisconsin's 131 private banks were in towns with fewer than 2,000 inhabitants, and 88 percent had under $200,000 in assets. After a decade in which the failure rate of private banks averaged 2 percent a year, in 1903 Wisconsin offered private banks a choice of incorporating or withdrawing altogether from banking. State charters were immediately taken out by 137, ten went out of business, and one was placed in the hands of a receiver. California required semiannual reports in 1887 and began to examine private banks in 1905. After 1913 it prohibited private banks. Texas never had fewer than 112 private banks in the 1880s, and by 1890, when national banks had become more numerous, there were 148 in Texas.

Not uncommonly, a private bank evolved into a chartered institution. In Tucson, the Jacobs brothers opened a general store and invested part of their capital in a money exchange in 1870. The next year they began lending greenbacks at 5 percent per month. In 1875 they were accepting savings deposits in addition to storing valuables in the store safe. In January 1879 the Pima County Bank opened in a corner of their store, the first to be incorporated in Tucson.

☐ Branches and Affiliates

The large number of commercial banks—some 27,000 at the end of 1913—was related to the rarity of branch facilities in the post–Civil War era. National banks, despite their label, were confined to a single location (unit banks) until 1922.

Banks began to show an interest in branches toward the end of the nineteenth century. In the early 1900s the comptroller rejected numerous applications for additional offices as contrary to the intent of the law, but allowed converting state banks to keep existing branches. In 1910 there were nine national banks with twelve branches.

Branching was seen as antithetical to free banking. Small bank owners feared that the competition of branch banks would crush them. H. Parker Willis insisted in 1902 that branches would actually "destroy the local money power which now practically stifles many forms of legitimate industry by a pressure of excessive interest rates, and by other even less justifiable means."[5] Most bankers would consider this view heresy. Not for them the finding of John A. James that in 1902 banks with less than $500,000 in their loan portfolio were significantly below minimum efficient size.[6]

Former Comptroller Charles Dawes was president of Central Trust Company of Illinois, opened in Chicago in July 1902 as a "big bank for small people." He told the Pennsylvania Bankers Association in 1903 that branch banking "would certainly not aid in building up our undeveloped country, and the newer sections of the United States." In 1905 Dawes described national policy to the Kansas Bankers Association: "to let the little men get on in the country, in order to let the little bank get into operation, in order to let the little manufacturer get into operation, and to not cut off from their credit those people who, starting from small beginnings, have brought us into this great prosperity which we all enjoy."[7]

The 1900 reduction in the minimum capital requirement for national banks diminished the urgency of branching as a device to bring banking to smaller localities without adequate facilities. As a result of pressure from small banks, the number of states specifically authorizing branching decreased from twenty in 1896 to twelve by 1910. Most important for the future was the 1909 law permitting branches throughout California.

In 1898 New York modified its 1844 branch prohibition and allowed New York City banks to locate offices anywhere in a unified five-county area of over 300 square miles. President William Nash of the Corn Exchange Bank viewed branch banking as "the permanent extension to small institutions of that support that is given to the Clearing House banks when they join together in financial panics and pool their resources for mutual protection."[8] As early as 1902, Nash's bank had absorbed seven existing banks and opened seven new offices. In 1913 Corn Exchange, with thirty-three locations, operated by far the largest branch network in the United States. In Michigan, following a 1909 ruling of the attorney general, most Detroit banks and some in Grand Rapids acquired branches.

Branches remained, however, very much the exception. In 1900 there were altogether 119, belonging to eighty-seven banks. By 1916, 292 banks had 548 branches, with half of them in the headquarters city.

As most states prohibited branches, bankers seeking close ties with other banks were "developing rapidly a system of joint ownership." Around the turn of the century, many leading non-national institutions were buying control or an interest in other banks. Chain banking, involving individual ownership of several banks, tended to evolve into group banking, in which a holding company owned several banks. Such arrangements were not uncommon in the Midwest, Northwest, and South.

The Union Investment Company of Minneapolis (organized around 1903) acquired a number of rural banks. In the early 1900s the president of the Continental National Bank of Salt Lake City organized a chain that spilled over from Utah into Idaho and Wyoming. By 1910 a Spokane holding company controlled about twenty-five rural banks in Washington and Idaho. William Witham built a chain in the South that became a holding company owning seventy banks by 1906, and 125 five years later.

Branch, chain, and holding company banks were not typical arrangements. In the years just prior to World War I, thousands upon thousands of locally owned, locally oriented, single-office institutions dotted the landscape—an important element in the setting of a land of a myriad small towns, soon to disappear. The United States "gives banking facilities under local control and direction to every little hamlet in this great country," the comptroller of the currency boasted in 1912.

☐   Trust Companies and Banking

As banks multiplied in the late nineteenth century, they also faced increasing competition from trust companies. Originally trust companies managed property placed in their care. Farmers' Fire Insurance and Loan Company, founded in 1822, was probably the first American corporation to act as a trustee. Renamed Farmers' Loan and Trust Company in 1836, this New York City firm was empowered to execute lawful trusts; it could not issue bank notes. Acquired by the National City Bank in 1929, it was consolidated with the bank in 1963.

The United States Trust Company was the first to be chartered exclusively as a trust company (in 1853) and remains a leader to this day. Its charter became the model for others in New York and for the state's general trust company incorporation law of 1887, enacted four years after Minnesota's. A number of states waited until the early twentieth century to pass general laws for trust company incorporation.

Pre–Civil War legislatures objected to combining banking with trust functions. Trust companies took advantage of the ambiguities surrounding the proper boundaries of banking to invade fields previously occupied by commercial banks. Depositors were writing checks against their balances with trust companies no later than 1857. In 1856 the United States Trust Company, the Buffalo Trust Company, and the New York Life Insurance and Trust Company handled almost 9,000 checks, which totaled nearly twice the amount they held on deposit at year-end.[9]

In the 1870s trust companies expanded the range of financial services offered; apart from their fiduciary function, they became indistinguishable from commercial banks by the late nineteenth century. Trust companies focused on a trust relationship with borrowers, lending on collateral such as warehoused bulk merchandise, stocks and bonds, and real estate.

After several trust companies failed in the panic of 1873, New York required regular reports to its banking department. In 1875 there were nine trust companies with 12 percent of commercial banking assets, in New York City. By 1900 there were thirty-one; their asset share had jumped to 32 percent.[10] By 1887 New York's superintendent of banks confirmed that there was very little difference between the business of trust companies and commercial banks. Nevertheless, *A Trust Manual*, published in 1898 by the Colonial Trust Company of New York, continued to deny this.

> A bank receives the deposits of the business community without
> interest and in consideration therefore agrees to distribute its

funds among its depositors as their several needs may require, and the available funds permit. The right to a discount is the compensation which a depositor receives for giving the bank the use of his deposits, and is to a certain degree, at least, dependent upon his average balance. On the contrary, the very idea of a trust company presupposes the payment of interest upon its deposits, and while therefore it is under no direct obligation to extend credit to its depositors, it is at all times ready and willing to extend such credit as is consistent with conservative, prudent banking. . . . While banks discounted notes, trust companies usually required collateral security. The trust company can support larger enterprise, and for a longer time. It can loan directly upon real estate which a bank is prohibited from doing.

Legal reserve requirements for trust companies were nonexistent or low. Keeping little cash on hand, trust companies were in a position to put their funds out at interest to a greater extent than banks. In May 1903 the New York City Clearing House began to require a 10 percent reserve for trust companies that wanted their checks cleared by a member bank. The trust companies gave up the clearing privilege rather than hold double the amount of reserves required by state law. Meanwhile, in 1903 commercial bankers opposed to trust companies organized the Bankers Trust Company, a fiduciary firm that would not compete with banks the same way existing trust companies did.

Trust companies chartered in the Civil War era had the authority to receive property of any kind for safekeeping. Safe deposit business was "a valuable adjunct to the business of a trust company," a 1910 manual of banking practice remarked.[11] The first corporation dedicated exclusively to this purpose was chartered in 1861 as the Safe Deposit Company of New York; it opened near Wall Street in 1865. Another eighteen corporations had received charters to serve New York City by 1901. In that year, the city had four independent safe deposit companies, and thirty-four affiliated with local trust companies and banks. National banks, prohibited from holding valuables for safekeeping by a comptroller's ruling in 1867, had to wait until 1927 for official authorization.

The number of trust companies more than tripled between 1900 and 1913, reaching over 1,800. Largely unhampered by legal restraints, their deposits (which paid interest on checking accounts) exceeded the total in state-chartered commercial banks. Their diversified activities, including investment banking, also contributed to their success. A Knickerbocker Trust Company brochure of 1901 explained that "the trust company of today, combining as it does every function of financial business, might well be called the department store of finance."[12]

Only states chartered corporations with trust powers until 1913. National banks would form alliances with trust companies. Under a gentleman's agreement, the Riggs National Bank in Washington, D.C., directed trust business to the nearby American Securities and Trust Company, while the latter sent commercial bank business to Riggs. The Philadelphia National Bank largely controlled the Philadelphia Trust, Safe Deposit, and Insurance Company. In 1891 the failure of the Spring Garden National Bank led to the closing of the associated Penn Safe Deposit and Trust Company in Philadelphia.

The Federal Reserve Act of 1913 authorized national banks to offer certain limited trust services for corporations. The Bankers Trust Company moved into commercial banking (1917). In September 1918 national banks could apply for a full range of trust activities. In 1935 the comptroller stopped reporting trust company statistics separately from bank statistics.

In 1913 locally owned, single-office banks studded the land; on average, there was one for every 3,600 Americans. Branching and holding company networks were still in their infancy. So prevalent and politically powerful had unit banking become that it retained its grip over the next half century.

8

Banks and the Means of Payment

Diffusion of banking facilities pro-
ceeded at an uneven pace in different parts of the country. The South
had 22,800 people per commercial bank in 1880, and 5,150 in 1909;
nationally the numbers were 8,500 and 4,250 respectively. The proportion of all money held by the public in the form of deposits soared from
55.5 percent in 1867 to 81.3 percent in 1900, and up to 88.2 percent in
1913, reflecting the spread of depository institutions.

☐ National Bank Notes

The 1863 law had the title "An Act to provide a National Currency,
secured by a Pledge of United States Stocks, and to provide for the
Circulation and Redemption thereof." Congress envisioned that, as
greenbacks were retired, national bank notes would become the sole
paper currency.

State bank notes, condemned by Secretary of the Treasury Salmon
P. Chase as "heterogeneous, unequal and unsafe," were still 85 percent
of all bank-issued currency in mid-1864. They disappeared from circulation once the punitive 10 percent annual tax took effect in mid-1866.
National bank notes exceeded $239 million in 1866 and climbed to $341
million by 1875, the high point until 1881. The $352 million of 1882
was not reached again until 1903. National banknotes were issued in

denominations as low as $1 and $2 until 1879, when $5 became the minimum.

Throughout the 1880s U.S. bonds sold above par, but national bank notes could be issued for only 90 percent of par. Government surpluses were used to retire bonds in the 1880s, raising their market price. Note issue became profitable once again as the premium declined in the early 1890s.

National bank notes outstanding between 1875 and 1900 were never more than 30 percent of the maximum amount permitted. In the South and West, where interest rates were higher than elsewhere, national banks issued almost no notes beyond the minimum based on required bond purchases. As rural interest rates declined, note issue became more worthwhile for these banks.

To encourage further increases, the 1900 Gold Standard Act authorized national bank notes for 100 percent of par value of bond collateral and allowed a bank to issue an amount equal to 100 percent of its capital—in both cases up from the previous 90 percent. National bank notes outstanding were only about 20 percent of the maximum allowed by law before 1890, 28 percent by 1900, but as much as 80 percent by 1914. Until 1905 the amount of capital stock of national banks constrained the volume of national bank notes outstanding; thereafter, it was the total of bonds eligible for the circulation privilege. By 1908 national bank notes in circulation were double the $300 million of 1900.

Per capita, national bank notes peaked at $8.22 in 1873, dropped to a low of $2.54 in 1891, then doubled by 1904; they were $7.36 in 1913. Alongside the $716 million of national bank notes in 1913 circulated $1 billion in gold certificates (receipts of Treasury-held gold), $469 million in silver certificates, and $337 million in greenbacks.

☐ Domestic and Foreign Exchange

National bank notes circulated at par. Remittances could therefore be made to any point in the United States at no more than the cost of transporting these notes, including insurance and forgone interest. Exchange between Chicago, St. Louis, or Cincinnati and New York City was frequently at par and rarely exceeded 80¢ per $1,000; before the Civil War the cost had been $10 or $15. Some $19.5 billion in domestic exchange was drawn, at a total cost of $11 million in 1890. At the 1859 rate of 1.9 percent, the expense would have been $195 million. In the early 1900s, 40¢ per $100 had become the usual shipping charge between New York and San Francisco. The reduced cost reflected improved transportation and communication, but the par feature of national bank notes was also important.

The money order business pioneered by the Post Office in 1864 and by American Express in 1882 troubled commercial banks in the interior in the 1890s and early 1900s. The American Bankers Association (ABA) developed a money order scheme handled by the American Surety Company that was used by almost 900 banks in 1909. American Express issued the first traveler's checks in 1891. National City Bank of New York began to offer its own checks in 1904. Other banks sold drafts on Bankers Trust Company in their own name under the auspices of the ABA.

Into the late nineteenth century foreign bills of exchange were sold mainly by institutions performing both mercantile and financial functions, continuing the antebellum pattern. Few national banks were in the foreign exchange business until around 1900. Some had "large and successful" foreign departments, the comptroller of the currency reported in 1904. National City Bank advertised in 1902 that it could pay out "any sum of money in any city of the world within 24 hours." Foreign bankers, however, financed most American imports and exports. "Though the status of the United States as one of the great powers in the political world is now universally recognized, . . . we have yet to secure recognition as an important factor in the financial world," the National Monetary Commission noted with dismay in 1912.

☐ Currency vs. Deposit Usage

In 1874 currency was used for at least half of the payments made in rural districts, but even in small cities the proportion in cash was no more than one-fourth. Payments in kind were still being made in many parts of the South and Southwest in the 1880s; western Iowa farmers used mostly currency and coin in the mid-1890s. In the nation as a whole (excluding New York City), almost 82 percent of total bank receipts were checks by 1881.

The "great lack of banking facilities in the sections which continually clamored for measures calculated to result in unsound currency" was noted by A. Barton Hepburn.[1] In smaller agricultural communities, national bank charters were unattractive, yet state banks could not issue bank notes. Rural America turned to greenbacks and later to silver as remedies. Congress refused to raise the $347 million limit on U.S. notes established in 1878, but it agreed to silver purchases that came to $500 million between 1878 and 1893. Per capita currency in 1900, at $15.65, was 22 percent above the 1870 average.

The return to gold convertibility of greenbacks in 1879 was widely (but mistakenly) expected to produce elasticity. Seasonal inadequacies were deplored for decades, but such inelasticity was inherent in the national bank note arrangement. To make matters worse, a bank that reduced its notes outstanding was prohibited from issuing more currency for another six months.

Charles Dunbar praised deposits as a type of currency that adapted itself "to the demand of the moment without visible effort." The farmer who distrusted checks or who lived far from a bank considered the Harvard economist's argument irrelevant. Currency was used to pay hired hands and local creditors, hence the farmer demanded currency for his crops. The fall harvest was a time of anxiety in the money market. The secretary of the Treasury noted in 1890 that "An amount of circulation which will be ample during ten months of the year, will frequently prove so deficient during the other two months as to cause stringency and commercial disaster. The crops of the country have reached proportions so immense that their movement to market, in August and September, annually causes a dangerous absorption of money. The lack of a sufficient supply to meet the increased demands during those months may entail heavy losses upon the agricultural as well as upon other business interests."[2]

Rural America increasingly resorted to checks as thousands of banks serving farmers opened after 1900. Nationally, the use of deposits as a vehicle of payment grew apace. Between 1867 and 1886 the proportion of currency to money balances held by the public dropped from 44 to 24 percent. In 1870 only $1.53 of adjusted commercial bank deposits existed for every dollar of currency held by the public. Comptroller Knox told the New York Chamber of Commerce in 1882 that "the use of coin and currency is almost nothing in proportion to the use of the modern instrument of checks which we find upon the remotest frontier." The deposit-currency ratio was 2.21:1 in 1882, twice that in 1900, and 7.19:1 in 1913. By 1909, 80 to 85 percent of the nation's business was conducted by check. At $68 per capita in 1900, commercial bank deposits were three and a half times the 1870 total, and over four times the amount of currency in circulation. Yet as late as 1909 defects in the note issue were the main topic of banking reform.

Misunderstanding of the monetary role of commercial bank deposits was by no means confined to the general public. Francis A. Walker's influential 1878 treatise on money limited the concept to specie, the (then inconvertible) greenback currency, and bank notes. Bank deposits, he insisted, economized on the use of money but did not serve the function of money—that is, "the final discharge of debts, full payment for commodities."[3] The Walker tradition dominated the period and appears, for example, in the 1914 edition of Joseph French Johnson's *Money and Currency*. Curiously, none other than Francis Walker's father had insisted in 1866 that deposits "discharge debts, purchase commodities, and perform all the functions of currency."[4]

☐ Checking Account Policies

By 1881 the business community's check usage was so extensive that over 90 percent of total receipts of banks were checks, drafts, and bills. Growing numbers of small checking accounts by 1910 reflected the "check habit" of the American people, as David Kinley called it.

Small-town banks had no minimum balance requirement. Some banks charged $2 a month to cover handling costs. By the early twentieth century, up-to-date banks in larger cities were increasingly analyzing the activity of deposit accounts for the purpose of gauging their profitability and requiring minimum balances.

At the 1884 ABA convention, representatives from a Kansas bank exhorted their fellow bankers not to render gratuitous services "such as making no charges for stationery or blanks, foreign exchange and collections, cashing drafts." Such appeals were in vain unless local banks agreed to cooperate. Buffalo appears to have been first, in 1881, to institute uniform collection charges. In 1899 the New York Clearing House established compulsory charges for out-of-town items. Some ninety-one cities had similar arrangements by 1912.

Under a system developed in 1899–1900 in Boston, the clearinghouse forwarded checks on the country banks of all the New England states to the drawing customer's bank for remittance at par (face value of the check). Checks drawn on the relatively few New England banks that refused to pay at par were subject to an exchange charge when a customer deposited those checks in a Boston bank. A number of major clearinghouses adopted the "Boston Plan" of par collection for banks in their area, including St. Louis, Kansas City, Detroit, Atlanta, and eventually New York.

To avoid paying a remittance charge to the bank on which the check had been drawn, banks developed elaborate check-routing arrangements. A check on a North Birmingham, Alabama bank deposited in a Birmingham bank four miles away traveled 4,500 miles over a fourteen-day period—from Birmingham to Jacksonville, Florida, to Philadelphia, back to Birmingham, and finally back to the North Birmingham bank. In this particular instance there were insufficient funds, so the check had to retrace the same route a second time.

☐ Interest-Bearing Deposits

Banks almost everywhere paid interest on deposits. The custom "has done more than any other to demoralize the business of banking," Comptroller of the Currency Knox stated in his *Annual Report* for 1873. A bank in good condition did not pay interest to depositors, the head of the Philadelphia National Bank admonished the 1884 convention of the American Bankers Association. "No genuine commercial bank should allow interest on deposits," H. Parker Willis, the leading banking professor of the age, insisted in 1917.[5] But the practice had become general in the post–Civil War era. Half of New York City's banks paid from 1 to 2 percent on out-of-town balances in 1886. In 1912, 2 percent was customary. The House Banking Committee was only the latest in an ancient line of critics when it denounced the "long standing evil which has drawn funds to places where they were not needed and away from those where they were" (1913).

As of mid-1909 deposits not bearing interest totaled only $1.1 billion. Interest was paid on $6.6 billion of nonsavings deposits and on $5.7 billion in commercial banks' savings accounts. Even the conservative Massachusetts Bank of Boston began to pay interest in 1907 on all accounts except active ones and those belonging to customers requiring accommodation. New York Superintendent of Banks Clark Williams (1907–1909) considered it his "clear duty to advocate throughout the State conservatism in the matter of the payment of interest."[6]

State reserve requirements for time deposits were generally lower than for demand deposits, but national banks had to hold identical reserves for both types. Some national banks therefore acquired a state-chartered savings affiliate. Thus, the First National Bank of Chicago sponsored the First Trust and Savings Bank, which was owned by the same shareholders. This "Chicago Plan," approved by the comptroller of the currency, was widely duplicated. By 1911 about half of all national banks offered savings accounts.

After the hardships suffered in connection with the failures that occurred during the panic of 1907, the idea of segregating savings deposits and requiring that these funds be invested more conservatively became more popular. New Hampshire had so legislated in 1891, as did

Michigan. Connecticut, Massachusetts, Rhode Island, California, and Texas also acted along these lines soon after the 1907 panic.

☐ Reserve Requirements and
Correspondent Banking

Deposit reserve requirements that were somewhat lower than those in effect just before the Civil War were among the 1864 amendments to the National Bank Act aimed at attracting state banks into the system. National banks in New York, as the central reserve city, had to carry a 25 percent reserve—just above the 23.8 percent actually held in 1860 but matching the standard that the New York Clearing House had adopted in 1860. In sixteen additional cities that also served as "redemption centers" for national bank notes (see Appendix), national banks could keep half of their 25 percent reserves in New York.[7] Other national banks ("country banks") had to hold 6 percent of their deposits as cash in vault; another 9 percent could be placed with national banks in the seventeen reserve cities. This 15 percent requirement was substantially below prevailing usage around 1859–60. Although the federal law did not call for greater reserves than had been customary, weak banks were forced to keep more than they had been accustomed to.

Well before the Civil War, bank reserves had been concentrated in New York. The National Bank Act recognized the city's position as the holder of underlying reserves of the banking system and reinforced it, making New York the sole central reserve city. Bankers' balances in New York increased over 250 percent in the ten years ending October 1870. Balances belonging to other banks kept in Wall Street banks rose from 13 percent of total assets in 1875 to 23 percent by 1895. First National Bank stood out, with 874 banks among its 1,076 accounts in July 1901.

After March 1887 the reserve classification in a populous city could be changed upon request of 75 percent of its national banks. Chicago and St. Louis quickly opted to become central reserve cities. By 1914 Chicago had $205 million in interbank balances, almost six times its 1887 total; St. Louis, with $66 million, had twelve times as much, but New York's $423 million was only thrice the 1887 total. In addition to the three central reserve cities, by 1914 there were forty-six reserve cities (see Appendix). Even so, a small number of national banks carried the bulk of bankers' balances. New York City remained "the clearing-house of the country," in O. M. W. Sprague's phrase. The "concentration of surplus money and available funds" in New York City was cited by the National Monetary Commission in 1912 as a major defect in the banking system.

The seven largest banks in New York City in 1890 made 26 percent of all loans by national and state banks there; by 1910 the top six made 46 percent of all loans. Here was grist for the mill of critics who discerned a "money trust."[8]

Payment of interest on bankers' balances was sometimes offered as an explanation for their concentration in New York City. Actually, in 1873 and in 1886 only about half of the banks paid interest. Others offered various free services, such as collection of out-of-town items. By 1891 most New York banks were paying interest; twenty years later Chemical Bank was the sole holdout. For that matter, banks outside New York also paid interest on deposits. What attracted funds to Wall Street banks was the financial preeminence of the great oceanbound metropolis.

Even when not required by law, banks held balances in major centers. The Pima County Bank in Tucson had accounts in San Francisco, St. Louis, Baltimore, and New York soon after it opened. Such balances facilitated the transfer of funds. The effectiveness of correspondent banking arrangements helps to explain why there was no strong branch banking sentiment in the post–Civil War era. Country banks developed "a feudal dependence" on large city institutions for counsel and assistance in the half-century before 1913.[9]

A bank could call on its correspondent for interbank loans, especially to meet seasonal needs, or in times of difficulties. Most borrowing took the form of notes payable by the bank, but because of public opinion and certain criticisms from the comptroller, it sometimes took the guise of loans to bank directors and officers, or sales of securities that were subsequently repurchased. From 1869 through 1882 interbank borrowing averaged below $9 million on any given day, rising to about $16 million from 1883 through 1892, and to $38 million from 1893 through 1914. Such loans increased available funds in a locality but not to any great extent. Loans from outside the region were 11 percent in the South, around 15 percent in the Pacific and Western states, and under 5 percent of the total in New England and other Eastern states, according to an 1898 estimate.[10]

In the early years, national banks held reserves considerably in excess of the legal requirements. By 1873, however, the fifteen smaller redemption cities were only two percentage points above the minimum. In New York the average reserve was near the minimum by 1883. Before 1900 national banks carried greater excess reserves than in later years, a course dictated by fear of panics and the unavailability of outside resources. As long as a national bank was deficient in reserves, it could not make new loans or dividend payments. Around 1900 the level and volatility of excess reserves declined. The Treasury tried to assist the banking system during periods of monetary stringency in the early 1900s.

Cash components of the legal reserve for national banks were rather inelastic in supply. Increases in urban bank reserves made necessary by calls from rural banks were mainly met by importing gold from abroad.

The National Bank Act requirement of reserves against deposits derived from antebellum laws of certain states. In turn, later state enactments drew on the 1864 amended federal law. By 1913 all but Illinois, Indiana, Maryland, Mississippi, South Carolina, and Virginia had reserve requirements, with Illinois the sole holdout to this day. Starting with Nebraska in 1889, six states called for a higher reserve against bankers' balances than for other deposits because of their greater instability. Under a distinction first made by New Hampshire in 1874 and followed in ten other states by 1911, time deposit reserve requirements (commonly 5 percent, as in the 1913 Federal Reserve Act) were made lower than for demand deposits.

As banks became more numerous, checks were used in ever rising volume as a means of payment. The public, however, was slow to recognize the shrinking relative importance of currency; its adequacy was a divisive political issue throughout most of the 1863–1913 period.

9

Bank Loans and Investments

□ Short-Term Commercial Loans: Theory and Practice

Proper banks made only short-term self-liquidating loans. As Comptroller of the Currency Knox affirmed (1875): "A bank is in good condition just in proportion as its business is conducted upon short credits, with its assets so held as to be available on brief notice." The funds to repay a commercial loan would be obtained before it matured in the course of producing and marketing goods, explained the American Institute of Banking's 1916 textbook. Important American financial writers in the pre-1914 era urged banks to confine loans to meeting the short-term needs of business and genuine commercial purposes. Such a policy was believed to avoid the dangers of speculative overtrading and overissue, while adjusting bank credit automatically. Banks were also called on to shun long-term real estate or fixed capital loans, as well as bond investments.[1] Banks departed more or less frequently from these principles, however. Comptroller A. Barton Hepburn's claim that "national banks do a purely commercial business" was more accurate as a description of the 1863 act's conception than of the reality of 1892. In 1904 "the larger portion of national banking business" was still related to discounting mercantile paper.[2] State-chartered and private commercial banks were likely to stray even farther from this ideal.

Around 1900 about half of the earning assets of commercial banks consisted of business loans mainly to small and medium-sized firms in manufacturing and trade on a short-term basis, financing working capital. Average maturity was sixty days, but renewals were frequent. Under the customary annual "clean-up," outstanding debt to a given bank was paid up for a time, often by borrowing elsewhere. Long-term business credits (essentially in the form of corporate bond holdings) were no more than one-fifth of the amount of short-term loans.

The "commercial credit" to which commercial banks supposedly were restricted was, however, a misnomer. Especially in smaller localities, many commercial banks made long-term loans to agriculture and industry. Bank credit was also a vehicle of permanent financing of corporations in the large cities. It is estimated that around 1914 only one-third of all bank loans represented commercial transactions. About half of all loans were for investment purposes; two-thirds of commercial bank credit went for fixed rather than working capital. Unsecured "commercial loans" did not in fact always represent "genuine commercial operations."[3] Banks began to look at the excess of customers' current assets over current liabilities, rather than at specific and actually completed business transactions, as the assurance for loan repayment.

Already before the Civil War, borrowers kept "compensating balances" with the bank from which they expected loan accommodations. The requirement spread afterwards as unsecured single-name paper became the basis for loans, bank operating expenses increased, and some bank customers resorted to open-market borrowing. The more conservative banks limited their lending as much as possible to customers with a continuing deposit relationship.

☐ Loan Limits by Law

National banks were not allowed to make unsecured loans to any one borrower in an amount exceeding 10 percent of the bank's capital. The purpose was to avoid monopolization of the bank's credit by a small group. In practice, about half the national banks (not always the same ones) violated the statute. Conscientious Quaker directors of a national bank in Pennsylvania qualified their affirmation to obey the law by adding, "except as to the limit of loans."[4]

State banks had higher (or no) lending limits. In 1906 Congress set the limit at 10 percent of capital plus surplus accounts. As of 1912, only thirteen national banks could lend as much as $1 million to a single party. After the law was amended, Comptroller of the Currency William Ridgely was prepared to revoke the charter of any duly warned bank that violated the law. The next comptroller, Lawrence Murray (1908–13), criticized only those banks whose excessive loans were considered unsafe or inadequately secured. By September 1909 some 15 percent of all national banks reported excessive loans. The Philadelphia National Bank accommodated the Pennsylvania Railroad by buying $1 million of its bonds with the understanding that the company would repurchase them on call or by a specific date.

☐ Credit Departments and Practices

As business became more complex, bank directors no longer had first-hand knowledge of all borrowers. Larger banks began to perceive the need for credit departments. Mercantile credit reporting agencies such as Dun and Bradstreet antedated the Civil War, but banks found that their information was too limited and unspecific for purposes of deciding on loan applications. Around 1883 the Importers' and Traders' National Bank of New York City organized one of the earliest credit departments, to investigate firms whose open market commercial paper it was considering for purchase. In 1892 there were said to be only six credit departments in the entire country, and barely ten by 1899 when the American Bankers Association convention voted to set up a model credit department in the secretary's office and to provide banks with technical information. Vice President James Cannon of the Fourth National Bank in New York City (a pioneer in the field) promoted the idea vigorously. Most major banks had a functioning credit department by 1911.

Traditionalists who kept credit files under their hats resisted these developments. In the early 1900s, when the First National Bank of Pittsburgh president (whose career had begun in 1852) discovered John Rovensky in the act of checking credits, he admonished him: "Johnny, don't you understand that these . . . are OUR customers; WE know them—other people may ask about them, but under no circumstance ought we to ask anybody about OUR OWN customers. Never do that again."[5]

Endorsements or guarantees for the notes of borrowers continued to be required; gradually, customers came to be considered on their individual merits. Banks extended a line of credit on the basis of the balance sheet submitted with the loan request. Financial statements, first used in the late 1870s, did not become common even in larger banks for another twenty years. In 1895 the New York State Bankers Association executive committee recommended that signed written statements of borrowers' assets and liabiltiies be obtained. In 1899 the ABA adopted a uniform property statement form. Financial statements came to be required in the recovery years after the panic of 1893, but thirty years later there were still persons who viewed the request for a statement to be a bad reflection on the borrower's credit standing.

☐ Loans to Agriculture

Rural unrest in the 1880s was partly related to the dearth of credit facilities to tide the Western farmer over the interval between planting and harvesting. Especially in frontier regions, farmers had to rely mainly on merchants, implement dealers, and commission men. In Lidgerwood, North Dakota, Emil Movius operated a farm implement business, general store, furniture store, lumberyard, and flour mill—all mainly on a cash basis. In the early 1890s he organized a state bank where customers could obtain financing. Loans were secured by chattel mortgages on horses, crops, and machinery, or by a real estate mortgage on land. Kinsley, Kansas, with two banks already in the 1870s, added a third in 1887. Its banks made some second mortgage loans but before 1900 were mainly interested in short-term loans on chattel or personal security.

Such loans, frequently renewed, were also made by national banks, which were prohibited by law from making real estate loans before 1913. The National Bank of Newberry, South Carolina, lent mostly to farmers on personal security or collateral, not on crop liens. National banks also circumvented the law by establishing loan offices that made long-term funds available.

Agricultural credit, particularly nonmortgage credit, was obtained mainly from local sources. Outside lenders, such as mortgage companies or individual investors, paid banks a fee for their services as agents. By 1914 short-term agricultural loans reached $1.6 billion, about 15 percent of all commercial banks' non–real estate loans. Nevertheless, farmers remained dissatisfied with the amount and terms of credit available to them.

☐ Real Estate Loans

The National Bank Act of 1863 forbade loans on real estate. So did state law in the Dakotas until the 1890s, in Oklahoma until 1905, and in Ohio until 1908. Various financial experts opposed long-term commitment of funds on the part of institutions with liabilities payable on demand. In practice, banks found it impossible to stay away from such commitments altogether. National banks, faced with competition from state-chartered banks, used indirect methods, with the complicity of the comptroller of the currency, to evade the ban. Sometimes a mortgage and trust company that shared the premises and management of the national bank was organized. Farmers were hostile because national banks were not allowed to lend on real estate securities. They were not placated by Comptroller William Trenholm's explanation that national banks were "exclusively devoted to the collection, the safekeeping and the employment in temporary loans of the floating capital of the country." The ban on real estate lending restricted the ability of national banks to serve "farmers and other borrowers in rural communities," the National Monetary Commission recognized in 1912.

Banks held almost $700 million of the $4.7 billion in farm mortgages outstanding at the end of 1913. In the 1910–14 period banks financed around 17–18 percent of farm mortgages. Nonfarm residential mortgages comprised about 4.5 percent of total commercial bank assets from 1900 to 1910. In 1900, 6.6 percent of new mortgages were placed with banks, and in 1912, 11.9 percent. This was the largest relative increase for any loan category. By 1913 commercial banks owned over 9 percent of total nonfarm residential mortgages outstanding.

□ Call Loans

Call loans, payable on demand, with stock exchange securities as collateral, grew rapidly after 1863. The First National Bank of New York decided in November 1864 to confine lending to loans secured by U.S. government bonds, except for loans to correspondent banks secured by bills receivable. By 1873, however, the bank was lending on railroad securities, too.

Call loans were about one-third of total loans of national banks in New York City in the 1870s, and almost half in the 1880s and 1890s. By 1913 the percentage fell back to one-third. Until 1904–13 (when security prices were in a downtrend), an amount just about equal to all deposits placed by correspondent banks with New York national banks (after the required reserve was set aside) went into the call loan market. Normally between 2.5 percent and 6 percent per annum, call loan rates soared in periods of stringency. As a rule, collateral had to be worth 20–30 percent more than the loan. Call loans were also made by certain investment banks, as well as by commercial banks outside New York City, the latter usually through their New York City correspondents.

Time loans with a fixed maturity, collateralized by negotiable corporate securities quoted on the stock exchange were also made by New York banks. From 1899 to 1906 about 60 percent of loans by New York national banks were thus secured.

□ Commercial Paper

Long-term credit evidenced by a signed note was the rule before the Civil War in the sale of goods by the manufacturer to the wholesaler, and by the latter to the retailer. This arrangement was replaced by discounts for immediate cash settlement as the war proceeded; a thirty-day limit on accounts receivable became widespread. The trade acceptance, already waning before 1861, lost further ground, shrinking to negligible amounts by 1900. Concomitantly, the commercial paper market—dealing in the unsecured promises to pay of well-known, sizable firms—developed more rapidly in the United States than elsewhere. In some of the larger cities of the South and Midwest, banks had begun to place surplus funds in the commercial paper market by 1860, but most of the paper continued to be held by banks in New England and the Middle Atlantic states in 1876. During the next twenty-five years the practice spread rapidly, except in the capital-poor South.

By 1900, in virtually every larger city, some banks had begun to buy commercial paper from dealers. Small country banks in the Midwest were also discovering this investment medium around 1900, and somewhat later in the South and far West. Favorable experience during the 1907 panic encouraged more banks to hold commercial paper. By 1913 all large cities had offices of commercial paper dealers or their representatives, which sold short-term obligations of 2,500 to 3,000 substantial firms.

Call loans made in the open market and commercial paper were two assets that banks acquired in the interest of diversification and liquidity. To round out their portfolios, they invested increasingly in securities issued by governments and the corporate sector.

□ Security Investments

After 1874 national banks with over $150,000 in capital could have as little as $50,000 in U.S. bonds; smaller banks were authorized in 1882 to have minimum bond holdings amounting to only one-fourth of their capital. Compulsory purchases of U.S. bonds by national banks finally ended in 1913. National bank holdings (mainly for note issue, but some as security for public deposits) dropped by more than half from 1873 to 1893. But commercial (mainly national) banks owned over half of the $1 billion of the outstanding interest-bearing federal debt in 1900, and 77 percent of the 1913 total. U.S. bonds constituted 5.2 percent of all commercial bank assets in 1900, but only 3.5 percent in 1913.

As borrowings of large corporations and state and local governments grew, bank holdings of their bonds increased dramatically. Securities other than those of the U.S. Treasury were 1 percent of total national bank assets in the 1860s, 4 percent around 1890, 8 percent by 1903, and over 9 percent a decade later. For all commercial banks, the ratio of nonfederal bonds to total assets was 12 percent in 1903 and 13 percent in 1913. Bonds were bought for current income in anticipation of capital gains, or sometimes in the hope of attracting the business of the issuing firms and government units. They were not considered liquid assets for seasonal or cyclical purposes.

Obligations of state and local governments, while only about 2 percent of the assets of all commercial banks, were some 10 percent of the total amount outstanding in the early 1900s. Banks owned over 13 percent of the larger and even more rapidly growing category of corporate bonds. These amounted to 6.7 percent of total commercial bank assets in 1900, and 9.3 percent by 1912. About half the corporate bonds were issues of railroads and other public service corporations. Perhaps one-fourth of railroad bond issues between 1860 and 1914 were bought by commercial banks. In 1914 security investments totaled 16.7 percent of bank assets.

☐   Investment Banking Functions

In order to obtain bonds at favorable prices, commercial banks became partners in underwriting syndicates. Acquisition of securities for the bank's own portfolio led to purchases on behalf of customers (particularly correspondent banks) and, in a few cases, to the development of a full range of investment banking activities.

The First National Bank of New York, a large-scale seller of U.S. bonds from its inception in 1863, remained active in securities after the Civil War. Under George F. Baker's leadership, the bank was allied with J. P. Morgan's operations, as was National City Bank under James Stillman. Several Chicago banks carried out investment banking functions. By 1891 the First National Bank of Chicago took an entire $1,276,000 issue of that city's bonds.

National banks were forbidden to act as full-range investment banks, the comptroller of the currency ruled in 1902. The First National Bank of Chicago's "well-organized and profitable" bond department found itself unable to deal in bonds secured by mortgages on real estate.[6] James Forgan organized a security affiliate in 1903, the First Trust and Savings Bank, a state bank owned by the identical shareholders. Two major New York City banks emulated the "Chicago Plan." The First National Bank of New York formed the First Securities Company in 1908 in response to criticism by the comptroller for holding $5 million in equities (mostly railroads). At National City Bank, Frank Vanderlip developed a general bond business and saw an opportunity in the investment market. James Stillman did not interfere, even when his cronies in the private banking houses began to protest. National City Corporation, organized in 1911, became the leading investment bank in the country in less than eighteen years.

Philadelphia banks participated in bond underwriting syndicates after 1900. To stimulate their patronage, they opened accounts with private Wall Street banks. Such ties strengthened J. P. Morgan's influence over finance and industry.

By the early 1900s the bond departments of certain major commercial banks were offering traditional investment banking services. Private banks engaged in investment banking also accepted deposits on which they paid interest; depositors were usually corporations, rather than individuals. J. P. Morgan had $160 million in deposits in 1912, about ten times the deposits of his main rival, Kuhn, Loeb and Company. Morgan also made short-term commercial loans, rarely for over $500,000, and financed foreign trade. The lines separating commercial and investment banking were becoming less distinct.

The retired first Comptroller of the Currency McCulloch reminded the American Bankers Association in October 1876 that "as banks are commercial institutions, created for commercial purposes, preference in discount should always be given to paper based upon actual commercial transactions. . . . It is no part of their business to furnish their customers with capital, nor should loans be made under any circumstances for operations in stocks, or to furnish facilities for stock operations." In practice, banks found it difficult to limit their lending activities so narrowly. They might have recalled McCulloch's advice in the aftermath of panic and failure.

10

Bank Failure
and Panic

☐ Bank Failure

The national banks' failure rate—6.5 percent from 1863 through 1896—
was low compared with the 17.6 percent of non-national banks. Creditors
of national banks recouped 75 percent of what was owed them; state
banks repaid only 45 percent. From 1891 to 1913, 367 national banks
failed, with liabilities of $182 million, and 1,702 non-national banks
failed, with over $622 million in liabilities. The fifty-year record through
the end of 1913 among the 10,472 chartered national banks was 538
failures; nineteen of these were subsequently restored to solvency. Dunbar's assessment of the system's first quarter-century applied as well to
the next: "It carried note issue and deposit banking side-by-side throughout the greater part of the country, under the management of a class of
remarkably sound institutions, giving to the community many of the
benefits of free banking with the minimum of its risks."[1]

Bank suspension before 1866 meant that a state bank was unable or
unwilling to redeem its circulating notes in specie; bank notes might
still circulate, but at a discount. National bank notes circulated at par,
regardless of the issuing bank's condition. After 1866 suspension involved a bank's inability to provide depositors with desired cash on
demand. There were panics in 1873, 1884, 1890, 1893, 1895, 1907, and
1914. Convertibility of deposits was suspended, except in 1884 (a panic
limited to New York) and 1895. During the 1893 depression, for exam-

ple, banks were forced to close en masse because of their inability to satisfy frightened depositors, except at ruinous sacrifice of assets. The comptroller distinguished between insolvent banks (turned over for liquidation) and illiquid banks temporarily closed but capable of resuming and paying creditors in full.

The comptroller's review of failures from 1865 through 1911 found that relatively few—13 percent—were the result of adverse business conditions. Fraudulent management and other criminal violations of the law accounted for over 36 percent. Loans in excess of the legal limit were found in 20 percent of the cases, while "injudicious banking" was the cause of 23 percent of national bank failures.

☐ Interbank Cooperation and Association

Specific internal weaknesses were often the cause of a bank's downfall, but a panic might undermine even well-managed institutions. To avoid this, bankers arranged to cooperate through the clearinghouse. In 1863 there were a total of six, with Cleveland's the only one west of the Alleghenies. Chicago (1865), St. Louis (1868), and San Francisco (1876) joined the growing numbers—twenty-four in 1883 and fifty-one by 1890. There were 162 clearinghouses in the United States in 1913, and two hundred thirty-three just three years later.

Beyond the original function of check settlements, some arranged to limit competition. For deposit safety, they set minimum reserves that sometimes were above the requirement for national banks. In panics, they undertook joint action.

The clearinghouse loan certificate, invented by George Coe, was used for the first time in November 1860. Banks needing aid deposited bonds and bills receivable with the New York Clearing House Association, as collateral for loans of up to 75 percent of their face value. The large-denomination certificates received in exchange were a joint liability of the clearinghouse banks and could be used in local settlements or balances due. There were three issues of certificates in New York in the course of the Civil War. Again in 1873, New York resorted to loan certificates, as did Philadelphia (already a user in 1861), Boston, Baltimore, Cincinnati, St. Louis, and New Orleans.

In 1893, $100 million of clearinghouse loan certificates were issued, including small amounts in such places as Buffalo, Pittsburgh, Detroit, Atlanta, and Richmond—but not in Chicago, where banks voted against their use, just as they had in 1873. Comptroller James Eckels welcomed the "invaluable" service rendered by the clearinghouses in the summer of 1893 because their efforts kept down the number of failures. Until 1893 loan certificates were exclusively large-denomination and were for members to use in settling debit balances at the clearinghouse. In 1893 the Atlanta clearinghouse issued the first small-denomination *circulating* loan certificate. Some $100 million of temporary extralegal currency appeared under nongovernmental auspices in 1893, representing a temporary 2.5 percent increase in the money stock.

Clearinghouse loan certificates were issued in various places in 1873, 1884, 1890, 1893, 1904, and 1907. In the panic of 1895 they were authorized but not issued in New York City. Only one instance of loss is recorded: Spring Garden National Bank did not repay the $170,000 issued by the Philadelphia clearinghouse in 1890.

In addition to lending to members during a panic, a clearinghouse might come to the aid of a particular bank in ordinary times. Baltimore's clearinghouse assisted the American National Bank twice in a twelve-month period (1899–1900), and St. Louis's aided the Missouri Lincoln Trust Company in September 1907. From time to time, clearinghouse members would come to the rescue of a failed bank's depositors to prevent a general loss of confidence locally. When three Chicago banks under common control failed at the end of 1905, James Forgan persuaded the clearinghouse to assume the losses. Chicago thereupon pioneered a clearinghouse examination of member banks, establishing a special bureau for the purpose. By 1913 nineteen other clearinghouses had followed suit at the urging of Comptroller of the Currency Murray.

□   Other Bankers' Trade Associations

Clearinghouses were organizations of local banks. Bankers were also active on the national and state levels. In 1876 a permanent national organization was formed (three years ahead of the British). Bankers met in October at the Philadelphia Centennial Exhibition; at a convention the year before in Saratoga Springs, New York, they had established the American Bankers Association. The American Institute of Banking (as it was renamed in 1907) was organized in March 1901 with the ABA's encouragement to further the training of bank employees. In October 1934 the ABA approved a graduate school of banking, which met for years on the campus of Rutgers University and more recently at the University of Delaware.

In 1884 the Bankers Association of the Dakota Territory was organized. In July 1885 the Texas Bankers Association was formed. Thirty years later, Rhode Island completed the roster of associations for the forty-eight contiguous states.[2] Alaska's was formed in 1949, and Hawaii's in 1961.

☐ Panics in the National Bank Era

Country national banks kept reserves in larger cities. Each fall rural communities demanded currency to move crops. As city banks reduced their call loans, interest rates would rise in the money market. "The system has produced disturbance and stringency every autumn for forty years, and panic after panic," the comptroller of the currency noted in connection with the events of 1907. All four deep depressions in the years between the Civil War and World War I (1873, 1884, 1893, 1907) accompanied a panic. Only the 1890 panic was not the prelude to a severe downturn in business.

Panic was associated with seven of the eleven business cycle contractions between 1863 and 1913. Exceptions were the economic declines of 1887–88, 1899–1900, 1902–1904, and 1910–12.

☐ The Panic of 1907

The panic of 1907 came as a great shock to American bankers. The 1907 economic downturn was worldwide, but imperfections in the banking system made it particularly acute in the United States; real net national product suffered an 11 percent decline between 1907 and 1909.

A run on the Knickerbocker Trust Company, the third largest trust company in New York City, on 22 October 1907, was followed the next day by a run on the second largest trust company. Secretary of the Treasury George Cortelyou quickly deposited $36 million in New York national banks. He did little beyond insisting that the private financial interests act in unison. Prominent Wall Street figures, led by the 70-year-old Morgan, met until the early hours of the morning in the library of his palatial Renaissance home in late October 1907.

Just as the situation in New York City was calming down, country banks made large demands on their reserve correspondents for currency. New York banks restricted the convertibility of deposits into currency on 26 October, and the clearinghouse began to issue loan certificates. In two-thirds of the cities with a population exceeding 25,000, banks restricted cash payments.

Over the years the banking system had become more vulnerable to shifts in the public's preference for cash. By 1907 for every dollar in currency there were $6 in deposits, compared with $2 in 1879. The ratio of deposits to vault cash in 1907 was double the 4.4:1 of 1879. The great rise in these ratios made banks increasingly sensitive to possible runs and quick to seek additional cash as a precaution. Conditions leading to the panic "were not due to the lack of confidence of the people in the banks, but more to a lack of confidence of the banks in themselves and their reserves," the comptroller of the currency noted at the time.

A contemporary economist, Wesley C. Mitchell, agreed that the payment restrictions and the consequent premium on currency were due more to "timidity in using bank reserves" than to their actual inadequacy. Had the New York banks tried to meet all demands in full, he surmised in 1913, the great scramble for cash probably would not have developed, and banks in smaller cities would have been in a position to avoid restriction. Mitchell criticized national banks for having made "a fetish of the reserve requirements. . . . Just at the moment of hesitation when timidity . . . spreads fear among businessmen and when boldness inspires confidence, the banks have been timid."[3]

Suspensions in 1907 ran to 1.22 percent of total commercial bank deposits (three to six times as great as in 1900–1906) and dropped back to 0.65 percent in 1908. Losses to depositors were 18¢ per $100 in 1907 (more than three times the amount of losses experienced earlier in the century), and 14¢ per $100 in 1908.

Restrictions on currency payments did enable many illiquid banks to survive. Once restrictions were in effect, however, the public distrust of banks was reflected in an 11 percent rise in currency holdings between September 1907 and February 1908 while deposits were declining by 8 percent. In early November 1907 currency rose to as much as a 4 percent premium over checks and remained above 1 percent until mid-December. The premium vanished by year-end. Early in 1908 the danger of further runs appeared to be over and restrictions on cash payment were eliminated.

In late 1907 the United States suffered "the most complete interruption of its banking facilities" since the Civil War, O. M. W. Sprague noted.[4] A record number of clearinghouses—some sixty—in every major city except Washington, D.C., resorted to the issue of some $256 million in loan certificates, which was two and a half times the 1893 volume.

Over twenty clearinghouses also sponsored small-denomination certificates, temporarily expanding the money stock by 4.5 percent. These "clearinghouse checks," endorsed by all the member banks, were sometimes as low as $1. Harrisburg, Pennsylvania's clearinghouse certificates of indebtedness carried the legend, "This check may be deposited but will not be paid in cash," translated into Polish, Hungarian, and Italian. New York's clearinghouse refused to issue "checks," fearing that they would circulate far from home. Major firms filled the gap by issuing printed payroll checks, usually in $5 denominations. Standard Oil's, drawn on the National City Bank, enjoyed a considerable circulation. Altogether, the public used over $250 million of these extralegal currency substitutes in 1907.[5]

The Aldrich-Vreeland Act of 30 May 1908 was a product of the recent financial debacle. National currency associations, each comprising at least ten national banks, were authorized to issue emergency notes. The notes circulated subject to a tax that escalated for every month they were outstanding. Conceived as a stopgap measure, the authority was extended until mid-1915.

The 1914 war crisis was the tenth occasion for the New York Clearing House to appoint a loan committee. Altogether, from 1860 through 1914, New York had issued $394 million in clearinghouse loan certificates.

New York State, which had raised trust company reserve requirements in 1906, raised them further following several unfortunate experiences during the panic of 1907. Under the 1908 law, trust companies had to keep 15 percent cash in their vaults—but only on demand deposits. In 1911 the New York Clearing House voted to admit to regular membership trust companies willing to keep an additional 10 percent in balances with clearinghouse banks. Most larger trust companies joined, ending decades of conflict with the traditional commercial banks. In Philadelphia, too, seven major trust companies joined the clearinghouse as full members in 1911.

The Los Angeles clearinghouse forced consolidation and liquidation, reducing the number of banks to around twenty. Such actions, and friendly cooperation, helped, but private efforts to protect the country's banks against panics were inadequate, as the comptroller of the currency insisted in 1907:

> If the experience of the country in the bank panics from 1857 to 1893 needed any further confirmation, the panic of 1907 has demonstrated beyond the possibility of denial that perfectly solvent banks—if independent, isolated units with no power of cooperation except through such voluntary association as their clearing houses—cannot protect themselves in a panic and save themselves from failure without such a suspension of payments as to produce disorder and demoralization in all the business of their customers.[6]

The studies and final report of the National Monetary Commission—established under the 1908 Aldrich-Vreeland Act—provided the materials for the debate that led to the Federal Reserve

Act of 1913. In addition to the Aldrich-Vreeland Act, Congress inaugurated the Postal Savings System, which opened for business 3 January 1911. Congress ignored calls for deposit insurance at this time, but eight states responded.[7] In December 1907 Oklahoma was the first to put a guarantee in effect. Early in 1909, Kansas, Nebraska, and Texas acted. Mississippi (1914), South Dakota (1915), North Dakota (1917), and Washington (1917) also instituted deposit guaranty plans. Only Kansas and Washington did not compel state banks to join. The comptroller forbade national banks to participate.

The president of the Kansas Bankers Association proved prophetic when he denounced the state law as "a mere bubble that will be punctured by the first ill will that blows."[8] The Kansas program, as well as all the other state schemes, succumbed to the heavy losses in rural banks. Oklahoma's plan was the first to go under in 1923, and Mississippi and Nebraska were the last, in March 1930.

11

Banking, Government, and the Economy

☐ Supervision

The Office of the Comptroller of the Currency instituted the policy of examining each national bank annually. Most states, however, subjected their banks to "very little interference and scarcely any espionage on the part of officials," the comptroller pointed out in 1884. New York did not examine its banks annually until 1884. By then only Indiana, Minnesota, and California had joined the five pioneering New England states (all except Rhode Island) in the practice of official "espionage." By the time of the comptroller's next survey in 1895, twenty-one more states had instituted regular examinations, and another fourteen did so between 1897 and 1908. Between 1912 and 1914, Arkansas, Kentucky, Mississippi, and Tennessee became the last four of the forty-eight contiguous states to introduce examinations.

Only fifteen states had distinct banking departments in 1895. An official with other functions (e.g., secretary of state, treasurer) had responsibility for supervising banks in twenty-one states. In 1902 the National Association of Supervisors of State Banks was founded "to promote the efficiency and effectiveness of the state banking system and state supervision." By 1913 there were twenty-nine state banking departments. The last of the forty-eight states to establish a specific agency for bank regulation was North Carolina in 1931.

Examination by public officials promoted public confidence in banks. For this reason the Wisconsin Bankers Association asked the state to assume this function in 1894. The Farmers and Merchants Bank of Los Angeles converted from being a state bank to a national bank in 1903, explaining that "a national bank is afforded government inspection."[1]

Already in 1865 the comptroller was writing to banks and requesting the correction of weaknesses revealed by the examiners. Comptroller Knox proudly contrasted "the excellent system now in operation" (1878) with the "generally lax system of bank supervision" found in the states before 1863. In 1884 the role of supervision was extended to include elimination of management difficulties at an early stage. By studying the causes of bank failures, Comptroller Henry W. Cannon suggested that national bank examiners use "such methods of examination as seemed to be best calculated to prevent repetition of such disasters, and to expose violations of law which led to the same." At the same time Cannon admonished national bank shareholders to "be more careful to elect men as directors and trustees who are competent and who will exercise proper care and supervision over the management of the affairs intrusted to them, who will select competent and honest officers, provide suitable rules and regulations for the conduct of the bank . . . and appoint regular committees of examination . . . not only to verify the accounts, but to keep a watchful eye over the association and the officers."[2] In short, owners and managers remained primarily responsible for a bank's soundness.

National bank examiners received a fee based on the bank's capital for each examination. This system encouraged superficiality. After over twenty years' experience in national banks, an Ironton, Ohio, banker told the American Bankers Association convention in 1887, "I found Examiners to be gentlemen of high character, yet they have one great fault. They are too fast." In the 1903 story "Friends in San Rosario," O. Henry called them "Uncle Sam's grayhounds." Many bankers complained to Comptroller Murray that "the first question that an examiner asked was what time the next train left town." Examiners economized on travel expenses by visiting banks along a regular route, thereby eliminating the element of surprise, so essential to a meaningful bank examination.

Political influence was "almost controlling" national bank examiner appointments, the head of the First National Bank of Chicago complained to the National Monetary Commission in 1908. In the state banking departments the problem was even more acute. Comptroller Murray admitted before the commission that "the supervision we have been able to give banks under the law as it stands has been ineffectual and inefficient and disastrous."[3] He proceeded to remove incompetents, rotate examiners, and insist on thoroughness.

The "more effective supervision of banking in the United States" was one of the purposes specified in the Federal Reserve Act of 1913. Examiners were placed on a salary basis, as all examining states, except Delaware and Illinois, had already done by 1910. A career system was established and the field force organized under twelve chief national bank examiners, who exchanged ideas that they passed along to the men under their jurisdiction. This contributed to a greater uniformity in procedures and practices throughout the nation. The act also made national banks subject to examination twice a year, which New York had been doing since 1905.

□ Federal Statutory Restraints

Under the free banking system of the United States, "any persons, however unfamiliar with [banking] principles, who [had] the necessary capital," could enter the business, as the report of the Monetary Commission of the Indianapolis Convention of Boards of Trade pointedly remarked in 1898. The National Bank Act, however, incorporated a number of safeguards. Among them were bans on lending on real estate, on lending in excess of 10 percent of the bank's capital to any one borrower, on investing in stocks, on allowing reserves against deposits to fall below the prescribed minimum, and on borrowing in excess of the bank's capital stock. In one way or another, however, one-third of all national banks managed to violate provisions of the law, Deputy Comptroller of the Currency Thomas P. Kane estimated. More than 25 percent were deficient in reserves, over 17 percent of national banks lent on real estate, and over 10 percent made loans in amounts over the legal limit to any one borrower.

□ The Federal Treasury and the Banks

The federal government's relationship with commercial banks went beyond examination and regulation. National banks were eligible to serve as internal revenue depositories. Tariff receipts, the bulk of federal revenues, continued to be held in the subtreasuries located in major port cities (see Appendix).

After the Civil War successive treasury secretaries viewed the deposit of public moneys in national banks as something to be done only in emergencies. Deposits were generally around $10 million in the

1870s (except during the 1879 bond refunding), and only somewhat higher in the early 1880s. Faced with surplus revenues that could not be used to retire Treasury bonds, Secretary Charles Fairchild made deposits that amounted to $54 million by 1888.

The Treasury came to the aid of the banks during several nineteenth-century crises. In the early 1870s bond purchases were concentrated to relieve autumnal currency difficulties associated with the movement of the crops. In the early 1900s Secretary Leslie Shaw enlarged the Treasury's role to anticipating and eliminating recurring autumnal stringencies even in ordinary times. Congress gave statutory recognition to his actions in 1907 by empowering the secretary of the Treasury to decide what collateral to require of depository banks; previously, only U.S. government bonds (in an amount equal to the deposit) were eligible. Moreover, customs receipts could also be deposited in national banks. Federal deposits were exempted from reserve requirements in May 1908.

By 1913 the secretary of the Treasury had developed a paternalistic attitude toward the banks when it came to government deposits, opening the government to the charge of discrimination and favoritism. The Treasury, however, understood the need to seek ways of minimizing the disruptive effects of its cash holdings on the money markets and the national economy.

☐ Many Banks, Few Branches

Large-scale extension of banking facilities to every corner of the nation marked the half-century that ended with the passage of the Federal Reserve Act. "Towns that barely supported a general store or a livery stable felt a burst of civic pride when some farmer or groceryman set himself up in the banking business," Raymond Moley remarked long after.[4] Several applications for the privilege of being the "First National Bank" might be submitted even before a town site was ready for settlers.

Local banks served over 7,000 communities in 1900. The 13,000 banks of 1900 grew to over 22,000 in 1908, and to 26,000 by 1913; most were minuscule, single-office operations. "Branch banking, as well as the establishment of banks of enormous capital, appeared to be regarded as contrary to the genius of banking in the United States, and both have been discontinued," a Philadelphia banker told the first convention of the Pennsylvania Bankers Association in 1895.[5]

The largest American bank at the turn of the century (National City Bank of New York) had total deposits of $130 million; the twenty-fourth largest had but $22 million. New York had seventeen of the top twenty-four banks; Chicago had two.

State banks (thought to be on the way out in 1866) were over two and a half times as numerous as national banks by 1913, and were especially prevalent outside the Northeast. The structural heritage of 1863—a dual banking system composed overwhelmingly of unit banks—proved remarkably durable.

☐ Technological Change

No major developments in the machinery used by banks occurred until the last quarter of the nineteenth century. The telephone changed ways of doing business, and adding machines became practical in 1888. Hanover Bank's bookkeepers verified adding machine results by hand, as it was not infallible.[6] Office procedures changed as various other machines became available shortly before 1900. By 1914 a truly up-to-date bank might use adding machines, punched-card tabulators, automatic typewriters, duplicating machines, and check-writing equipment. Improved models were offered from time to time, but no really new equipment appeared until the electronic computer in the mid-1950s.

☐ Banker Aloofness

President Woodrow Wilson reminded his ABA audience in September 1908 that "the bank is the most jealously regarded and the least liked instrument of business. . . . The people regard [banks] . . . as belonging to some power hostile to them."[7] Bankers were often considered aloof and forbidding. The first instruction Governor William Larrabee gave the manager of his First National Bank of Elkador, Iowa, in 1883 was not to solicit business from anyone, lest he put the bank under obligation, making it more difficult to refuse the customer when he requested a loan. The Merchants National Bank of Boston did not allow employees to solicit deposits, thus discouraging the notion that a depositor was entitled to a line of credit. Franklin Haven (president of the bank until 1883) deemed it an honor for someone to open an account with Merchants. Would-be depositors in the Bank of New York needed a card of introduction and were received as if the bank were doing them a favor.

Bankers had been of the opinion that nothing would be gained by going after each others' customers. Local solicitation was also considered unethical. Percy Johnston (later to head Chemical Bank) learned this lesson when he visited clients of another Louisville bank. He was guilty of disturbing "a nice gentlemanly relationship" that had always existed among that city's banks.[8]

☐ Reaching out for Customers

By the end of the century, however, bankers were actively soliciting correspondent business by mail and in some cases sending out traveling representatives. No longer was it beneath their dignity to seek new business. National City Bank of New York had never solicited an account until Frank Vanderlip arrived. He began by contacting various national banks of his acquaintance, adding 365 accounts in his first year (1901). James B. Forgan complained in 1906 that New York and Philadelphia banks were "soliciting business from our Chicago merchants on wide open principles." By around 1912 every large bank had a new business department.

Advertising began to appear. In May 1906 *Bankers Magazine* initiated a banking publicity section that discussed advertisements analytically. Woodrow Wilson amused his audience of bankers at their 1908 convention with the remark that "the banks have turned away from their old time modesty and reserve and have now gone into advertising."

To attract a new group of wealthy depositors, the Second National Bank of New York opened a women's department in 1871, as did the Fifth Avenue Bank soon thereafter. The National Bank of Commerce in Kansas City boasted in January 1899 that its "Ladies Department" was "the first of its kind in the West." The Portland Trust Company had the first on the Pacific coast in 1907.

☐ Meeting Competition

Many banks considered the competition to be too keen. In 1914 a Maryland banker complained, "So numerous have country banks become that a state of competition exists, so excessive as seriously to threaten the welfare of the banks, and to a material degree, demoralize the people through too cheap credit."[9] James Stillman, of National City Bank hailed the news that the rival National Bank of Commerce had come under Morgan-Ryan-City Bank control. On 16 February 1910 he wrote Vanderlip: "At least you should be able to get the larger banking interests to adopt conservative and businesslike methods in a broad co-operative manner, and stop the unbusinesslike and unprofitable methods . . . and meeting the terms of small institutions for fear of losing business."[10]

☐ Department Stores of Finance

Banks responded to significant competition from trust companies by emulating their broad range of activities, taking on time deposits and investment banking as well as trust functions. "Department store banking" was a phrase in use already in the early 1900s to describe this comprehensive diversification.[11] Factors, discount houses, and commercial credit and personal finance companies arose or expanded their services in fields not provided by banks.

Commercial banking's share of total assets of all American financial intermediaries reached a peak for the twentieth century of 53.5 percent in 1912, slightly above 1900's 52.8 percent. Life insurance companies had 13 percent, having grown significantly in the preceding fifty years. Mutual savings banks (confined to the Northeast), with a 12 percent share, had lost ground; savings and loan associations—formidable rivals after 1950—were a mere 3 percent of the 1912 total.

☐ Interest Differentials Narrow

By 1914 most regional interest rate differentials had narrowed. With improvements in transportation and communications, transfer costs fell. Sources of financing increased in local markets. Rates fell faster in states with lower capital requirements and easier chartering laws. Commercial paper across the country grew in volume. Substantial firms increasingly resorted to securities financing.

☐ Banks, the Money Stock, and Failures

Lending and investing activities of commercial banks were responsible for generating the greater part of the U.S. money supply, which included the public's holdings of coin and currency plus all types of commercial bank deposits. From 1867 to 1879 the money supply grew very slowly, averaging 1.3 percent a year and actually falling in five of the twelve years. From the resumption of specie payments in 1879 to the inauguration of William McKinley eighteen years later, the money stock increased very unevenly but averaged 6 percent annually. Widespread clamor for government action to expand the money supply accompanied the deflation of under 1 percent a year from 1879 to 1897, though this represented an improvement over the 3.5 percent yearly deflation estimated for 1867–79.

From 1863 through 1913 there were ten deflationary years when at least 1 percent of all commercial banks failed: 1876–79, 1884, 1885, 1893, and 1895–97. The two worst years were 1878 when 3.1 percent were swept away and 1893 when 5.8 percent closed their doors. Depositors suffered losses, but never national bank note holders.

From 1897 to 1914, in contrast, money growth averaged 7.5 percent and prices rose over 2 percent a year. The acceleration was traceable in good measure to the great increase in world gold output, which added to the reserves of the banking and monetary system. During these years of inflation, the rate of bank failure was never as high as 1 percent. Yet the panic of 1907 clearly revealed that the mechanism was flawed. Recurring panics caused by defects in banking law and practice *could* be avoided, according to Wesley C. Mitchell, an outstanding American authority on business cycles. "Elasticity of lending power is needed more than elasticity of currency," he suggested in 1913.[12] The Federal Reserve System set out to provide both kinds of elasticity.

The Security Bank opened 14 July 1908 as National Farmer's Bank in Owatonna, Minnesota, a town of 5,500 some sixty-five miles south of Minneapolis. Designed by Louis Sullivan, the building is a National Historical Landmark. *Courtesy of the Minnesota Historical Society.*

Part III.

Banking from 1913 to 1945

12

The Federal Reserve System's Early Years

☐ Deficiencies in the Old Order

Having a central bank ran against the American grain. Centralization would either bring politics to banking via complete governmental control, or bring banking to politics through Wall Street domination, as was widely feared. Consequently, banks had remained "individualistic in the highest degree," the House Banking Committee noted in 1913.

Certain central bank functions were being performed before 1914, albeit inadequately. Correspondent banks in major cities made loans available, but their capacity for lending diminished just when country banks faced the greatest need. Clearinghouse loan certificates expanded reserves on certain occasions, but only on a local basis. The Treasury placed deposits with national banks to ease a crisis, as in 1907, but it had no power to conduct regular operations with commercial banks.

Reformers concentrated mainly on making the currency elastic. Federal Reserve notes would eventually replace the bond-secured national bank notes. Currency alone, however, would not "meet the need for a more effective supply of deposit credits"; in periods of stress banks suffered from an "inability to convert good assets into a medium that can be used in making payments," the House Banking Committee recognized. Accordingly, in the long title of the Federal Reserve Act of 1913, "to afford means of rediscounting commercial paper" appeared just after, "to furnish an elastic currency." This represented the first attempt to deal directly with the "long recognized rigidity of our credit system," J. Lawrence Laughlin noted. The University of Chicago professor stressed that "wider and deeper than the inelasticity of our currency has been the inelasticity of our credit system."[1] Provision of "a sound and elastic supply of currency and credit" was thus a major purpose of the 1913 act.

The main ends sought were clearly stated in the Senate Banking Committee majority report: "to give stability to the commerce and industry of the United States; prevent financial panics or financial stringencies; make available effective commercial credit for individuals engaged in manufacturing, in commerce, in finance, and in business to the extent of their just deserts; put an end to the pyramiding of the bank reserves of the country and the use of such reserves for gambling purposes on the stock exchange."

The national banking system had failed to "afford any safeguard against panics and commercial stringencies or any means of alleviating them," the House Banking Committee stated. The one point on which there was general agreement among bankers and the public was that the measure would "render a recurrence of financial panic impossible," as the Denver *Rocky Mountain News* editorialized at the time the bill was enacted.[2] In November 1915 Federal Reserve Board Chairman Charles Hamlin assured the Western Economic Society that "we will never have any more panics."[3]

Indeed, there was no panic in the first major business downturn after the establishment of the Federal Reserve System, despite the sharp 44 percent drop in wholesale prices and a 32 percent shrinkage in industrial production. At the business cycle peak, January 1920, deposits were 7.05 times the currency holdings of the public; at the trough in July 1921, the ratio was 7:1. There was no scramble for cash on the part of commercial banks; their loans contracted as the Federal Reserve banks reduced their credit.

□   Discount Facilities

Banks belonging to the Federal Reserve System (member banks) could now obtain funds outright at an interest rate known in advance and uniform for all, unlike correspondent banks, which charged what the traffic would bear when lending on secured collateral. The rediscount rate was to be fixed "with a view of accommodating commerce and business," according to a phrase in the statute attributed to Woodrow Wilson. H. Parker Willis, the banking expert who had worked on the measure for then Representative Carter Glass, explained that "credit will be more simply available, cheaper and more equitably open to all."[4]

By relating rediscounts directly to the volume of goods bought and sold, Federal Reserve notes and commercial bank deposits would "adjust themselves to the needs of trade," Willis's teacher J. Laurence Laughlin reasoned.[5] The Federal Reserve Board was confident (1923) that "there will be little danger that the credit created and contributed by the Federal Reserve banks will be in excessive volume if restricted to productive uses," that is, "credit in the service of agriculture, industry, and trade."

☐ Correspondent Balances and Reserve Centralization

The forty-nine major national banks in New York, Chicago, and St. Louis feared very substantial declines in correspondent bank balances, which had represented about half of their total deposits. To ease the adjustment, reserve deposits were gradually transferred to the Federal Reserve banks over a three-year period ending 16 November 1917.

Country banks had become accustomed to receiving 2 percent interest on balances kept with correspondents, some $930 a year on average, representing 7.7 percent of their net income. Typical reserve city banks received $15,250, over 12 percent of their net. Federal Reserve banks, however, paid no interest. By way of compensation, the required reserve was reduced below the percentage under the National-Bank Act, enabling banks to earn interest on the released funds. The system's ability to provide member banks with liquid funds was thought to make the previously higher requirements unnecessary. The national banking system's classification of "central reserve city," "reserve city," and "country bank" remained the basis for differential reserve requirements for demand deposits until 1972.

☐ Federal Reserve Banks and Member Banks

Multiple Federal Reserve banks would ensure "local control of banking, local application of resources to necessities," the House Banking Committee reported. Member banks, the sole shareholders in each district's Federal Reserve bank, selected six of the nine directors and received up to 6 percent dividends on their stock.

The reserve banks, confining their dealings to commercial banks, would "do for existing banks what an ordinary bank does for its customers," the House Banking Committee pointed out. As bankers' banks, Federal Reserve banks served member banks by holding their surplus funds, lending to them, processing their deposits and providing remittance facilities.

At the start, men with previous experience in commercial banking were largely in charge of the Federal Reserve banks' operations. The system's early days reflected "a great deal of commercial banker mentality, as distinct from direct banker influence."[6] Even the system heads cultivated the view that the Federal Reserve banks had been created primarily to serve the interests of member banks.

☐ Multiple Reserve Banks

Localities vied for the distinction of possessing a Federal Reserve bank headquarters. Preferences revealed by a poll of all national banks prevailed, except for Cincinnati, which lost out to Cleveland. Two major financial centers, Baltimore and New Orleans, were relegated to branch status, together with fourteen other reserve cities. Of the forty-nine reserve cities in 1913, only seven were selected to be headquarters of a district Federal Reserve bank. New York, Chicago, and St. Louis, the only three central reserve cities, were natural choices. Richmond and Atlanta were designated for headquarter banks, although neither had been a reserve city, as was the case with nine branches: Buffalo, Birmingham, Charlotte, El Paso, Jacksonville, Little Rock, Memphis, and Nashville (see Appendix).

Multiple reserve banks would avoid "a very high degree of centralization" and ensure "really independent institutions, likely to look to one another for aid only under emergency conditions," the House Banking Committee stated. The system "is not a central bank. It is a regional system," the Federal Reserve Board's annual report carefully noted in 1921. Each reserve bank was independent in its operations and policies, subject only to general supervision by the Federal Reserve Board in Washington.

The district banks were expected to develop into regional money and capital markets. The paradoxical result of setting up twelve district banks (the maximum possible) rather than eight (the minimum allowed by law) was to ensure New York's continued dominance—contrary to the wishes of Congress.

In 1913 Americans envisioned the "Fed" as a source of emergency assistance to commercial banks rather than as an agency to execute monetary policy. The discovery that uncoordinated purchases of U.S.

government bonds by twelve Federal Reserve banks had disruptive effects on the securities market led to the creation of a coordinating committee in May 1921. A year later the Open Market Investment Committee for the Federal Reserve System was placed under the supervision of the Federal Reserve Board. Even then, Carter Glass (considered by many to be the father of the Federal Reserve Act) insisted that the Fed was not a central bank. In 1935 he reminded fellow Senators that in 1913, "instead of a central banking system, the Congress decided to create a regional reserve banking system . . . with a large measure of local authority and a Federal Reserve Board charged, not with conducting a central bank system, but charged merely with supervisory power to see that these regional Reserve banks complied with the law."[7]

The new arrangement represented an evolution from the clearinghouse, "for the most part . . . merely putting into legal shape that which hitherto has been illegally done," Senator Owen pointed out (1913).[8] The most fundamental concept of the 1913 act, uniting the nation's banks, had been borrowed from the clearinghouse practice of emergency pooling of reserves.

☐   Banker Hostility

That the legislation was evolutionary did not make it more palatable to most bankers, who would have been satisfied with a measure limited to providing relief in emergency situations of credit stringency. The *New York Times* raised the specter of "absolute political control over . . . banking in a bill which reflected . . . the rooted dislike and distrust of banks and bankers that have been for many years a great moving force in the Democratic party, notably in the Western and Far Western states."[9]

☐   Membership in the Federal Reserve System

President Wilson signed the measure on 23 December 1913. By 2 April 1914, 7,471 banks had agreed to join. Only fifteen relinquished their national charter, while another thirteen failed to become members by the December 1914 deadline.

State-chartered banks stayed out of the system. Of the 8,500, only fifty-three had seen fit to join the system by June 1917, when the law was amended to make it more attractive for state banks. But that summer only thirty-six more became members. At least as important as the 1917 amendment were fears of a drain of bankers' reserves because of

America's participation in World War I, and the calls to patriotism from high-level officials. By the end of 1918 a total of 930 state banks had responded; member banks had 63 percent of all commercial bank deposits, well above the 42–43 percent share between 1914 and 1916. In 1922 a record 1,600 state banks were members. The vast majority preferred to remain outside, collecting interest on reserves with correspondent banks (until 1933) and charging exchange for clearing checks, while keeping fewer required reserves.

☐ World War I

War broke out in Europe in midsummer 1914, some fifteen weeks before the Federal Reserve banks were ready to open. During the ensuing panic, bankers did not suspend cash payments, thanks to the emergency currency issued under the Aldrich-Vreeland Act. Almost 2,200 national banks joined national currency associations. At the peak—24 October 1914—$384 million of their notes were outstanding (about one-fourth of the amount of currency in the hands of the public before the war began). Within two months $217 million was redeemed, and all but $200,000 was redeemed by July 1915.

U.S. government bonds represented only 2.9 percent of all commercial bank assets in mid-1914. Banks reduced their holdings of U.S. bonds slightly from 1913 to 1916, but they had over 78 percent of the outstanding total in 1916.

A 1916 amendment to the Federal Reserve Act viewed at the time as "a technical alteration of no great importance,"[10] developed into a significant departure from the "real bills" approach of the 1913 act. The amendment authorized the discounting of paper secured by U.S. government securities. At the time only $300 million of these securities were not serving as collateral for national bank notes.

Banks increased U.S. bond holdings threefold from 1916 to 1918. By mid-1919 government bond holdings peaked at $4.9 billion, totaling 11.5 percent of all bank assets. Over half of their combined investment portfolios consisted of federal securities. Commercial banks further assisted the Treasury's war requirements by making large advances to finance acquisition of U.S. securities by citizens responding to the slogan "Borrow and buy." The Fed established a preferential rate on member bank borrowings secured by U.S. bonds, and member banks were encouraged to borrow at little or no net cost. Banks thus overcame their longstanding aversion to rediscounting.

During the period of direct American participation in World War I

(April 1917 to November 1918), bank loans and investments rose by \$7 billion. Banks were asked to consider a borrower's relation to the war effort. Nonessential industries were to be denied credit.

Reflecting the sharp wartime rise in the demand for American farm output, short-term bank loans to agriculture soared from \$1.6 billion in 1914–15 to a peak of \$3.9 billion in late 1920 through early 1921. Meanwhile, banks had over \$1.4 billion in farm mortgages by the end of 1920, twice as much as six years earlier. Federal Reserve notes were under \$400 million when the United States entered the war. Six months later they exceeded the \$700 million in national bank notes. By mid-1918, the new paper money constituted half of the currency held by the public and amounted to \$2.6 billion by the end of 1918. At this juncture Californians relaxed their long-standing hostility to paper money, turning in gold coins for Federal Reserve notes.

In September 1918 a leading Chicago banker and early supporter of the Federal Reserve idea, Edmund Hulbert, whose experience went back to 1875, told the American Bankers Association that he could not remember "any four-year period since I have been a responsible officer of a bank when I had less anxiety as to the possibility and certainty of meeting all calls from depositors and borrowers as I have during the last four years."[11]

With the assistance of the Federal Reserve banks, gigantic financial transactions were now executed smoothly and simply. "War finance on our present scale," Benjamin Anderson wrote in 1920, "could hardly have been carried out by the old machinery." To the Chase National economist, this represented "a supreme vindication of the federal reserve system."[12]

13

Banking in the 1920s

☐ Business Lending Declines

From 1900 to 1920 business borrowing from banks increased as a fraction of total business funding, only to drop in the next fifteen years. Banks provided 32.1 percent of net short- and long-term debt at the end of 1920, but nine years later they provided only 23.3 percent. As a share of total bank assets, however, business loans and securities combined in 1928 were one percentage point above the 36 percent share in 1900.

Short-term loans declined in relative importance, despite the Federal Reserve Act's encouragement of such loans. Loans eligible for rediscounting at the Fed fell from 32 percent of all national bank loans in 1920 to 20 percent by 1929; as a proportion of total national bank loans and investments, eligible loans dropped from 24 percent to 12 percent. Business loans declined from 47 percent of all bank loans and investments in 1922 to only 33 percent in 1929. The 1920 commercial loan total ($15.5 billion) was not surpassed until 1929. Faced with reduced demand for loans by creditworthy businesses, bankers turned to other areas. Security and real estate loans combined exceeded the amount of commercial loans by 1923.

Vigorous speculation in inventories at rising prices followed the armistice of 11 November 1918. Producer prices then tumbled 40 percent in the year ending July 1921, inflicting heavy losses on inventory holders. Hand-to-mouth buying became an ideal, as improved transportation and control techniques facilitated greater efficiency in inventory management. After 1922 both inventories and accounts receivable—traditionally financed by banks—declined.

Banks curtailed lending in 1921–22, *after* prices had collapsed. Even so, business loans in 1922 were almost double the total in 1915. Banks formed creditor committees in 1920–21 to avoid bankruptcy proceedings. Collections were deferred to enable the reorganization of promising firms. Businesses that could not obtain renewals or pay off loans came under banker control. To businessmen, this became a lesson in the desirability of attaining independence from bank financing. Earnings retained out of substantial profits served as an important source of funds. The Wall Street boom facilitated bond and stock flotations (especially in 1927–29) which were used for working capital.

The trend toward borrowing from long-term investors rather than banks was especially marked among larger firms. The largest corporations often had no outstanding bank loans. The current assets of 729 (mainly successful) larger businesses rose 32 percent from 1922 through 1928, but their bank loans fell 37 percent. To avoid the risk of insolvency during a cyclical downturn in earnings, bank debts were repaid.

Small and medium-sized enterprises, not in a position to retain as great a proportion of their profits or to sell securities, received about three-fifths of commercial loans in 1920, and three-fourths in 1930. Unlike large borrowers who could shop around for the best terms, smaller firms were expected to keep an ample deposit balance and to have their entire line of credit with a single bank on a permanent customer basis. Banks wanted customers to secure their explicit permission before going to the commercial paper or general acceptance market. Some businessmen complained that banks were meddling excessively in the affairs of borrowers who were neither insolvent nor likely to get into any kind of trouble.

In most large cities, especially those where the booming industries of automobiles, steel, machinery, and electrical equipment were located, bankers bemoaned the disappearing large borrower. In smaller centers the number of good industrial and commercial borrowers shrank when many merged into larger firms. In rural localities the withering impact on local merchants of chain stores, mail-order houses, and shoppers who motored to large cities for sizable purchases also adversely affected bank lending.

Around 1912 banks in larger cities began to organize new business departments in order to seek out promising relationships. All over the United States bankers began to hawk credit. Jesse Sprague reported that "in many cases credit was forced on one."[1] Even so, in mid-1929 bank loans of all types were only 25 percent above the speculative level of 1920.

☐ Credit Departments

Most larger and medium-sized banks opened credit departments in the 1920s and 1930s. The Federal Reserve insisted that a bank have financial statements for firms whose paper was rediscounted. Even more important in inducing more comprehensive record-keeping was the corporate income tax, first imposed in 1913.

Credit departments coupled with clearinghouse examinations tended to raise standards of creditworthiness. When a Minneapolis holding company, First Bank Stock, asked subsidiary banks to install credit files in the 1920s, the country bankers balked. Credit information no longer could be viewed as a trade secret for the exclusive use of senior bank officials. Loan officers reviewing business balance sheets and earnings reports tended to focus on a small number of financial ratios, leading to some degree of standardization of credit policy among banks.

Countywide credit bureaus sponsored by the Wisconsin Bankers Association consolidated information about borrowers in a given area; fourteen were organized or under way by mid-1927. They discovered that, on average, one out of seven Wisconsin borrowers had been receiving credit from more than one bank without their knowledge.

☐ Short-Term Agricultural Credit

From a peak of $3.9 billion in mid-1920, short-term loans to agriculture dropped over 20 percent by mid-1923. The $2.6 billion outstanding in the late 1920s was not reached again until 1952. Banks supplied 90 percent of all non–real estate loans to farm households from institutional sources, while federal agencies provided no more than 2 percent.

By May 1920 farm prices were two and a half times the 1913 level, but fell by more than half over the next thirteen months. The collapse was (erroneously) blamed on lack of credit accommodation. Agitation for new sources of intermediate credit (up to three years) resulted in the Agricultural Credits Act of 1923. Twelve federally owned (until 1968) intermediate credit banks were organized to rediscount notes of commercial banks, agricultural credit corporations, and livestock loan companies, as well as to lend directly to cooperative marketing associations. Banks made very little use of the system, even during the distressed 1930s, as the profit margin for guarantors of farmers' notes was deemed too small.

☐ Farm Mortgages

The bank share of farm mortgages, under one-fifth before 1915, was close to one-fourth during most of the 1920s. As certain short-term bank credits were consolidated, total farm mortgage debt was at a peak of $10.8 billion at the start of 1923. Banks held 10 percent of the 1930s $9.6 billion total; life insurance companies held more than twice as much.

The federal government entered the field of systematic lending for the first time in July 1916. A law that aimed to furnish capital for agricultural development provided for twelve federal land banks to make first mortgage loans through cooperatively owned farm loan associations. By 1927, the holdings of federal land banks surpassed those of commercial banks, and in 1930 represented over 12 percent of all farm mortgages.

Privately owned joint-stock land banks—also authorized by the 1916 law—held under 7 percent of all farm mortgages outstanding at their peak in 1927. Many of the eighty-eight organized before 1932 failed; others had to resort to drastic measures to avert failure. The successful California Joint-Stock Land Bank, started in 1919 by the predecessor of the Bank of America, made long-term credit available at 6 percent.

Both types of land banks organized under the 1916 law obtained loanable funds by selling bonds secured by first mortgages. They were separate from commercial banks and were not associated with currency schemes, unlike the colonial and pre-1861 land banks. After 1933 joint-stock land banks made no further loans, and they were liquidated completely by 1951. Federal land banks were converted to private ownership in 1947.

☐ Urban Real Estate Lending

After 1913 national banks could lend on real estate, at first, only on "improved and unencumbered farm lands" for up to five years. In 1916 nonfarm property became eligible for one-year first mortgages, increased to five years in 1927. State-chartered commercial banks continued to make the bulk of real estate loans.

Urban and suburban construction activity was a major force for prosperity. Banks held 11.7 percent of the 1929 total of nonfarm mortgages on one- to four-family dwellings, and 8.4 percent on dwellings for more than four families. Aggregate bank-held real estate loans of all types doubled between 1920 and 1929.

The commercial bank share of the sharply rising volume of non-farm residential mortgages increased from 8.8 percent in 1920 to 10.7 percent in 1929, at which time they represented 8 percent of bank assets, double the 1920 proportion. Mortgages extended by banks were for two to three years in the early 1920s, and by 1930 for three and a half years, usually for up to about half of the market value of the property.

☐ Loans to Consumers

The variety of borrowings offered consumers after 1920 was labeled "the most spectacular and most novel development in the field of credit" in a scholarly review of *Recent Social Trends*. National City Bank of New York (the largest bank in the country) was not the first to establish a personal loan department, but its example, set in 1928, was followed by 200 banks within a year. Many departments were discontinued in the early years of depression, but some 157 operating in 1938 had been opened before 1930, and over half before 1925.

Bank installment loans to consumers, a mere $25 million in 1920, reached $204 million in 1930, 6.8 percent of all consumer installment credit. Noninstallment loans grew from $285 to $837 million during this decade. A beginning had been made; by 1930 consumer loans amounted to 3 percent of all commercial bank loans.

Symbolically, the first bank in Richmond, Virginia to offer consumer loans (in 1927) located the department in the basement. The generally silent President Calvin Coolidge expressed approval of consumer installment borrowing in 1926. Such credit, Professor Edwin Seligman concluded in 1929, "will be recognized as constituting a significant and valuable contribution to the modern economy."[2]

Sales finance companies (making mainly auto loans), consumer finance companies, and Morris Plan "industrial banks" (started in 1910 and concentrating on small loans to wage earners) were responsible for most of the upsurge in personal loans. The satisfactory experience of these lenders (themselves heavy borrowers from banks) taught banks that personal loans were both safe and profitable.

☐ Bankers' Acceptances and Commercial Paper

In 1913 national banks were authorized to issue bankers' acceptances for transactions arising out of foreign trade, and in 1916, out of domestic trade. The Federal Reserve banks encouraged the use of this credit instrument, whereby a bank guaranteed a customer's draft and agreed to make payment if the named firm failed to meet its obligation. Federal Reserve banks maintained a preferential buying rate, progressively lowered standards of eligibility for purchase, endorsed acceptances sold to foreign central banks, and entered into repurchase agreements with dealers.

In the early 1920s there were several hundred accepting banks but only 164 by the end of 1930. Most of the business was done by fifty major banks. The $1 billion of bankers' acceptances outstanding in 1920 was not surpassed until 1927. The peak $1.7 billion in 1929 rivaled the volume in London, previously the main source for bankers' acceptances.

Between 1916 and 1924 Federal Reserve banks bought from 25 percent to 60 percent of the bills drawn—and somewhat less in the next seven years, owning 22 percent at the end of 1929. Subsequently, they held their buying rate slightly above the market rate. Commercial banks buying bankers' acceptances were secure in the knowledge that these could be sold to the Federal Reserve banks when necessary. Accepting banks came to hold over half the shrunken volume after 1932—$400 million outstanding in 1935, and only $210 million in 1940—whereas in 1929 they held only 11 percent.

Commercial paper, used by about 4,400 borrowers, was at a peak of $1.3 billion in 1920. Beginning in the mid-1920s, more financing was done through the upstart bankers' acceptance market. In the venerable commercial paper market, volume was down to $334 million by 1929.

☐ Brokers' Loans in the Great Bull Market

Call loans had served as the main type of secondary reserve for banks before 1914. As war loomed and European investors sold vast quantities of securities, the New York Stock Exchange closed on 31 July 1914. Until trading was partially resumed four and a half months later, call loans that were secured by investment securities could not be liquidated, creating a prejudice against relying on them as secondary reserves. Bankers' experience during 1920–21 dispelled this bias because they could turn stock market loans into cash, whereas supposedly self-liquidating commercial loans turned out to be frozen.

The hope of sponsors of the Federal Reserve Act that banks would devote less of their funds to financing the security markets was not realized. Loans on security collateral were 27.5 percent of total national bank loans in 1915, 28.8 percent in 1925, and 34.6 percent in 1929. From the end of 1928 to mid-1929 member banks decreased the proportion of loans on securities only slightly, from 39.3 percent to 38.1 percent. Not all such loans, incidentally, were for Wall Street speculation.

Common stock prices rose 50 percent between 1923 and 1926, and again from 1926 to 1928, climaxed by a further gain of 25 percent in the first nine months of 1929. Member firms of the New York Stock Exchange required a minimum margin of 20 percent for most of the 1920s and raised the margin to 25 percent in mid-1929—which meant that a customer could borrow three-quarters of the purchase price of a stock.

Nonbank lenders (mainly nonfinancial corporations) became very important sources of funds in the call loan market toward the end of the 1920s, providing 70 percent of the $9.2 billion total of loans to brokers and dealers in late October 1929. In mid-October member banks in New York City reported brokers' loans of $1.1 billion for their own account, $1.8 billion for out-of-town banks, and $3.9 billion "on account of others." Nonbank sources were responsible for 85 percent of the increase in the preceding year.

These lenders recalled over one-third of their funds in the last week of October as stock prices tumbled. New York banks filled the gap created by this withdrawal. Lenders suffered few losses as the call loans to brokers had been amply secured. But banks sustained heavy losses on security loans to nonbroker customers, especially on loans secured by stock of other banks. Loans made by member banks to brokers had ranged from 9 percent to 14 percent of total loans in the late 1920s. Brokers' loans reached a peak of 7.2 percent of total loans and investments of member banks at the beginning of 1929, dropping to 4.3 percent by the end of 1930.

Preventing speculation "from making undue inroads upon the preserves of legitimate business finance"[3] was seen by Willis as one of the Federal Reserve's main responsibilities. The Fed was concerned that the absorption of funds in stock speculation would raise the cost of credit for legitimate uses. Member banks seeking discounts at the central bank (as over half were at one time or another in 1929) would be admonished if they held collateral loans while in debt to the Federal Reserve. Actually, loans secured by stock collateral did not decrease funds available for other uses or raise interest rate levels. As the New York Federal Reserve Bank explained to the Senate in March 1920, call money rates "do not determine and have not exerted an important influence on the rates for commercial borrowings; it is the universal custom of the banks to satisfy first the commercial needs of their customers." As long as call loans were important, however, they aroused widespread doubts and misgivings.

☐ Federal Funds

A new money market instrument, federal funds, was developed in the 1920s.[4] These bankers' balances at a Federal Reserve bank might be bought (borrowed) or sold (loaned out), depending on a commercial bank's reserve position and needs. Because of depressed conditions, some New York City member banks had excess reserves, while other banks were borrowing at the discount window of the New York Federal Reserve Bank in the early summer of 1921. Borrowers found it to be less troublesome to buy federal funds instead of seeking rediscounts.

Local markets for federal funds developed also in Boston, Philadelphia, Chicago, and San Francisco. Volume averaged $40–80 million a day, in the early 1920s, rising to a minimum of $100 million, and sometimes as much as $250 million, in the late 1920s. Despite this sharp growth, the federal funds market was quite small compared with other open-market instruments in the 1920s. In 1928–29 the federal funds rate was often above the Federal Reserve discount rate not only because some borrowers lacked eligible paper but because others wished to avoid criticism at the Federal Reserve for borrowing. The federal funds market almost disappeared during the Great Depression; it revived somewhat between 1937 and 1942 and enjoyed a resurgence in the 1950s.

☐ Security Investments

"Bonds for secondary reserves," a popular slogan in the 1920s, was based on the view that their ready salability made bonds desirable. Conservative country bankers, eager to diminish their dependence on local loans, invested in corporate bonds. Corporate bonds, 8 percent of total assets of all banks in 1920, were up to 11 percent by 1930. Utilities and manufacturing in particular accounted for the portfolio growth of $1.3 billion between 1922 and 1929. Bank holdings were 12.4 percent of all corporate bonds outstanding in 1929, slightly below the 1912 proportion. Bank holdings of all types of medium- and long-term debt of nonfinancial corporations combined was over 8.4 percent of the $19 billion outstanding in 1920, and 9.5 percent of the $30 billion outstanding in the 1930s.

Bank holdings of U.S. government bonds equaled 1919's $4.9 billion once again in 1928, remaining at this level until the latter part of 1930. Banks owned almost 29 percent of the outstanding federal debt in 1929, compared with 65 percent of a very much smaller total in 1912. At

7 percent of total bank assets in 1929, holdings were double the 1912 proportion. Among national banks, the proportion of federal bonds *not* held for the purpose of securing national bank notes rose from 3.2 percent in 1913 to 30.3 percent in 1930, clear evidence of their increasing popularity as secondary reserves.

Banks owned some 12 percent of the total state and local government bonds outstanding in 1929, just as in 1912, but as a share of bank assets, government bonds increased from 2.4 percent to 3.1 percent between these years.

Foreign securities represented only 2.3 percent of national bank investments before World War I. As New York became a major marketer of such securities, bank holdings rose to $1 billion by 1929, representing 1.5 percent of bank assets and about 7.7 percent of national bank investments. Many foreign issues went into default when international trade plummeted in the early 1930s.

Altogether, security investments beyond the more traditional sectors of government, railroads, and public utilities rose from 39 percent of all holdings in 1921 to 49 percent in 1930. Favorable experience from 1922 through 1928, when loss charge-offs by national banks related to securities were below loss rates on loans, encouraged banks to purchase securities.

☐ Securities Underwriting

Large commercial banks' expertise in securities was extended to underwriting new issues, the main activity of regular investment banks. The new issue volume in 1927, at $10 billion, was twice the level of the early 1920s; it reached $11.6 billion in 1929. Commercial banks originated 22 percent of all new security issues in 1927 and more than twice that proportion by 1930. In those two years bank participation in new issues represented 37 percent and 60 percent of the dollar total. By 1930 commercial banks had the greater part of the new issue business of bonds.

While 386 banks engaged directly in the securities business, security affiliates operated by 180 commercial banks were used to engage in activities closed to the banks themselves. National City Bank's National City Company was the leader. New York's Chase National Bank, Guaranty Trust, Bankers Trust, and Equitable Trust, as well as Chicago's Continental Illinois, First National of Boston, and Detroit's Union Trust were also prominent participants through affiliates. In most cases the affiliate took over from an established bond department. As investor preference turned to common stock around 1924, many banks made the shift.

☐ Banks as Department Stores of Finance

The concept of banks as financial department stores was around before 1914, but it was not until after 1920 that the practice became widespread, especially in cities. By diversifying their services, banks aimed to achieve more rapid growth of earnings.

Beginning in 1915 a national bank could open a trust department after securing permission from the Federal Reserve Board. A total of 1,294 national banks had such permits in 1920, and almost twice that number had permits by 1930—about one-fourth of all national banks, including most of the sizable ones. Safe deposit boxes were offered by some national banks even before the 1927 McFadden Act specifically authorized this activity. The same was true of underwriting activities. Thus, an up-to-date bank of the late 1920s was "equipped to render any form of financial service . . . a composite of the old commercial bank, savings bank, trust company, bond house, insurance company, safe deposit company, and mortgage house."[5]

☐ Service Charges on Checking Accounts

Banks popularized small checking accounts by reaching out to households, including those of industrial workers, with the slogan, "Pay by check and have a receipt." They later discovered that such business could be unprofitable because of handling charges. Half of the accounts in nine Minnesota country banks had balances of less than $50 in 1930.

Analysis of customers' accounts and the imposition of service charges had been proposed in the late nineteenth century, but they became important only in the 1920s. By 1929 over 500 localities were imposing service charges, and many more would have were it not for severe competition conditions. At least some banks in forty states imposed service charges—50¢ or $1—when the balance fell below $50 or $100.

☐ Par Collection of Checks

High (if not excessive) check collection charges had been imposed on American business by cartel agreement or in the name of business ethics.[6] The Federal Reserve was expected to change this practice. By the end of 1916 some 16,000 banks—including a great proportion of nonmembers—were on the par list. To encourage maximum use of their clearing facilities, Federal Reserve banks eliminated all charges for check collection.

There were still 10,000 nonpar banks at the end of 1918 when a vigorous drive to make par collection universal got under way. After a year there were 3,996 nonpar banks, and by the beginning of 1921, only 1,755 remained out of 30,253 commercial banks. The Fed confronted uncooperative banks with demands for payment over their counter in currency at full value. Under pressure from Congress, Federal Reserve banks discontinued over-the-counter collection of nonpar bank checks in 1923. The nonpar list quickly expanded to almost 4,000 by the end of 1925. In 1930, 18 percent of all banks were nonpar.

□ Time Deposits

The Federal Reserve Act of 1913 explicitly authorized national banks to assume time deposit liabilities with a lower reserve requirement. Time deposits were almost one-third of total deposits, excluding those owing to banks and the U.S. government, by 1912; this proportion rose to over 40 percent by 1930, with national banks showing the sharpest gain.

In 1927 the Federal Reserve Board expressed concern over "the constantly growing tendency to transfer what are in effect demand deposits into so-called time certificates or savings accounts." Commercial banks encouraged the transfer and advertised heavily for "savings deposits." Some banks (especially in large cities) allowed customers to write checks against time deposits.

Time and savings deposits held by individuals at commercial banks doubled between 1921 and 1929. The $15 billion of these deposits at commercial banks in 1929 equaled the combined total held in mutual savings banks and savings and loan associations.

□ Decreased Interbank Deposits

Correspondent bank deposits declined considerably in the 1920s. Member bank deposits held in other American commercial banks represented 14.4 percent of their total deposits in 1915, but fell to half that figure in 1920, and to 6.2 percent by 1930. Interbank deposits for all commercial banks combined dropped from 15 percent of total deposits in 1914 to slightly over 10 percent in 1920, and remained near that percentage during the decade.

□ New York's Position

As holder of domestic bank balances, New York became slightly more important after 1914 relative to other financial centers. In 1925 all but fifty-five of Georgia's 655 banks kept a New York bank account, as did 515 of California's 644 banks.

Sponsors of the Federal Reserve had sought to diminish Wall Street's power but did not have much success. New York City had 1.2 percent of the nation's banks, but 25.4 percent of total bank assets in 1900; the 1929 shares were 0.5 percent and 22.6 percent, respectively. National City Bank became the first billion-dollar bank in the United States in 1919. Following major mergers, Chase National became the world's largest bank in May 1930. Eight of the nation's twelve largest commercial banks were headquartered in lower Manhattan in 1930. As of 1932 the New York money market had actually increased in relative importance over some decades earlier.

□ Federal Deposits and the Independent Treasury

Public monies were received and disbursed by 850 national banks in 1913, twice as many as in 1908. As late as mid-1920 there were 587 public depositories. Not until January 1916, over a year after the Federal Reserve banks opened, did the Treasury Department make much use of those twelve banks for business previously handled by the depository national banks.

Federal Reserve banks were not originally intended as a substitute for the subtreasury system. As events unfolded, however, the superfluity of the old arrangement became apparent. Between October 1920 and February 1921 the nine subtreasuries were finally closed; most of their monetary and depository functions were turned over to the Federal Reserve banks. Ever since the Civil War, the role and significance of the Independent Treasury System had been diminishing gradually, but it lingered on for seventy-five years. Even after 1921, the Treasury Department found it necessary to use several hundred national bank depositories in localities that had considerable federal government business but no Federal Reserve branch.

□ Rediscounts

Banks learned to use the Federal Reserve as a source of funds during World War I. The rediscount rate (kept moderate at the request of the Treasury) moved from 4.75 to 5.5 percent in January 1920 and reached 7 percent in June. Over the next five months the volume of rediscounts grew by an additional $263 million, cresting at $2.8 billion at the end of October, a level not reached again until mid-1973. Wesley Mitchell, the business cycle authority, noted that in the face of the violent contraction of economic activity in the eighteen months ending in mid-1921, "the Federal Reserve System proved its strength by averting" a bank suspension, such as the nation's pre-1914 experience would have led one to expect.[7] As Alexander Noyes commented, "At no time during this period of shaken credit and strain on bank resources was there any such run on the banks as occurred in 1907, 1893 and 1873. With the Federal Reserve's machinery of note-issue on commercial paper operative, there was no panic of bank depositors, no hoarding of money, no issue of clearing-house certificates, no 'premium on currency.' "[8] As the economy unwound from its speculative binge, rediscounts decreased, dropping below $1 billion in January 1922 for the first time since June 1918. Borrowing next exceeded $1 billion in May 1928, and in most months thereafter until the end of 1929.

Federal Reserve officials did not dispute the appropriateness of borrowing for seasonal, temporary, or emergency needs but opposed banks' taking advantage of the generally prevalent differential between money-market rates and the rediscount rate, or remaining continuously indebted to the district bank. During the 1920s the system did succeed in sharply reducing seasonal stresses in the money market and the corresponding seasonal movements that had earlier characterized interest rates.

□ Clearinghouse Agreements and Competition

It was not a legitimate function of a clearinghouse to force members to pay identical interest rates on deposits, New York's clearinghouse manager had testified in 1912. When Wall Street raised the rate on bankers' balances to 3 percent in early March 1918, banks in other cities followed suit. Federal Reserve denunciation of this type of competition led to an agreement by the New York City Clearing House on 19 March 1918 to reduce the rate to 2.5 percent and to link it thereafter to the rediscount rate (the practice in London). Disagreements prevented the clearinghouse in Baltimore from regulating interest rates before 1927. Detroit's clearinghouse (like most others) had a maximum somewhat above New York's; it also enforced uniform charges for small deposit accounts and collection services. Cleveland and New York banks had gentleman's agreements not to encroach on a neighborhood already dominated by another bank. Detroit lacked such an understanding, and excessive branching led to low profits and even losses in several locations.

Clearinghouse regulation of interest paid on deposits plus minimum exchange charges had been instituted to eliminate cutthroat competition. Notwithstanding uniform schedules and regulations, a scholar of the 1920s described the situation in most cities as one of "wholesome competition."[9]

□ New Banks

By 1920 there was one bank for every 3,500 Americans, including "spite banks" sponsored by feuding local groups. In 1920 Rockland, Wisconsin (population 120), boasted two banks. Nationally, over 46 percent of incorporated banks were in places with fewer than 1,000 residents; over 40 percent had less than $250,000 in loans and investments. Of the 6,109 charters granted from 1921 through 1929, states issued 79 percent and the comptroller of the currency only 21 percent. He rejected 30 percent of the applications for new national banks. There was a marked tightening after 1925; Comptroller McIntosh believed that "there is too often a desire to organize banks in localities where the communities are amply served and which would not support new institutions with a likelihood of any fair measure of success."[10]

Another barrier was erected as some states banned the organization of any new private banks, although they permitted existing ones (some 3,500 in 1919) to continue. Texas took this step in 1923, and Georgia in 1930.[11] Many banks chose to incorporate when states instituted the supervision of private banks. In Ohio private banks declined from 216 in 1913 to 144 in 1920, and to thirteen by 1936. Illinois, with 667 private banks in 1914, approved a public referendum in November 1918 that required their incorporation by the end of 1920.

The trend toward lower capital requirements climaxed around 1900 and was reversed in the 1920s. In 1920, 28 percent of incorporated banks still had no more than $25,000 in capital.

Bankers sought legislation requiring a demonstration of need before new banks could open. As early as 1889 Pennsylvania's bank charter law incorporated the need criterion, as did New Jersey's a decade later. New York inserted a "public convenience and advantage" provision into its law after the panic of 1907; another five states added such a test by 1909. Seven years after Texas enacted a public necessity test, an annual average of fifty-four charters were granted, compared with 130 in the previous eight years. To bankers, the wisdom of such a policy became increasingly evident after 1920, but enacting it usually happened slowly. Thus, Virginia's banking division recommended the needs test in 1911 and the Virginia Bankers Association recommended it in 1912, but not until 1928 was the chief bank examiner empowered to refuse a charter application. By 1938 a needs test was the law in thirty-eight states, and most also considered the purpose or integrity of the applicants.

New bank formation slowed in the 1920s. Together with the closing of unsuccessful banks, this brought the population per bank in 1930 to 5,000, 40 percent above the 1920 level.

□ Mergers

Despite the organization of over 6,000 new banks during the 1920s, by 1930 there were 6,600 fewer banks. Mergers as well as failures accounted for the decline. The desire to avert outright failure prompted many combinations, especially in the South and the West. Acquisition of branches was another powerful motive to merge. Urban banks aiming to expand the range of their services took the merger path, while commercial lenders sought out specialists in savings or trust activities. A 1918 law facilitated direct consolidation of national banks; by 1927 national banks could consolidate with state banks.

Each year from 1900 through 1909, about seventy banks were acquired; twice as many were acquired from 1910 through 1918. The annual average for 1919–20 was 180; for 1921–25, 330; and for 1926–30, 550. Total assets of merged banks peaked at $1.8 billion in the second quarter of 1929, with 130 banks involved.

Some acquisitions reflected a drive for greater size, which would enable banks to better serve large business customers. Two California banks owned by Giannini were combined late in 1930 to form the Bank of America National Trust and Savings Association. The larger component, the Bank of Italy, had already become the largest bank west of Chicago, only sixteen years after its founding in 1904.

The 100 largest banks had about one-fourth of all U.S. bank assets in 1920, and around one-third a decade later. In most metropolitan areas by 1929, the two to four largest banks controlled over half of the assets, and in smaller cities an even greater proportion. Mergers were largely responsible for this concentration of bank assets.

□ Branching at Home

Branches represented 4 percent of all commercial bank offices in 1920, and 13 percent a decade later. Just over 3 percent of all banks had branches in 1930; most of these had but a single branch office.

Increasing auto traffic and downtown parking problems also prompted the spread of branches. Intracity branches tripled between 1920 and 1930. A majority of all branches were in places of 100,000 or more inhabitants: New York, Detroit, Los Angeles, and Philadelphia alone had over one-third of the total. Two-thirds of all branches in the nation at the end of 1929 were in the states of these metropolises, plus Ohio.

Out-of-town branching grew more rapidly than in-city branching after 1925. Even so, fewer than one-third of all branches were outside the head-office city by 1930; half of the national total were in California.

The Federal Reserve Board's suggestion that national banks be allowed to open branches in the city or county of their head offices aroused the American Bankers Association to vote against any form of branch banking in 1916. The 1922 ABA convention resolution asserted that "branch banking is contrary to public policy, violates the basic principles of our Government, and concentrates the credit of the nation and the power of money in the hands of a few." By 1930, however, the membership had accepted "community-wide branch banking in metropolitan areas and county-wide branch banking in rural districts where economically justifiable." At this time, ten states allowed city or contiguous territory branching, and nine others allowed it statewide.

To meet the challenge of state branch banks, Comptroller of the Currency D. R. Crissinger in 1921 authorized national banks in states that permitted chartered banks to branch to open tellers' windows limited to accepting deposits and cashing checks. National bank branches were authorized for the first time in 1927, but only in the head-office city of those states that permitted branching; a majority did not. Banking Committee Chairman Lewis McFadden (ex-president of the First National Bank of Canton, Pennsylvania) assured fellow representatives that the measure was really "anti-branch banking . . . severely restricting [its] further spread." President Herbert Hoover reaffirmed in 1929 that "one of the fundamentals of the American credit system" was that bank credit "be subject to the restraint of local interest and public opinion."

Giannini spoke out for nationwide branch banking before the House Banking Committee in 1930. His holding company had bought a large Wall Street bank in 1928, twenty-four years after organizing an institution in California that developed into the giant Bank of America. The holding company, Bancitaly Corporation, was renamed Transamerica (today's First Interstate Bancorporation), a name that reflected its objective. Though Giannini's goal was not to be achieved, he could boast the largest branch system in the country. His Bank of Italy had 287 branches at the end of 1929, while the largest network in New York City comprised only sixty-seven.

☐   Foreign Branches

Giannini also talked about "world-wide department store banking" offering every phase of financial activity in 1929; it arrived forty years later under Citicorp auspices. The first overseas branch was opened in 1887; by 1914 there were twenty-six, half of them in the Far East. In 1913 national banks were authorized to open branches outside the United States. By the end of 1920 there were 181 foreign branches of U.S. banks (a total not seen again until 1965), the majority of them in Latin America. Overseas branches were down to 107 in 1926 and numbered 110 in 1939.

National City Bank of New York had the largest number for many decades. Its eighty-three foreign branches from China to Belgium contributed 30 percent of its total profits in 1930.

☐   Chain and Group Banking

By 1930, ninety-four of Chicago's 206 banks, representing about half of Chicago's banking resources, were associated with chains or (in a few cases) holding companies. Dozens of banks opened in new sections of Chicago and its suburbs following World War I, more or less closely linked to the downtown giants; they lent heavily on real estate, to their subsequent regret.

In the late 1920s chain banking declined in relative importance, while holding companies, sometimes called "group banking," became more popular as a way to link banks. The stock market boom facilitated the financing of acquisitions, while pressures faced by rural banks made them eager to join. Most of the major holding companies over the next thirty-five years were organized in the late 1920s in states with limited or no branching.

The Eccles brothers organized the First Security Corporation in 1928, with seventeen banks in Utah, Idaho, and Wyoming that were no more than "an overnight train ride away" from Ogden, Utah, because they wished to keep in close touch with each one. Some, like the Minneapolis-based Northwest Bancorporation and First Bank Stock Corporation, bestrode many states along the northern tier; other group banks, like the Marine Midland Corporation in New York and Banc Ohio (both founded in 1929), kept their bank subsidiaries within the boundaries of one state.

Holding companies sought safety in diversification. The spread of bank holding companies was startling to some, but then the stock market crash ended prospects of further expansion for decades to come.

☐ The Dual Banking System

Advantages previously enjoyed by state-chartered banks in fiduciary activities, time deposits, and real estate loans were reduced in 1913. Nevertheless, in 1919 the national banks' share of total commercial bank assets fell below 50 percent for the first time since 1865, sinking to 44.4 percent by 1926. This occurred despite the conversion of 2,828 state and private banks to national charters from 1900 through 1920; many did so to escape from the burdens of deposit guaranty schemes instituted by several states. The all-time peak of national banks was 8,244 in mid-1922.

The McFadden Act of 1927 was intended "to put new life into the national banking system," the House Banking Committee explained. Federally chartered banks gained increased powers to invest in and underwrite securities, make real estate loans, open branches, and lend a larger amount than previously to one borrower. The Senate Banking Committee was satisfied that the measure modernized the National-Bank Act "along the lines of conservative banking, and without any deviation from the high standard which has been set by the national banking system."

Defections continued, however, because the 1927 act did not remove all the competitive disadvantages suffered by national banks. By 1929 the national bank share of all commercial bank assets was 43.7 percent—slightly less than in 1926. During the 1920s, 127 national banks with assets of at least $5 million (which was large in an era when the median bank size was less than one-tenth this amount) had converted to state banks.

Senator Glass viewed the dual banking system as "an almost insuperable obstacle in the way of sound banking legislation." In the same year (1931) a Federal Reserve Committee found that the dual banking system hampered "effective standards of supervision" and maintenance of "proper standards" for Fed membership and promotion of "sound banking policy." Nevertheless, member banks had 64.3 percent of all bank deposits in 1920, and 69.8 percent a decade later, despite reductions of reserve requirements in some states after 1913.

□ Bank Supervision

With the abolition of the fee system in 1913, examiners were required to spend as much time as was needed "to acquire a thorough knowledge" of a bank's condition, the comptroller of the currency reported in 1915. "Constructive guidance" was offered, in addition to verification of the bank's condition. Comptroller John Pole saw his primary function as that of a bank supervisor. Federal supervision in the 1920s reflected "a reasonable degree of intrusion into the affairs of banks."[12]

The 1920s saw a marked upgrading in the quality of state banking departments. Overall, state examinations had not been as effective as federal ones in protecting depositors and bank shareholders. Yet there occurred a "progressive improvement" in the 1920s and 1930s; much of the credit belonged to the high standards of the national banking system.[13]

□ Failure

Notwithstanding improved government supervision and the general prosperity from 1921 to 1929 (except for two minor cyclical downturns), almost one-fourth of the banks operating in mid-1920 had suspended by the end of the decade. On average, at least one bank closed every day of the year; in 1926 as many as 2.7 banks closed each day. Small-town banks and banks with large farm mortgage portfolios were hit especially hard. The annual rate of bank failure, 1.97 percent, contrasted sharply with the 1.06 percent rate in commercial enterprises. From 1892 to 1920 businesses had failed more frequently than banks.

From 1921 through 1929 over 5,700 banks, holding in excess of $1.6 billion in deposits, suspended operations—a number far in excess of the total for the preceding fifty-six years. The suspension rate from 1898 through 1920 was never as high as 1 percent; from 1921 through 1929 it was as low as 1.3 percent only in 1922.

The situation did not arouse much concern at the time. Disappearance of small, weak banks was expected to strengthen the banking system. Failures, in the Federal Reserve view, resulted from bad management and war-induced dislocations. In no year did losses to depositors exceed 0.23 percent of all deposits.

☐ Overview of the Twenties

A popular explanation of the high failure rate was that there were too many banks and too few bankers. The minute size of many institutions compelled the banker to assume multiple roles. In Castlewood, South Dakota in 1927, A. E. Dahl was bookkeeper for a time as well as teller, janitor, and insurance agent, "besides doing many other duties around the bank."[14]

As commercial loans stagnated, a "radical transformation" was under way. Most of the growth in loans was on security and real estate collateral. In the mid-1920s bankers were being advised to advertise for business. Banks aimed to attract more households as well as more commercial enterprises. Large banks reached out for the business of significant customers in other major centers. In rural areas, credit facilities may have been backward in 1916, but not a dozen years later. Federal instrumentalities had made a difference.

The increase in the ratio of capital to total assets from 11.7 percent in 1920 to 14.5 percent in 1930 gave a deceptive appearance of strength in the banking system. The ordeal of the Great Depression would prove to be too much for thousands of banks of all sizes.

14

A Crumbling Industry

□ Rising Tide of Failures

In November 1930, just thirteen months after the great crash on Wall Street, more than twice as many banks closed as in any previous month. December was even worse—352 banks, holding about 0.75 percent of all deposits in American banks, went under. The largest bank to fail up to that date, the Bank of United States, accounted for half of the December deposit total. The misleadingly named bank in New York City was founded in 1913 and had ranked twenty-eighth in the nation at the end of 1929.[1] January and February 1931 saw an encouraging decline in failures, but they moved up again in March. After a June rise, they declined in July and August.

Great Britain's abandonment of the gold standard in September 1931 set off a tidal wave of uncertainty and a large outflow of gold to Europe. Banks eager to strengthen their cash position sold large quantities of bonds; U.S. government securities declined 10 percent and high-grade corporates declined 20 percent in just the few months prior to January 1932. That winter saw "the most desperate scramble for liquidity" hitherto experienced.[2] In the six-month period August 1931 through January 1932, over 1,800 banks, with $1.4 billion in deposits (some 4 percent of the U.S. total) suspended.

Suspensions in 1931 were almost four times the average number for 1921–29; deposits in closed banks exceeded the aggregate for those nine years. One-tenth of the nation's banks suspended in 1931. Many surviving banks adopted a policy of restricting credit. Banks sold bonds and reduced their loans, while deposits contracted by 16 percent in the second half of 1931.

In October 1931 President Hoover urged large banks to establish the National Credit Corporation. The cooperative venture fizzled after a few weeks of lending $135 million against security collateral not usually accepted. In January 1932 the president signed a bill creating a major new federal lending agency: the Reconstruction Finance Corporation (RFC).

From 1930 through 1932 bank loans dropped 44 percent; deposits declined by 30 percent. Year after year the economy shrank: real GNP fell 9.9 percent in 1930, 7.7 percent in 1931, and 14.8 percent in 1932. Nonagricultural product prices dropped over 23 percent from 1929 to 1932; farm products tumbled by 53 percent.

The calamitous deflation brought down the banking system and the economy. If the Federal Reserve had taken early, vigorous action, deflation could have been slowed or stopped. As holders of the nation's ultimate reserves, however, they felt responsible for keeping the Federal Reserve banks liquid and solvent. Years later Dr. Emanuel Goldenweiser, the Fed's chief research economist during the 1930s, wrote, "Commercial bank concepts were simply being applied to a central bank [to which they are not relevant]."[3] Money supply regulation was definitely not a primary objective.

Until February 1932 amendments constricting statutory rules may have prevented the Federal Reserve from lending to otherwise sound banks. The Federal Reserve Act was interpreted "rather liberally in efforts to help out member banks known to be fundamentally sound but in difficulties," according to Goldenweiser.[4] Many member banks, however, found credit more readily available at a correspondent bank than from the Federal Reserve.[5] Except in the last part of 1931, member bank borrowings were a fraction of the 1928 and 1929 volume, amounting to 5–10 percent of eligible paper, excluding Treasury bonds, and 2–3 percent if the bonds were included. Low short-term money-market rates may have deceived the Federal Reserve Board into believing that an easy monetary policy was being pursued.

Meanwhile, the RFC in its first eleven months authorized almost $900 million in loans, assisting over 4,000 banks in their struggle to remain open. Congress hampered the RFC's usefulness after August 1932 by ordering the release of the list of borrowers each month. Many banks sorely in need of help stayed away from the RFC because of pride and/or fear of depositor runs. RFC loans were short-term and had to be secured with quality collateral.

In addition to making advances to enable banks to remain open, the RFC lent $80 million to closed banks during the Hoover administration. In 1933, between mid-March and October, the RFC disbursed over $900 million to depositors in 2,421 closed banks. In October 1933 the Deposit Liquidation Board was formed to speed up these operations. By the time it ceased to function in early 1936, the board had enabled many thousands of depositors to receive payment sooner and had aided in the reorganization of hundreds of banks.

Despite the cumulative deterioration of the economy, suspensions in 1932 (1,453 banks) were 37 percent below the 1931 total, and deposits in closed banks were 58 percent lower. Yet 1932 hardly qualified as a year with a "normal" failure rate, as Hoover misleadingly described it.

☐ The Tragic Holiday

To ease pressure on the banks, a number of Midwestern communities had declared moratoriums on their obligation to pay deposits on demand, many on the pretext of celebrating the bicentennial of George Washington's birthday in 1932. Nevada declared the first statewide moratorium for twelve days starting 31 October 1932. Michigan's governor declared a statewide bank holiday, 14–22 February 1933, that had to be extended. Two Detroit giants, the Guardian Union group and First Wayne, never did reopen, but after liquidation, depositors received back everything owed them plus 5 percent interest.[6]

In January 1933, for the first time since the beginning of the Depression, the public showed a preference for gold in its craving for cash. At the peak on 4 March, $626 million in gold coin and $763 million in gold certificates were held outside the Treasury and Federal Reserve banks. Of that $1.39 billion, $300 million was acquired between 15 February and 4 March. This represented "something more than the hoarding of currency which reflects a distrust of banks; . . . [it represented] a distrust of the currency itself . . . inspired by talk of devaluation of the dollar and inflation of the currency," as the head of the Federal Reserve Board of New York noted privately at the time.[7] An international run on the dollar developed in the second half of February 1933, which exhausted the Federal Reserve Bank of New York's gold reserves. In the nine days ending 3 March, the twelve Federal Reserve banks lost $425 million in gold.

Three-fourths of the $1.63 billion increase in currency in circulation between 15 February and 4 March occurred in the week of 27 February. Panic accelerated in the first three days of March. Deposit withdrawals were at the rate of 10 percent a week—over $800 million on 2 and 3 March alone. In the early hours of Saturday, 4 March, Governor Herbert Lehman, prodded by the New York Clearing House and the Federal Reserve Bank of New York, ordered a bank holiday in the Empire State; Illinois quickly followed. Most of the nation's correspondent banks were now closed.

As Franklin Roosevelt took the oath of office at noon on 4 March, banks all over the country, except in Pittsburgh, were either closed by state order or were restricting depositor withdrawals. The new President's first official act was to declare a four-day moratorium (later extended to nine) on 5 March.

The "Bank Holiday" was the culmination of no fewer than five panics in the early 1930s. On 6 March 1933, for the first time ever, banking activities were suspended simultaneously all across the United States, and all state-chartered banks—not just member banks—were under orders from Washington. Withdrawals were permitted only for emergency situations and routine payments. Depositors were philosophical; the public seemed to regard the bank holiday as a joke.

Roosevelt announced the schedule of reopening of licensed banks in a nationwide radio address Sunday evening, 12 March: the very next morning in the twelve Federal Reserve bank headquarters cities; 14 March in some 250 other cities with recognized clearinghouses; and 15 March in all other localities. Every bank wishing to open had to apply for a license certifying its soundness.

Roosevelt assured the public that only sound banks would be permitted to reopen and appealed for a return of currency hoards to the banks. The President told listeners that it was "safer to keep your money in a reopened bank than under a mattress." Roosevelt's reassuring words, calm strength, and bold actions put an end to the panic.

Three days after the Bank Holiday ended, Winthrop Aldrich, the head of the Chase National Bank, wrote to a Minneapolis banker, "Confidence has been restored . . . and the people are again willing to trust the commercial banks."[8] The public flooded the banks with currency; over $1.2 billion was returned to the Federal Reserve banks. By mid-May only about $250 million of the more than $1.5 billion in currency withdrawn between 7 February and 4 March was still outstanding.

Referring to Roosevelt's inaugural address, disenchanted populist Senator William Lemke complained, "The President drove the money-changers out of the Capital on March 4th—and they were all back on the 9th." That was the day Congress rushed through the Emergency Banking Act, which reopened the nation's banks under continued private ownership.

On 1 January 1933 there were 17,796 commercial banks in operation. In the first ten weeks of the year, 447 suspended, merged, or liquidated. At the conclusion of the Bank Holiday (15 March), some 11,878 of the 17,349 in business twelve days earlier were licensed to reopen. As of 12 April there were 4,215 with about $4 billion in deposits without a license. Over 1,100 unlicensed banks were liquidated in 1933. At the end of 1933 some 1,900 banks, with $1.25 billion in deposits, representing less than 4 percent of all commercial bank deposits, awaited reorganization.

Public opinion held bankers mainly responsible for the depression and for depositors' losses. Despite the existence of the Federal Reserve, the banking system was not panic-proof, contrary to the assurances of experts made over a stretch of twenty years.

□   Deposit Insurance

Deposit insurance was a tangible bulwark for a badly shaken public in need of more than verbal reassurances. Texas bankers had pointed to the failure of all eight state schemes as an argument against federal legislation:

> We of Texas know what a nightmare and mockery and basically unsound thing this guaranteeing of deposits is. We have had about 18 years experience and the good and solvent banks in our state were taxed $25,000,000 to pay for the mistakes and mismanagement and crookedness of people who should never have attempted banking. All Texas bankers have long since agreed that such a scheme will not work—that it encourages more and poorer banks and more and poorer bank managers.[9]

Public clamor for deposit insurance won the day, however. The Banking Act of 1933 (the Glass-Steagall Act) enabled banks to qualify for insurance on a showing of bare solvency, based on intrinsic rather than prevailing market value of assets. All member banks as well as most state nonmembers of the Fed became insured. They represented 97 percent of all deposits. Effective 1 January 1934, the first $2,500 in a deposit account was insured. The limit was raised to $5,000 in August 1934, fully protecting over 98 percent of all depositors in insured commercial banks.

When permanent arrangements went into effect on 23 August 1935, 93 percent of commercial banks with 98.6 percent of deposits were insured. The annual premium was now set at 0.0833 percent of total deposits, based on losses experienced by the banking system in noncrisis years over the seven decades ending in 1933. Banking reforms, it was expected, had eliminated the likelihood of crisis years.

The Federal Deposit Insurance Corporation (FDIC) was set up against a backdrop of 4,000 suspended banks in 1933—28.2 percent of all banks—involving $3.6 billion in deposits, and eventual depositor losses of over 15 percent of that total. Losses from 1865 to 1935 came to $3.5 billion—half of that in the years 1920–33.

Before the FDIC, depositors experienced long delays: the drawn-out liquidation process consumed a large part of the failed bank's assets in legal fees. From January 1934 through the end of 1940, the FDIC aided or closed 355 distressed banks. Mergers were arranged that assured payment in full to holders of $353 million in deposits in 129 banks. The other 226 banks were placed in receivership. Depositors lost only $3 million out of total deposits of $86 million. In the seventy years before the FDIC, losses had averaged 20 percent of deposits in closed banks; under the FDIC losses were under 1 percent of the total deposits in all closed banks.

☐ Postal Savings as a Haven

In the wake of actual and anticipated bank failures, many Americans turned to the post office. Deposits in the postal savings system were under $200 million in 1930 but reached $1.2 billion in mid-1933, held in some 7,100 post offices across the United States. Leaflets reminded postal patrons in the early 1930s of the availability of these government-guaranteed deposits.

Taxpayers were maintaining "at an enormous expense a system that unfairly competes and is tearing down our banking structure," Texas bankers were told in February 1933.[10] One argument for depositor insurance was that it would eliminate the need for the postal savings system. The original $2,500 ceiling on insured deposits matched the maximum that could be held in a postal savings account. When the deposit insurance ceiling was raised to $5,000 in 1934, bankers thought that government-sponsored competition would be brought to an end. Instead, deposits stabilized at around $1.2 billion for the rest of the decade.

☐ Capital Infusions

The Emergency Banking Act authorized RFC investment in preferred stock and capital notes. Many commercial banks added to their capital in order to qualify for deposit insurance. The FDIC's objective was a capital base (adjusted for losses) equal to at least 10 percent of deposits. In 1940 over 20 percent of insured commercial banks, with almost two-thirds of deposits in all insured banks, had less than 10 percent.

When National City Bank sold $50 million of preferred stock to the RFC in December 1933, it wrote off $24 million in loans at the same time. Continental Illinois, called the "promoter's bank" in the 1920s, was greatly weakened by the collapse of the Insull utility empire in the Midwest. In October 1933 the RFC bought $50 million in preferred stock to bolster the Chicago giant. By mid-1935 (when this particular program ended), 7,115 banks, almost half the banks in the country, had been strengthened to the tune of $1.1 billion, equal to one-third of the capital of all banks as of mid-1932. RFC losses and charge-offs turned out to be insignificant. The same was true of the $1.1 billion in RFC loans to 4,922 open banks.

Bank capital traditionally consisted of common stock supplemented by retained earnings. By the end of 1934, however, preferred stock totaled almost 11 percent of the capital funds of member banks and subordinated notes and debentures made up another 2.5 percent. To restore depleted capital funds, the RFC bought $782 million of preferred stock from 4,202 banks and $434 million in capital notes or debentures issued by 2,913 banks; by mid-1935 it held one-third of the capital in the banking system. These emergency devices were later retired.

Shareholders in national banks had always been required to contribute an additional amount, up to the par value of their stock, to pay off creditors in the event of failure. By 1930 all but ten states had similar provisions, usually in the form of "double liability," as in the 1863 National Bank Act. Altogether, the comptroller of the currency had collected $180 million from stockholder assessments of $329 million in 2,822 national bank receiverships since the first one in 1865. To encourage investment in bank stock after the collapse, the banking acts of 1933 and 1935 eliminated double liability on newly issued stock. National banks were required to accumulate retained earnings equal to at least the par value of the capital. The states followed suit.

☐ Deposit Rate Ceilings

The spirit of reform engendered by the spectacle of a tottering banking system affected the controversial practice of paying interest on interbank deposits. After the panic of 1857, the New York Clearing House suggested a ban, arguing that otherwise a bank would be compelled to "expand its operations beyond all prudent bounds." Already in March

1858, forty-two of the forty-six member banks agreed to abolish interest payments on correspondent deposits. Again in the aftermath of the panic of 1873, clearinghouse members were urged not to pay interest.

The hope that the establishment of the Federal Reserve would lead to a rechanneling of funds away from the Wall Street call loan market was not realized. Bankers' balances no longer counted toward member banks' legal reserves, but they were convenient for making investments and loans outside the immediate locality of banks in the interior, and they continued to serve as a highly liquid, income-yielding asset until 1933.

There was a widespread (but erroneous) notion that "the payment of interest on demand deposits has resulted for years and years in stripping the country banks of all their spare funds, which have been sent to the money centers for stock speculation purposes," as Senator Carter Glass alleged.[11] Accordingly, the Banking Act of 1933 forbade the payment of interest on demand deposits. This provision had little practical significance in June 1933 because New York Clearing House members had earlier reduced their rate to 0.25 percent. In the long run, however, the statutory ban on demand deposit interest affected interbank and business deposits adversely.

The eight states with a guaranty scheme had placed a limit on interest payments on time deposits to forestall anticipated aggressive rate competition, which might push paying banks into risky, unsound assets. Interest had averaged around 2 percent of total member bank deposits in the 1920s, declining to 1.5 percent by 1932. As earnings fell during the early 1930s, bankers advocated a reduction in interest payments; apparently loan rates were falling faster than deposit rates.

The 1933 law empowered the Federal Reserve Board to set a ceiling on time deposit rates offered by member banks "in order to put a stop to the competition between banks in payment of interest, which frequently induces banks to pay excessive interest and has many times over brought banks into serious trouble," said the chairman of the House Banking Committee, expressing a widely held belief that still persists despite lack of supporting evidence. Time deposit rate ceilings applicable to all insured commercial banks (Regulation Q) had no operational significance for banks until around 1950.

☐ Separating Investment Banking from Commercial Banking

Another significant reform that grew out of the banking collapse was the separation of corporate business security underwriting from commercial banking. The sharp decline in volume and the heavy losses sustained after the stock market collapse prompted commercial banks to rid themselves of these operations. Winthrop W. Aldrich, newly appointed head of Chase National Bank, was convinced that "the spirit of speculation should be eradicated from the management of commercial banks."[12] To the dismay of the Wall Street private banks, he also urged (and Congress agreed) that investment bankers be forbidden to take deposits. In March 1933 Aldrich announced that Chase Securities was to be separated from the bank, as did the new leadership at National City Bank. Impressed by the speed with which the two largest American banks accomplished their severance, Congress ordered the divorcement of investment from commercial banking to be completed within a year of the passage of the Banking Act on 16 June 1933.

The liquidation of the First Security Company by the First National Bank of New York marked the end of the oldest Wall Street affiliate, one that had joined with Morgan and National City in underwriting securities of leading railroads and industrial firms. Morgan's investment banking functions were turned over to the newly organized partnership of Morgan, Stanley and Company. The firm's commercial banking operations continued under the historic name J. P. Morgan and Company until the 1959 merger that created the Morgan Guaranty Trust Company. The former security affiliate of the First National Bank of Boston became the separate investment house, First Boston Corporation.

Most private bankers remained in investment banking. Firms like Kuhn, Loeb and Company and J.&W. Seligman discontinued their deposit activities, a role earlier assumed largely to suit customers' convenience.

The Senate banking committee had generalized from a few isolated cases. The record of security affiliates was certainly no worse than that of the investment banks, which previously had dominated the new issues market. A study covering 1921–32 found no significant difference between all issues of the eight largest affiliates and the eight largest private investment banks. "The belief in the utter financial depravity of integrated as compared with specialized investment banking is a myth," George W. Edwards concluded.[13]

Commercial banks were permitted to continue to underwrite general government obligations (federal, state, and local). Over the years they have played an active role in these markets.

Some critics feared that divorcement would diminish the availability of underwriting facilities at a time when encouragement of business investment was so urgently needed. Elimination of banks from the ranks of corporate security underwriters had the effect of hindering business recovery to some (unknown) extent. At the same time, investment banks continued to depend on commercial banks for financing their operations.

☐ Overbanking and Other Factors in the Collapse

Overbanking contributed to the large numbers of failures of the 1920s and early 1930s. "There were too many banks, and competition among them was too sharp," the chairman of the FDIC testified in 1955, pledging his agency to work to prevent the recurrence of such a state of affairs. Within the city limits of Chicago, 318 new banks were launched between 1921 and 1935; 263 of these failed or disappeared by merger by 1935. Erie, Pennsylvania (population 116,000), had ten banks; five went under in 1933.

It cost less to start a bank in the early 1900s than to buy a good farm. Brunswick County, Virginia, exemplified the rural situation. Its first bank opened in 1890; by 1921 there were six: four in the county seat and two others in towns with under 400 inhabitants. Of the nine established after 1890, only three were still open at the end of 1933.

Leading local businessmen had traditionally viewed the role of bank president as the pinnacle of their careers. Senator Glass was not alone when he argued that a lack of "real bankers" had been an important factor in the failures.

The 1933 law repealed the 1900 provision authorizing national banks with only $25,000 in capital. Over the period 1921–31 over 59 percent of suspended banks (state and national) had no more than $25,000 in capital. The minimum for national banks was restored to $50,000.

Between mid-1931 and mid-1932 bond prices tumbled as deposit withdrawals compelled banks to liquidate securities in a demoralized market. Losses on bonds and securities owned by national banks were under 1 percent in every year from 1922 through 1929, 1.1 percent in 1930, 2.5 percent in 1931 and 1932, and 3.2 percent in 1933. Deterioration in the quality of loans and investments (measuring their quality at the time they were added to the bank's portfolio) was not a major cause of bank failure—at least not after 1930, Milton Friedman and Anna Schwartz have insisted. Federal Reserve policies, they argue, failed to provide commercial banks with additional reserves to meet the demand for additional currency; such reserves would have prevented a multiple contraction of deposits.

Currency proved to be elastic. In February 1933, the amount of

Federal Reserve notes in circulation was double the total of the late
1920s, and their share of total currency in circulation had risen from 37
percent to 54 percent. But currency was not at the heart of the problem.
If the Federal Reserve banks had bought large amounts of U.S. government bonds in the last half of February, the March 1933 crisis might
have been averted.[14]

Few American industries were more adversely affected than banking by the sharp business contraction that began in mid-1929. Deposits
had expanded by $18 billion between 1921 and 1930, only to decline by
$19 billion in the next three years. Suspended banks accounted for $7
billion of this shrinkage. Losses to depositors were 1 percent of deposits
in all commercial banks in 1931, and over 2.2 percent in 1933. The
severe business downturn brought down countless banks. Their failure
in turn spelled disaster for the overall economy, as credit availability
diminished.

The 1933 panic came at the very end of the contraction phase of the
business cycle. Earlier panics had occurred at the beginning of a cycle
and had ushered in business decline. How mistaken the 1931 edition of
the *Encyclopedia of Banking and Finance* proved to be when it stated,
"This country is now thought to be panic-proof."

The nightmare of the early 1930s haunted bankers and supervisors
for the next quarter of a century. Viewing the debacle as a banking rather
than a monetary phenomenon, the agencies followed a "policy of keeping
banks and banking practices within the bounds of rightful competition,"
as the FDIC explained in 1955.[15] Bankers, too, remained cautious.

15

Reconstruction and War

BANKING IN THE UNITED STATES FARED worse than in any other major industrialized economy during the Great Depression. At the low, bank credit (loans plus investments) was 38 percent below the 1929 level, compared with a 20 percent average decline in thirty-eight other nations. Reflecting the upheaval of the early 1930s, cash plus U.S. government obligations rose from 23 percent of assets in 1929 to 39 percent in mid-1933, to 52 percent in mid-1937, and to over 61 percent at the end of 1940. Total loans, almost 58 percent of total assets in 1929, shrank to less than 26 percent in 1940, while capital accounts declined from 14 percent to under 10 percent of total assets. Bank loans in 1940 were half of the 1929 amount. Adjusted for inflation, 1929's loan volume was not reached again until 1951.

☐ Business Loans

From March 1933 to September 1934 a famous Chicago district survey found "a genuinely unsatisfied demand for credit on the part of solvent borrowers, most of whom could make economically sound use of working capital."[1] The banking crises from 1930 to 1933 deepened and lengthened the Great Depression. For small businesses, farmers, and households, credit was expensive and more difficult to obtain. This squeeze, Ben

Bernanke has argued, reduced aggregate demand and prolonged the economic decline.[2]

Bankers' reluctance to make risky loans was often criticized privately at board meetings of the New York Federal Reserve Bank in the early 1930s. RFC Chairman Jesse Jones (a former Houston banker) publicly denounced bankers' conservatism on many occasions, urging them to accommodate all deserving borrowers. Jones sent all banks a circular letter in July 1938, as the economy wallowed once again in recession, stating that too many banks were waiting on the sidelines instead of lending. As long as banks were not meeting all legitimate demands for credit, government would be forced to lend, he warned. The next day the president of the American Bankers Association replied that banks were "making every effort to find suitable borrowers" and pointed to the banks' obligation to protect depositors by finding truly bankworthy loans.

Fewer than 9 percent of manufacturing firms surveyed for the years 1933 through 1938 experienced difficulties in obtaining loans: 5.1 percent reported that loans were refused, and 3.7 percent faced restrictions. The National Industrial Conference Board found the adverse decision to be "fully justified" in a substantial number of cases; in others, earnings and capital merited a loan.

Loans to business began to slowly increase after a $15 billion low in 1935, when they represented 31 percent of total bank assets. Though business activity in 1936–37 was nearly equal to that of 1928–29, business loans remained well below the earlier level. In 1940 business loans and corporate securities combined were 18 percent of bank assets, half of the ratio in both 1928 and 1900. Banking's share of net corporate debt (long- and short-term) was 23.3 percent at the end of 1929, but only 14 percent a decade later.

Around 1900 business loans to finance working capital requirements of mainly small and medium-size firms in manufacturing and trade represented about half of total assets, but not quite 25 percent by 1940. Firms with assets under $5 million received about three-fourths of business loans. Over 80 percent of the dollar total was unsecured in 1940.

☐ Lending Innovations

A far-reaching "technical revolution" in debt financing began in the 1920s and accelerated after 1933.[3] Banks devised new ways of meeting the needs of small and medium-sized firms for short- and intermediate-term credit. Techniques developed earlier for consumer installment financing were adapted for business lending.

A wider range of collateral was now acceptable. Accounts receivable financing exceeded $800 million by 1940; banks provided 40 percent of the total. Unlike the practice of factors, who earlier had the field to themselves, banks did not notify the borrowers' customers of their involvement in most cases. Installment financing of commercial and industrial equipment was pioneered by commercial finance companies. Banks overtook them by 1940 with $200 million of such loans.

Field warehouse receipts were the basis for 2 percent of commercial and industrial loans by the end of 1941, slightly less than the amount of commercial bank loans secured by receivables. About one in eight banks was making the former type of loan, while one in four engaged in accounts receivable financing around 1940.

Far more significant quantitatively than the innovations in collateral, term loans had an original maturity of more than one year and generally incorporated provisions for amortization. Used only in negligible amounts in 1933, the $2.2 billion of term loans outstanding by the end of 1940, constituted nearly one-third of banks' commercial and industrial loans and about 12 percent of all their loans. Term loans in the late 1930s were increasingly made in smaller amounts to lesser businesses. By 1941 over half of them went to firms with less than $5 million in assets. Previously, banks had made short-term loans with implied renewals at maturity. George Moore of National City Bank pointed out that "the apparent increase in term lending was really an illusion."[4]

The lengthened maturity came to be approved by the supervisory authorities. In September 1934 a joint federal-state bank examiners' conference agreed not to criticize as "slow" a loan whose payment was reasonably certain, whatever its maturity, but many examiners continued to raise the traditional objections. The Banking Act of 1935 recognized that changes in business finance had significantly shrunk the short-term self-liquidating paper eligible for rediscount privileges under the original Federal Reserve Act. By broadening the class of eligible paper, Congress wished to encourage longer term lending in the hope of stimulating business recovery. Banks were now free to establish policies appropriate to their circumstances; federal banking agencies welcomed less liquid loans.

The trend toward longer average maturities, already under way in the 1920s as a result of bank purchases of corporate bonds, was accelerated by the development and spectacular growth of term loans. Whereas 57 percent of all loans matured in ninety days or less in 1913, only 30 percent did in 1940. Almost half of bank credit to nonagricultural, nonfinancial business in 1940 had an initial maturity exceeding one year. On the eve of World War II, banks held 3.1 percent of the short-term debt of nonfinancial business and 3.5 percent of their debt due in a year or more. Term loans totaled 53 percent of the latter.

With the decline in current assets as a proportion of total business assets after 1920, especially from 1929 to 1935, the demand for short-term business loans weakened. Firms were anxious to retire short-term debt. Others refinanced long-term bonds at the prevailing low rates on term loans, avoiding the delay and registration expenses involved in meeting Securities and Exchange Commission requirements for public offerings.

Even the sharp business downturn of 1937–38 produced no serious defaults on term loans. They turned out to be satisfactory, profitable, and safe. Yet as late as 1945 probably a majority of experts continued to assert that only short-term loans were appropriate for banks.

☐ The Prime Rate Arrives

The prime rate—the interest charged on short term bank loans to corporations with the highest credit standing—came to the fore around 1934 after short-term interest rates had dropped sharply. In June 1935 and again in 1937, the Committee on Credit Practices of the prestigious Association of Reserve City Banks affirmed that the minimum loan rate should be equal to the interest on bankers' acceptances plus the selling charge—at the time, 1.6875 percent. The prime rate remained, however, at 1.5 percent from 1934 through 1947. Competition prevented bankers from getting the higher rate.

☐ Farm Loans

Production credit associations, federally sponsored short-term lenders, came into existence in 1933. Together with Commodity Credit Corporation loans and various other emergency programs designed to deal with the 63 percent decline in farm prices between August 1929 and March 1933, federal agencies (direct and sponsored) provided 30 percent of short-term, non–real estate farm loans outstanding by January 1935, and over 50 percent two years later. The commercial bank share of all institutional loans of this type fell from 98 percent in 1930 to 58 percent by 1940.

Thanks to the federal land banks, mortgage loans were available to farmers at lower interest costs, with more liberal maturities and loan sizes. The land banks' $2.15 billion peak mortgage volume in 1936 was 30 percent of the total outstanding. Commercial banks had 10.1 percent of the 1930 aggregate, and only 8.4 percent in 1940.

Federal agencies held an amount equal to only 4.7 percent of total agricultural loans of all types made by all private institutions in 1930, but 58.2 percent by 1940. Federally sponsored agencies (like the federal land banks) participated even more, holding loans amounting to 26 percent of the private total in 1930 and 87.9 percent by 1940.

Though bank lending to agriculture increased by over $300 million between 1935 and 1940, it remained below the 1911 total. Not until the late 1940s was the $3.5 billion of 1930 matched again. Commercial banks, the source of 29.7 percent of all agricultural credit in 1913 and 23.9 percent in 1930, provided only 15 percent in 1940.

☐ Government Loans to the Private Sector

Direct loans from the federal government (a vestige of World War I's War Finance Corporation) came to 0.1 percent of the $112 billion net business debt in 1930. In 1940 the federal share was 1.1 percent of the $81 billion outstanding.

RFC loans to business aggregated $3.2 billion from 1934 (when the agency was first authorized to lend in this field) until 1953 (when it was superseded by the Small Business Administration). One-third of this total was made available before 1941. Bank participation through loan-sharing or federal guarantees was encouraged.

Although RFC loans were restricted to firms unable to obtain credit from private sources, federal activities did compete with and restrict the markets of private lenders. The government extended loans "so secured or of such sound value as reasonably to assure repayment" (in the words of the 1932 RFC Act). But they represented more than ordinary risk, and rates were below what was necessary to cover full costs. Loans went mainly to medium-sized manufacturers for one- to ten-year periods. These amortized term loans stimulated commercial banks to expand in this field.

The Export-Import Bank, opened in 1934 to encourage American foreign trade, had over $130 million in direct business loans outstanding by the end of 1940. Unlike the RFC, the Export-Import Bank is still operating.[5]

Federal agency loans reached a high point in relative importance in 1940, when they amounted to 4.8 percent of the combined total of net private, state, and local government debt, contrasted with 0.3 percent a decade earlier. Federally sponsored agencies (mostly in agriculture and housing) already had 1 percent of the combined total in 1930, but their share grew much less rapidly thereafter, reaching only 2.2 percent by 1940. In the peak year, 1934, federal loans and loan insurance combined were 9 percent of the depression-shriveled GNP, but by 1940 were only 3.2 percent of a much larger GNP.

Government's expanded role in lending displeased bankers. The New York Trust Company citing the $6.04 billion in loans held by the government—an amount equal to 28 percent of commercial bank loans as of mid-1938—deplored the fact that the federal government was "conducting the largest banking operation in this country, if not in the world."[6]

☐ Federal Government Mortgage Activity

Federal home loan banks, established in 1932 with government-supplied capital (which was repaid by 1951), served to buttress faltering savings and loan associations. The Home Owners Loan Corporation—set up in 1933 to refinance defaulted mortgages and liquidated without loss in 1951—enabled over one million families to retain their homes; it also strengthened financial institutions by removing $3.1 billion in bad loans previously on their books.

The Federal Housing Administration (FHA), by far the most significant New Deal housing measure, opened in 1934. By 1939 over one-third of all private nonfarm housing starts were FHA-insured: 37 percent of all one- and two-family homes and 21 percent of multi-family dwellings, representing altogether 20 percent of all nonfarm mortgages under $20,000. Commercial banks made one-third of all FHA-insured home mortgage loans from 1935 to 1952. In 1938 the Federal National Mortgage Association was created to establish a secondary (resale) market for FHA-guaranteed mortgages. The federal agencies popularized amortized mortgages with periodic repayment of part of the principal and encouraged longer maturities and an increase in the loan-to-value ratio.

Urban housing mortgage loans from the federal agencies, $2.4 billion at the end of 1940, were $600 million below the mid-1936 peak. Federal farm mortgages, at $2.5 billion, were $400 million below their high at the end of 1936. By 1940 commercial banks had $600 million more than the federal government agencies in urban mortgages but remained far behind in farm mortgages.

□ Real Estate Loans

Bank holdings of nonfarm residential mortgages fell by almost 25 percent between 1929 and 1934, before climbing to a record $3 billion in 1940—one-eighth of the total mortgages outstanding. These mortgages comprised 4.6 percent of all commercial bank assets in 1930, and 4.2 percent in 1940. Increasingly, banks financed residences rather than business real estate. Dwellings were the basis for 42 percent of total bank mortgages for three decades until the mid-1920s, for 56 percent by 1930, and for 74 percent by 1940.

The Banking Act of 1935 continued the trend toward more liberal mortgage lending powers for national banks. Commercial banks had overtaken mutual savings banks in mortgage lending on one- to four-family houses by 1940, and the gap between the two subsequently grew.

□ Consumer Lending Becomes Important

Banks operated 1,222 personal loan departments at the end of 1938, of which 1,065 opened after 1929. Carrying 2–3 percent of all consumer installment paper in 1929, commercial banks had 10 percent in 1936, and over 26 percent by 1941.

In 1933 fewer than 1 percent of banks were lending to persons on the basis of character and income. Many banks acquired their first experience with consumer loans in extending home repair and modernization financing under the National Housing Act of 1934. By the end of 1935 over 6,000 banks were making FHA-insured modernization loans. Even after FHA coverage on these Title I loans was reduced from 20 percent to 10 percent of a bank's portfolio, most continued to make them. Banks had over 42 percent of the total held by all institutional lenders in 1941.

Many banks went into other types of consumer lending as well. Beginning in 1935 the Bank of America (which had been offering low-cost loans in small sums from the time it opened in 1904) announced on radio, billboards, and newspapers its willingness to finance autos. Commercial banks' auto installment loans were over $600 million in 1940, fifteen times the 1930 volume, but still under one-third of the total outstanding. Over half of the banks' personal loans carried an endorser's signature. Single-name, chattel mortgage loans remained the specialty of personal finance companies.

In 1940 banks had fifteen times more money in all types of consumer installment credit than in 1930. Although only about one-tenth of the nation's banks were in the field to an important extent, over one-fourth of those with over $10 million in loans and investments were involved. While banks greatly increased personal installment loans during the 1930s, their single-payment consumer loans in 1940 were $200 million below the 1930 total of $836 million. Other financial institutions increased their single-payment loans from $118 million to $164 million during the 1930s.

☐ Brokers' Loans

Insufficient legal authority hampered the Federal Reserve Board's strong desire to discourage "speculative" loans in the late 1920s. Member banks not seeking discount accommodation, nonmember banks, and nonbank lenders in the call loan market were all outside the Federal Reserve's jurisdiction until 1933. The appearance of excessive security loans had been "an outstanding development in the pre-panic period" in the view of the Senate Banking Committee. Accordingly, the Banking Act of 1933 aimed "to prevent the undue diversion of funds into speculative operations." Brokers' loans were thought to divert short-term funds into the financing of capital improvements and to deprive the commercial sector of its due proportion of credit. The Federal Reserve banks were therefore asked to ascertain whether bank credit was being used excessively for speculative purposes. Moreover, member banks could no longer place call loans "for the account of others," (nonbank lenders), a prohibition already instituted by New York City banks in November 1931.

These measures, intended to affect the supply of funds for security loans, were less significant than a provision in the Securities Exchange Act of 1934 that empowered the Federal Reserve to set margin requirements for all lenders (not merely member banks). Since May 1936 all commercial banks have had to follow Regulation U when making loans for the purpose of buying and carrying securities. This practice was yet another attempt by Congress to constrain credit diversion into speculation. As the Federal Reserve Board of Governors pointed out in May 1988, however, "The use of credit to finance purchases of stock does not reduce the amount of credit available to industry, commerce or agriculture. The borrowed funds . . . are transferred to the seller, who reinvests the proceeds."[7]

Banks ceased to use brokers' loans to adjust their reserve position. After 1933 brokers were handled like other bank borrowers. Call loans dwindled into insignificance, usually amounting to less than $1 billion in the 1930s.

☐ Bank Investments

The 1920s had been marked by "overinvestment in securities of all kinds," according to the Senate Banking Committee. The maximum amount that national banks could invest in nongovernmental obligations of any one borrower was reduced in 1933, and further lowered to 10 percent of the bank's capital and surplus by the Banking Act of 1935. The comptroller of the currency (who had previously required only that investments be marketable) began to control their quality, ruling out "speculative issues" in 1936.

Relative to bank loans, total securities went from 40 percent in 1929 to 100 percent in 1934, and to 140 percent in 1940. U.S. government bonds alone came within 5 percent of total bank loans in 1940. Survivors of the debacle of the early 1930s craved safety and liquidity. U.S. government obligations, over half of total bank investments already in 1933, reached almost 70 percent by 1940. State and local government bond holdings increased by more than 70 percent during the 1930s, exceeding bank-owned private-sector bonds in 1940 for the first time; the difference widened greatly in subsequent years.

Bank holdings of private corporations' bonds declined by half during the 1930s. Term loans combined with bank investments in business securities, however, showed a growth of 50 percent over the same period. Bank holdings of medium- and long-term debt of nonfinancial corporations actually rose from 9.5 percent to 13.1 percent of the total outstanding.

Most bankers disliked the New Deal and its deficits but esteemed the bonds that financed much of Roosevelt's program. In 1940 federal bonds were almost one-fourth of all bank assets. In mid-1930 banks owned 30 percent of all U.S. government bonds outstanding, and in 1940 38.6 percent of a much larger total.

First introduced in 1929, Treasury bills (obligations maturing in less than one year, generally ninety days) became the dominant element in the money market by the early 1930s. At times, banks held half or more of the total bills outstanding. The same was true of Treasury notes. Bank ownership of (longer term) U.S. government bonds was around 30 percent of the total.

Heretofore, as in the second half of 1932, open market operations had been used to influence the level of bank reserves. In December 1934, however, Federal Reserve banks were authorized to make maturity swaps in their portfolios to help maintain stability in the government bond market or to assist the Treasury's financing operations. The following spring they bought some long-term bonds to keep the market orderly. In April 1937 transactions necessary for "preserving an orderly market" were authorized. A year later the Fed sought to avoid too rapid or too great a rise in bond prices. A stable government bond market thus developed into a concern of the Federal Reserve.

☐ Swollen Excess Reserves

Commercial bank demand for liquidity in the 1930s was reflected in increased holdings of cash equivalents (as well as of short-term U.S. government securities). Over and beyond the legally required reserves held at the Federal Reserve, the total of vault cash, cash items in the process of collection, and balances at all banks constituted 13.5 percent of member bank assets in 1929, 17 percent in 1933, and 28 percent in 1939. Enormous gold inflows into the United States pushed excess reserves of member banks to $2.8 billion at the end of 1935, to over $5 billion in 1939, and to $7 billion at the end of 1940, when they almost equaled the amount of required reserves. Treasury bills yielded only 0.05 percent in the spring of 1934 and did not offer more than 0.35 percent until 6 May 1942, except in May 1937 when the interest reached 0.74 percent.

The inflationary potential of the unprecedented swelling of excess reserves alarmed the Federal Reserve. The Banking Act of 1935 authorized the doubling of reserve requirements from the previous ratio. Flexible ratios "to prevent injurious credit expansion and contraction" replaced the nineteenth-century concept (in the original Federal Reserve Act) of fixed reserve requirements for the purpose of providing a liquid safeguard of deposits. Between August 1936 and May 1937 the Fed used its new powers to the fullest, bringing the excess down to 14 percent of requires reserves. The severe economic downturn in 1937–38 (attributed by monetarist economists to this action) led to somewhat lower reserve requirements in April 1938. Despite higher reserve requirements, excess reserves were 4.1 percent of total assets of member banks at the end of 1936, and as much as 10.6 percent in 1940.

☐ Currency and the Banks

Federal Reserve notes surpassed national bank notes by 1918 and were three times as great in 1933. Despite the growing importance of Federal Reserve notes, at various times in the 1920s national bank notes exceeded the 1913 level of $715 million. Over $650 million were outstanding in the early 1930s and over $900 million were outstanding in 1933 and 1934. The U.S. government bonds that backed them were retired as of 1 August 1935. Thus ended a century and a half of activity, long after provision of currency ceased to be a major function of privately owned commercial banks.

Even the retirement of all national bank notes did not signify the achievement of Willis's ideal of "a single uniform currency, provided by federal reserve banks, resting upon an adequate gold reserve issued only for commercial paper, and expanding and contracting as business requirements made it needful."[8] Silver certificates lingered on until the end of the 1960s; U.S. notes (greenbacks) still circulate today. Moreover, the link between Federal Reserve notes and gold and commercial paper was severed long ago.

Rigid collateral requirements of the Federal Reserve Act had "prevented the Reserve System from adopting a monetary policy that was clearly in the interests of combating the prevailing deflation" when gold left the United States in 1931–32, the House Banking Committee recognized. After untoward delay, U.S. bonds owned by the Federal Reserve banks were made eligible in 1932, but only temporarily because of misgivings about this departure from principle. In 1935 the arrangement became more permanent. Subsequent modifications in the law at long last made Federal Reserve notes truly elastic.

☐ Time Deposits in Relative Decline

Currency held by the public rose over 34 percent from 1930 to 1933, while deposits held by individuals, partnerships, and nonbank corporations declined sharply—almost 38 percent in the case of demand deposits and over 42 percent for time deposits. In 1933 time deposits amounted to 42 percent of the total, excluding interbank and government deposits.

Commercial bank time deposits increased by only one-third from 1933 to 1940. Not until early 1944, amidst the high saving of wartime prosperity, was the $20.2 billion of 1930 seen again. Banks became uninterested in time deposits during the depression years; some 400 did not accept them at all by 1940. Interest paid dropped from an average of 3.2 percent in 1930 to 2.4 percent in 1934, and to 1.3 percent by 1940.

☐ Postal Savings Competition

Some competition for time deposits came from the Postal Savings System. The FDIC chairman expressed the hope that postal savings would soon be limited to bankless communities. In mid-1935, however, only 21.4 percent of post offices that accepted deposits were in such towns. Few places with first- and second-class post offices had no banks.

After 1933 total postal deposits stabilized at around $1.25 billion for the remainder of the decade. The all-time record of $3.4 billion in postal savings deposits was in mid-1948. Decades after the need had passed, the system was finally discontinued in 1966.

□ Service Charges on Demand Deposits

Demand deposits held by individuals, partnerships, and corporations other than commercial banks surpassed the previous peak of mid-1930 six years later, and were over 31 percent greater by 1940. This substantial growth occurred in the face of the 1933 prohibition on interest payments, and service charges.

In 1931 perhaps half of all the accounts in banks were being carried at "an actual loss," the ABA's Bank Management Commission estimated: "It is difficult to free public thinking of the old idea that banks are institutions for 'free service.' "[9] The National Recovery Administration (NRA) gave much impetus to the movement for service charges on demand deposits. By 1935 94 percent of the banks responding to an ABA questionnaire had adopted service charges. As the decade ended, few well-managed banks failed to levy them.

Just as minimum balance requirements became widespread, special checking accounts (with no minimum balance) made their appearance. A New York City bank began to offer such accounts at 5¢ a check in 1935. Bankers feared for the soundness of the plan, but by 1950 over one-third of the nation's banks offered it.

□ Cooperation through Clearinghouses

City clearinghouses numbered 362 in 1925, 391 in 1931, and 351 in the late 1930s. Smaller towns and country districts began to organize regional clearinghouses under ABA guidance in the late 1920s. Regional clearinghouses increased from 56 in 1931 to 233 in the late 1930s, at a time when the NRA inspired the organization of trade associations in many other industries as well.

Thus, the Arkansas Bankers Association code of sound banking practices (adopted in 1931) was left to the fifteen regional clearinghouses for interpretation; within each region, service charges would be uniform. Wisconsin regional groups had begun to do the same even earlier, in addition to agreeing on uniform charges on small loans and on a reduction of interest paid on time deposits. The state banking department began to work with these regional groups in the 1930s; by 1945 most banks in a particular Wisconsin district had a uniform schedule of service charges.

□ Persistence of Nonpar Banks

Checks drawn on nonpar banks could not clear through the Federal Reserve. At the end of 1940, 2,715 banks, 18 percent of all commercial banks (mainly in the Midwest and the South), were not yet on the par list and derived some revenues from exchange charges.

□ New York's Position and Correspondent Balances

In the years after the banking collapse, New York gained notably in deposits held by the public (excluding governments and banks) as corporate balances found their way to the Wall Street giants. New York City banks held around 20 percent of the nation's total deposits in the 1920s, 23.6 percent in 1933, and 27.4 percent in 1939—well above the 1900 position of 25.4 percent. By 1945, however, New York's share was down to 22 percent.

Correspondent balance shifts were responsible for some of these changes. As large excess reserves accumulated in the 1930s, the proportion of interbank deposits to total deposits—10 percent in 1930 and 10.8 percent in 1933—rose to 16.8 percent by 1940. With explicit interest payment ruled out by the Banking Act of 1933, various correspondent services were offered as compensation for deposit balances. Interbank deposits in New York City member banks were 38.4 percent of the national total in 1930, 40 percent in 1934, and a striking 51.6 percent in 1939, but they dropped sharply by 1945.

□ New and Insured Banks

The Banking Act of 1935 marked the official end of free banking, less than a century after the movement began. Before the comptroller of the currency could charter a new bank (or the FDIC insure a state nonmember bank), several factors, among others, had to be considered: "future earnings prospects" and "the convenience and needs of the community

to be served by the bank." Such standards had already been used by
several states, as well as by the comptroller at times. The FDIC hailed
the 1935 law as an aid "to prevent a recurrence of the evil which is to be
greatly feared . . . the return of the overbanked condition of the early
twenties."[10] In the 1936–45 decade, altogether 535 new banks opened,
less than one-fifth of the 1921–35 average pace. As many as one-fifth of
the banks chartered from 1936 to 1945 opened without FDIC protection
for their depositors. Subsequently, the proportion of noninsured banks
became negligible.

The chartering of new national banks in the quarter-century beginning in 1936 went "to the extreme of unduly restricted approval," according to a study prepared at the direction of the Office of the Comptroller of
the Currency.[11] Well into the 1940s the United States was "seriously
underbanked," an ABA-sponsored monograph suggested.[12] Between
1930 and 1935 the number of commercial banks declined by one-third.
The further net decrease of 934 in the next four years brought the total to
the lowest level since 1903. The 7,400 average population per banking
office in 1940 was more than double the 1920 figure.

☐ Mergers

Mergers in the early 1930s reached an all-time high of 1,567 in the
years 1930–31. In the next two years, half as many mergers occurred.
These figures do not include numerous takeovers of suspended banks by
sound ones. The desire to avert failure prompted many combinations.

After 1933 mergers abated further, averaging under 200 a year for
the rest of the decade, and under 100 a year from 1941 through 1945.
From 1935 through 1945, 153 mergers were arranged with the financial
aid of the FDIC, thereby giving complete protection to over $395 million
in deposits.

☐ Branching Spreads

Acquired banks were often turned into branch offices in states where
branching was permitted. Between 1931 and 1935, twelve of the
twenty-two states with unit banking laws decided to allow branches. A
number of other states expanded the territory in which branching was
permissible. In New York the state was divided into nine districts in
1934, each comprising several counties; New York City banks remained
confined to the city's five counties. Communities that would otherwise
have been bankless benefited.

Not even the collapse of the early 1930s could move Congress to authorize national banks to branch beyond the extent to which state banks were allowed. National banks could not branch in a unit banking state; there were still ten unit states in 1935. Capital requirements for branches remained onerous until 1952.

Between mid-1930 and the end of 1933, the branch total declined (by 736) for the only time in the twentieth century. By the end of 1940, 741 branches had been added. Head-office city branches fell by one-third during the 1930s, while out-of-town offices increased 70 percent.

The number of banks with at least one branch grew by 200 between 1930 and 1940, when they represented 7 percent of the total. Until the mid-1930s unit banks had the bulk of assets. On the eve of World War II, their share was down to 47 percent.

□ Chains and Holding Companies

In 1931 there were 176 chains, each controlling at least three separately chartered banks, with 908 affiliates and some 2 percent of the U.S. deposit total. About the same deposit share was held in 1939 by ninety-six chains with a total of 424 affiliates. Most chain banks were located in unit banking states.

Group banking declined in the early 1930s, when a number succumbed to failure. By the late 1930s, and for a decade thereafter, holding companies with at least three banks had 7 percent of all banking offices and 11 percent of all deposits.

The Banking Act of 1933, the first federal effort at regulation, covered only holding companies with member bank subsidiaries. To obtain a permit to vote its member bank stock, a holding company was subjected to examination by the Federal Reserve Board. Few (only twenty in 1948) actually came under the board's supervision.

□ Dual Banking Survives

State-chartered banks had over half of all bank assets from 1920 to 1933. Subsequently, national banks regained the lead, though they remained far fewer in numbers.

Mainly as a result of the sharply higher failure rate of state nonmember banks, the member bank deposit share increased from 70 percent in 1930 to 80 percent in 1933—and to a peak of 85 percent in 1942, remaining above 80 percent until 1971. Roosevelt was not inclined to compel banks to belong to the Federal Reserve System.[13] By being FDIC-insured, however, 90 percent of state banks came under federal jurisdiction. The new agency's bank examination policies had the effect of raising standards among nonmember banks.

State banking departments improved their examinations under FDIC prodding; typically, however, national bank examiners were more competent. This was one factor in A. E. Dahl's decision to apply for a national charter in Rapid City, South Dakota, where every one of the state banks had closed in the early 1930s. Dahl also felt that there was less politics in the national banking system.[14]

☐ Supervisory Examination Reforms

Before the Great Depression, supervisors evaluated banks based on the ideal of liquid, open market paper, marketable securities, and self-liquidating loans to commerce, industry, and agriculture. In September 1931 Comptroller John Pole instructed national bank examiners not to charge off bonds rated in the top four grades, regardless of their market price, unless there had been a default. This pioneering approach in the direction of "intrinsic" valuation was hailed at the time by the Senate Banking Committee. Pole understood that "present conditions demand sympathetic treatment." In July 1932 he complained that some examiners did not "fully appreciate the extremely abnormal business conditions and the weakened condition of the securities market at this time."

In July 1938, with a major recession as background, the three federal banking agencies, as well as the National Association of Supervisors of State Banks, agreed to emphasize intrinsic value rather than liquidity in future examination of loans. Similarly, bonds would be judged on their "inherent soundness" rather than on daily market fluctuations. Marketable securities with a reasonable risk would be valued at cost. The "slow loan" category, used for over two decades for those that did not conform to the concept of self-liquidating loans, was replaced by Classification II, whereby "a substantial and unreasonable degree of risk to the bank" had to be involved. As long as ultimate repayment was "reasonably assured," loans would not be so classified.

The 1938 agreement thus dealt with the recognized tendency of examiners to be hypercritical during depressions and more easygoing in good times, thereby exerting undesirable procyclical influence on bank credit extension. The stress on soundness rather than liquidity was also reflected in the uniform examination report form adopted by the federal agencies in 1938 and used in a majority of states as well. Chairman Marriner Eccles wrote to President Roosevelt on 24 June 1938 that the new approach of the Board of Governors would "stop the deflationary trend resulting from contraction of bank credit under the pressures of previously prevailing bank examination policies and restrictive investment regulations."[15]

As late as 1941 however, bankers complained to the Senate Banking Committee that their loans and securities were being more severely criticized by examiners than at the end of the 1920s. Thus, the Bank of America had to contend with the classification of its innovation, economically desirable accounts receivable and factoring loans as "slow" or "doubtful."

The federal agencies hoped that the 1938 changes would "afford the banks a broader opportunity for service to the community and for profitable outlet for some of their abundant, idle funds." The main impact was felt only after World War II.

□ Return to Profitability

J. S. Douglas, an early foe of the New Deal, voluntarily closed his Bank of Clemenceau (Arizona) in 1933, in protest against Roosevelt's policies. He felt that "no honest man can remain in the banking business."[16] The industry suffered net losses in 1933 and 1934. Banking became profitable once again in 1935. Net profits over the next five years averaged a 5.7 percent return on capital. By 1939 Continental Illinois National Bank was able to retire $50 million of RFC-owned preferred stock with earnings from long-term U.S. government bonds.

In June 1940 a spokesman for the ABA reported that banks "have never been in a sounder financial condition." He assured the Senate Banking Committee that "whatever the demands of this country and no matter how great the credit requirements may be in this emergency which seems to lie ahead, the chartered banking system is able, has the resources, has the attitude, has the interest and the desire adequately to serve the credit needs of business and industry in this country."[17] By 1940 banking had recovered significantly from the trauma of the early 1930s, under a president who, as a lawyer and businessman, had "run away from banking."

□ Wartime Business Loans

Banks made a minor contribution to business financing during World War II. As industrial output more than doubled from the beginning of 1940 to mid-1945, commercial and industrial loans increased 18 percent.

These loans almost paralleled the 45 percent rise in output in the rearmament years 1940–41, but in the following eighteen months, as the U.S. military effort assumed gigantic dimensions, bank credit for civilian industries declined over $4 billion, offset only partially by a $2 billion increase in loans for war production. In mid-1945, in the final stage of the war, commercial and industrial loans were slightly below the 1941 total.

About 55 percent of the manufacturing plant and equipment added during the war years was built at public expense for private operation. Government loans and guarantees were further significant sources of war production financing. The RFC made over $1 billion in loans, mostly at the request of the armed forces. V-loans to war contractors were government guaranteed in whole or in part. War procurement agencies also provided working capital through advances and prepayments on government contracts—$2.2 billion at the 1943 peak.

Total loans actually fell from $21.7 billion at the end of 1941 to $18 billion by mid-1943. The 1941 level was restored by the end of 1944, but in mid-1945 loans were only 16.2 percent of total assets. With the end of fighting, reconversion activities brought total bank loans to $21 billion at the close of 1945.

☐   Agricultural Loans

Farm output expanded almost 20 percent from 1940 through 1945, yet short-term loans from all institutional sources (excluding crop price support loans) were only $2.5 billion—about the amount that banks alone had made available in 1918. Bank loans to agriculture at the end of 1945 were $100 million below the 1941 figure.

The 69 percent increase in farm mortgage debt from 1915 to 1920 had set the stage for difficulties in the postwar era. From 1941 to 1946, however, wartime prosperity enabled farmers to prudently reduce their mortgage debt by 22 percent. At the end of 1945 banks had 11 percent of outstanding farm mortgages.

☐   Nonfarm Mortgages

Nonfarm residential mortgage debt at the end of 1945 was slightly below the 1941 level, and $3 billion less than at the end of 1930. Bank holdings were about the same in 1945 as in 1941, but represented only 2.1 percent of total assets—just slightly higher than the 1900 proportion. In 1945, 80 percent of all bank mortgage holdings were for residences, up from 76 percent in 1941. For the first time ever, at the end of

1945, total bank holdings of all kinds of nonfarm residential mortgages exceeded those held by mutual savings banks.

□ Consumer Credit

In September 1941 consumer credit from all sources came under Federal Reserve regulation as an anti-inflationary measure. Regulation W, together with wartime prosperity and the unavailability of autos and other consumer durables, plus the high rate of personal saving, brought about a 70 percent decline in two years from the $1.7 billion consumer installment loans in commercial banks at the end of 1941. By the end of 1945 there was a slight increase to $740 million. Noninstallment consumer bank loans were just under $700 million at the end of 1941, and again four years later.

All in all, because of very limited demand from the private sector, bank loans were a minor factor in the economic expansion associated with rearmament and war. The federal government, however, was a very different story.

□ Flood of Federal Securities

Commercial banks played a major role in financing World War II by lending to other bond buyers, by handling three-quarters of the war loan campaign sales volume, and above all by adding enormously to their own portfolios. Banks bought almost 40 percent of the $187 billion borrowed by the federal government from private sources (excluding the Federal Reserve and government trust funds) between July 1940 and the end of 1945. Commercial banks held 34.2 percent of the federal debt in 1941, and 33 percent four years later. In addition, almost 60 percent of the $9 billion increase in bank loans from 1940 through 1945 went to finance security acquisitions, mostly U.S. bonds.

To encourage bank buying, reserve requirements and deposit insurance assessments against war loan accounts were eliminated. Thanks to a Federal Reserve purchase guarantee, Treasury bills (yielding 0.375 percent) were made risk-free. Bills ceased to be a money-market instrument as the Federal Reserve came to hold three-fourths of the entire amount outstanding by mid-1945. Banks invested in 0.875 percent certificates of indebtedness, knowing that they could borrow at a preferential discount of 0.5 percent if in need of reserves. Almost 45 percent of the government securities acquired by banks from 1941 through 1945 matured within a year. Government obligations maturing in more than ten years amounted to one-third of bank holdings in 1941, but only one-tenth in 1945.

U.S. government bond holdings went from 40 percent of total bank loans and investments at the end of 1939 to 73 percent six years later. For the first time ever, interest income from investments exceeded income from loans in 1943. Whereas from 1934 to 1941, 45 percent of current operating earnings derived from loans, in 1945 banks derived that proportion of their earnings from federal bond interest.

The commercial banking system used up excess reserves inherited from the 1930s. The $22.5 billion increase in Federal Reserve holdings of government bonds provided additional reserves that enabled commercial banks to acquire whatever federal securities were not sold to other investors. The volume of U.S. bonds bought between mid-1940 and mid-1945 was equal to banks' total assets in 1940. Thanks to Federal Reserve support of government security prices, banks did not fear significant loss or the inability to meet subsequent unforeseen needs for liquidity. Half or more of total bank assets from 1943 to 1947 consisted of Treasury bonds; at the end of 1945, they were 57 percent of the total.

□ Bank Prosperity

Despite large tax payments, profits doubled as total assets increased 103.5 percent between 1941 and 1945. Since 1870 the rate of return on total national bank capital had averaged 7 percent; 1945's record of almost 11 percent was not surpassed until 1969. By retaining the bulk of earnings after 1943, banks strengthened their capital. The $8.9 billion in capital at the end of 1945 was 45 percent above the decimated 1933 level but still below the $9.2 billion peak of mid-1930.

The ratio of capital to total assets—10.3 percent in 1939—had been decreasing since 1875 (when the series began), reaching a low of 5.5 percent in 1945. On the other hand, the ratio of capital to assets other than cash plus U.S. government obligations was 25.5 percent in 1945—about the same as in the late 1930s. Assets rated substandard by bank examiners represented 48.2 percent of adjusted capital as recently as 1939, but came to only 7.6 percent in 1945, the lowest level since the beginning of deposit insurance.

□ Structural Developments

At the time of the bombing of Pearl Harbor, there were just under 14,300 banks operating, 300 more than there would be at the end of the war. The number of branches remained at around 3,700. Wartime shifts of population and activity brought significant changes in the location of deposits. New York and Chicago had twenty-five of the eighty-nine banks with deposits over $100 million in 1939, but only thirty-four of the 180 in 1946.

By the end of World War II the ravages of the Great Depression had been repaired. Banks were in a strong position to meet the demands of the postwar economy.

16

A Turbulent Era

TWO GREAT WARS AND THREE OF THE SE-
verest downturns in the history of American business buffeted banking
in the thirty-two years from the founding of the Federal Reserve to the
end of World War II. A seriously weakened and shrunken banking
system survived the Great Depression, gradually rebuilt earnings and
capital, and attained new heights of prosperity by the mid-1940s.

During both world wars, the Federal Reserve, established for the
purpose of serving member banks, was turned into a Treasury instru-
mentality. Thanks to military spending and inflation between mid-1914
and mid-1920, bank assets more than doubled, compared with 40 percent growth in the preceding half-dozen years. Relative to GNP, however, bank assets, which had risen from 61.6 percent in 1908 to 65
percent in 1914, dropped to 54.7 percent in 1920.

Following a very sharp readjustment from January 1920 to July
1921, the economy surged upward until mid-1929, but the role of banks
as direct lenders diminished. The growing importance of time deposits
encouraged banks to increase security holdings as well as to make larger
loans secured by stocks, bonds, and real estate. Secured loans, 39.2
percent of total bank loans in 1920, were 54.1 percent by 1928. Even so,
the United States remained "par excellence the land of the unsecured
loan based on a showing of a financial statement and other evidences of
financial capacity and integrity."[1]

Prosperity turned out to be impermanent. As real GNP declined by one-third, total bank assets shrank by 37 percent from 1929 to 1933. Despite the retention of two-thirds of annual net earnings, the $3 billion capital shrinkage was not restored until 1945.

Many families found themselves outside the financial network in the 1930s. The bleakness of the Depression in the South was recalled by writer A. R. Ammons: "There was no money. There were no coins. We traded chickens and eggs in town for salt, sugar, baking powder, fatback."[2]

By 1920 a bank director enjoyed as much prestige as a member of the local school board or a 32d degree Mason. But during the Depression banking became "a discredited, hampered, and governmentally hen-pecked occupation," Willis observed at the end of 1933.[3] The leading public relations expert of the period noted in 1935 that "the public is ready to believe the worst about the banker."[4]

Although thousands of banks disappeared, the unit banking arrangement remained intact, partly because of deposit insurance. Its leading sponsor, Congressman Steagall, told a receptive audience, the National Association of Supervisors of State Banks, in September 1936, "Community banks built up out of community pride and community spirit for the promotion and development of community life constitute the mudsill of the Nation's economic structure."[5]

The total of 14,126 banks in 1945 was 13,000 below the number in 1915, but as had been true for 150 years, most were small, independent institutions. Branches were almost five times as numerous in 1945 (3,723) as in 1915, but most communities had no branches. Commercial bank offices increased from 26,660 in 1915 to a peak of 31,259 in 1922, then shrank by 45 percent over the next eleven years. Not until 1967, when the population was 80 percent above that of 1922, was 1922's office total surpassed. Supervisory authorities held the view that, before the collapse, "there were too many banks engaged in unregulated and unrestricted competition," as the chairman of the FDIC told a congressional committee in 1955. Few new banks were chartered after 1929.

The FDIC—the outstanding innovation resulting from the banking collapse—was called on to protect some 1.3 million depositors from 1934 through 1945. The 398 insured banks that were closed had aggregate deposit liabilities of about $500 million. Only 2,000 depositors suffered losses because they had accounts in excess of $5,000.

Diversification efforts, notable in the 1920s, persisted in the 1930s. In the field of investment banking, retrenchment was initially a result of declining security flotations, but later was imposed by government under the Banking Act of 1933.

Low earnings and swelling excess reserves in the late 1930s led bankers to modify lending practices and extend new types of accommodation, most notably, the term loan. Lending directly to consumers, as well as indirectly through advances to consumer finance and commercial finance companies, reached significant amounts. Nevertheless, bank loans at the end of 1940 were about half the 1929 total. About half of the earning assets consisted of federal, state, and local government securities.

As banks expanded the scope and nature of their lending, they found themselves increasingly in competition with other financial institutions. The commercial bank share of total assets of all depository institutions was just over 79 percent in 1929 and 1939. Government credit programs grew markedly. At the high point in 1940, loans from federal agencies were 4.8 percent—and from federally sponsored agencies, another 2.2 percent—of total indebtedness of the private sector and state and local governments combined.

Already in 1933 bank holdings of federal obligations surpassed the business and agricultural loan total. As banks acquired tens of billions of dollars' worth of U.S. government bonds during World War II, the enormously swollen excess reserves of the late 1930s shrank to less than $1.5 billion (under 10 percent of member banks' total reserves) by the end of 1945. The bank share of net corporate debt (long- as well as short-term), already down to 14 percent at the end of 1939, was 13.7 percent five years later. Loans of all types were less than one-sixth of total bank assets in 1945.

As of mid-1945 the comptroller of the currency described the functions of the national banking system as "the handling of the Nation's current funds, the investment of those funds in Government securities and Government-guaranteed loans, the direct creation of credit for governmental use, and the performance of certain quasi-governmental services."[6] U.S. government securities owned by banks were over three and a half times the amount of their loans. Some observers doubted whether banks would resume the commercial lending function in the postwar economy.

Survivors of the debacle of the early 1930s remained chastened. Comptroller of the Currency James J. Saxon described bank managements as "ultra-conservative-plodding, unimaginative, and dull," with a "collective indisposition to innovate."[7] All this was to change in the 1960s, thanks in part to his leadership.

Manufacturers Hanover Trust Co. Manhattan branch, Fifth Avenue and Forty-third Street. Completed in 1954, the award-winning design featured a seven-foot-wide vault door just inside the glass wall on the avenue side. Gordon Bunshaft, the Skidmore, Owings & Merrill architect in charge of the project, noted that the walls of aluminum and glass "broke the masony-fortress psychology of branch banks up to then." *Courtesy Manufacturers Hanover Trust Co.*

Part IV.

Banking since 1945

17

Structural Change and Functional Growth

THREE MAJOR STRUCTURAL DEVELOP-
ments barely visible in 1914—domestic branching, holding company
expansion, and overseas activities—swept the banking industry after
1945. Branching extended a bank's retail activities in its headquarters
state. Holding companies enabled institutions to deliver a growing
variety of financial services unrestricted (until 1956) by intrastate and
interstate restraints on branching. Overseas branches and subsidiaries
became a major vehicle for growth of most major banking organizations after 1965. A few years later, foreign institutions invaded the
United States on a large scale, opening new facilities and acquiring
important American banks as well.

☐ New Bank Formation

For decades after the formal end of free banking in 1935, federal chartering authorities were skeptical when evaluating the need for a new facility. Fewer than 2,100 new commercial banks opened from 1935 through
1961. The total was three times as great from 1962 through 1988, and
new bank formation as a percentage of existing banks returned to the
average rate of the 1920s.

Over 90 percent of the banks that opened between 1945 and 1988 had deposit insurance; 761 did not. Today, except in Texas, North Carolina, and Washington, states require FDIC insurance before a bank may open. Thus, ultimate federal control of new entry is almost complete. In 1945, 93.8 percent of all commercial banks were insured; in 1988, 98.1 percent were insured.

In October 1980 the Office of the Comptroller of the Currency announced a significant policy shift reflecting the agency's experience that "a strong organized group with solid financial backing and a well-conceived and developed operating plan generally is able to establish and operate a successful bank even in the most economically distressed or most highly competitive markets." Previously, economic and competitive characteristics of the community to be served by the new bank were emphasized in evaluating applications. Over the next eight years, 54 percent of the 2295 newly opened institutions had national charters. Approval did not mean that the organizers were guaranteed a profit. Now the marketplace would govern entry decisions "to the greatest extent possible."

□ Bankers' Banks

The very limited geographic scope of branching prompted the development of correspondent bank relationships, which linked many thousands of financial institutions scattered all over the United States into a somewhat interrelated network, reducing the inconveniences created by the absence of nationwide branch banking. A few hundred banks—located in New York, Chicago, San Francisco, and regional centers—service many thousands of banks. The facilities of the large institutions have enabled respondent banks, no matter where they are located or how small they are, to offer depositors and borrowers a wide range of services.

As many correspondent banks became subsidiaries of far-flung holding companies, respondents complained about a deterioration of service and, in some cases, competition in the local service area from the big city bank. Independent bankers began to organize jointly owned bankers' banks, particularly in states with numerous unit banks. The first, the Independent State Bank of Minnesota (1975), serves almost 500 institutions. The Bankers Bank in Oklahoma City (1986) was the twentieth to be organized. Bankers' Bank of Kansas, N.A. (1988) was started by four national and twelve state banks. It participates in extensions of large loans, check clearing and remittances, debit and credit cards, and it engages in some securities transactions.

☐ Minority Banks

Banks catering to special groups were chartered in the 1960s and 1970s. The U.S. Treasury has classified fewer than 100 banks as "minority," qualifying them for special government deposits. Eight were women's banks, scattered across the land from Greenwich, Connecticut, to Los Angeles. After two years San Diego's Women's Bank, finding its name a deterrent to business, chose to become California Coastal Bank. The oldest such bank, First Women's Bank, opened in Manhattan in 1975. The last opened in Rockville, Maryland, in 1979. Now that antidiscrimination laws are in effect and women want to join the mainstream, the concept of a women's bank may be obsolete. First Women's became First New York Bank for Business in 1989.

The oldest existing minority-owned commercial bank, Consolidated Bank and Trust Company, was started by blacks in Richmond, Virginia, in 1903 as St. Luke Penny Savings Bank. The largest, Freedom National Bank, opened in Harlem in 1964. The number of black banks declined from fifty in 1979 to thirty-six in 1988.

The National Negro Bankers Association, organized in 1927, had fourteen charter members. It became the National Bankers Association in 1948 and broadened into the trade association for ethnic minority banks in 1972. Other ethnic groups eligible for the federal Minority Deposit Program are Hispanic-American, Asian-American, American Indian, Eskimo, Aleut, and multiracial.

Sponsors of minority banks feel that existing institutions are not serving their needs. On the whole, minority banks have been below average in profitability and have a high rate of failure.

☐ Private Banks

Unincorporated banks can no longer open for business. About 5,500 private banks—whose owners were personally liable to creditors—were doing business at their peak in 1904. That number fell to just over 1,000 by 1924, to 685 in 1929, to 330 in 1933, and to only 57 by 1940. Today, fewer than ten remain. By far the largest private bank, Brown Brothers, Harriman and Company, dates back to 1818. In addition to Wall Street, it has offices in Philadelphia and Boston and holds a seat on the New York Stock Exchange.

☐ Mergers

Long-established institutions were among the 1,503 commercial banks acquired by merger in the 1950s. In 1955 Chase National Bank joined with the smaller Bank of the Manhattan Company under the latter's 1799 charter to form Chase Manhattan Bank, the largest combination of the decade.

Competitive factors, as well as banking criteria already in the 1956 Bank Holding Company Act, were incorporated into the Bank Merger Act of 1960. Both laws were intended to prevent significant anticompetitive changes. Between 1960 and 1988 over 5,000 banks were acquired by other banks or bank holding companies. Under the 1966 amendments to the earlier laws, the three federal agencies deny acquisitions that would restrain trade, unless "the anticompetitive effects of the proposed transaction are clearly outweighed in the public interest by the probable effect of the transaction in meeting the convenience and needs of the community to be served."

The Antitrust Division of the Justice Department saw fit to challenge some forty mergers and acquisitions approved by the requisite banking agency. The merger of two sizable banks in the same geographic market was all but impossible after a 1963 Supreme Court decision prevented Philadelphia National Bank from combining with Girard Trust Company. In 1970 the Supreme Court prohibited the joining of two New Jersey banks headquartered across the street from each other. The proposed $41 million institution would have had 19.3 percent of the commercial bank assets in the Phillipsburg-Easton area.

When an institution did not serve the same market as the acquiring bank, proposals were sometimes denied or litigated on the ground that the acquirer could have entered the market in a less anticompetitive manner. This "potential competition" doctrine was uniformly rejected at the district court level and did not succeed on appeal by the Antitrust Division to the Supreme Court. After 1981 the Board of Governors of the Federal Reserve System did not deny a single acquisition on these grounds.

A more permissive attitude toward combinations arose in the 1980s as thrifts began to offer more banking services. Wells Fargo, the third largest organization in California banking, was allowed to acquire Crocker National, the fifth largest, in May 1986, after divesting branches in seven markets where competition would have been substantially affected. Giant out-of-state acquisitions by holding companies have been allowed since 1981. BankAmerica purchased the troubled Seattle-First National Bank in 1983; Florida's SunBanks acquired the Trust Company of Georgia in 1984; Chemical Banking Corp. of New York joined ailing Texas Commerce in 1987 to form the fourth largest banking organization in the United States; Security Pacific in California bought Ranier in Washington State; and North Carolina's NCNB combined with the failed First Republic Bank in 1988 to form the largest bank in Texas. Mergers of giant banks have also increased; twenty-four with at least $1 billion in assets were acquired from 1982 through 1984 alone. A hostile takeover of Irving Bank Corporation by Bank of New York in 1988 (creating the twelfth largest banking organization) was a first.

A variety of considerations have prompted acquisitions. The acquiring firm may wish to strengthen retail activities by branching, to follow customers to the suburbs, to gain economies of scale, or to be in a position to make larger loans. Incentives for the acquired bank include the substantial premiums over the market price of their shares that shareholders might receive, or the dim profit prospects that the institution fears as an independent. Over 400 mergers since 1945 involved failing banks.

☐   Branch Banking

Branch expansion is a powerful inducement for acquisitions. Nevertheless, unit banks were in the majority until 1987. "Commercial banking in this country is primarily unit banking," the Supreme Court noted in June 1963. This statement could not be applied to deposit volume around 1935 and no longer described the number of offices by 1964, soon after the Philadelphia National Bank decision was written.

The dominant tendency since 1930 has been to ease restrictions, but eight decades after the passage of California's 1909 law, a majority of states do not allow unrestricted statewide branching. In 1930 twenty-three states prohibited all branching. Banks with branches were 1 percent of the total in 1900, 2 percent in 1921, and 8 percent at the end of World War II—but 50 percent in 1987.

Unit banks had 72 percent of all offices in 1945 and operated half or more until 1959. Branch offices exceeded the number of head offices in 1964. Banks with at least one branch operated 76.6 percent of the 60,034 offices at the beginning of 1988, compared with 28.2 percent of 17,958 offices at the end of 1945. Branches numbered 4,000 in 1945, 8,000 in 1957, 16,000 in 1965, 32,000 in 1977, and 46,667 by the end of 1988.

The total number of offices steadily diminished from late 1922 until 1945, except in 1933–34 when many suspended banks reopened. Even 1935's shrunken total, 42 percent below that of 1922, was not exceeded until 1949. The mid-1922 aggregate of almost 32,000 offices was matched in 1968.

Population per office was double the 1920 ratio of 3,400:1 by the mid-1930s. A twentieth-century peak of 8,000:1 was reached in the early 1950s. At the end of 1960 there was one office for every 7,500 people, about 200 more than at the end of 1945. The striking upsurge of branching nationwide reduced the average population per office from 7,300 in 1945 to 4,000 in 1987 (about where it stood in 1907), notwithstanding enormous improvements in transportation since the horse-and-buggy era.

From the 1933 Bank Holiday until the end of 1951, three-fourths of the increase in branches was outside head-office cities, as was two-thirds of the net growth in the next two decades. Head-office city branches, at least 50 percent of the total through 1936, were 43 percent in 1945, and down to 29 percent by 1986. Meanwhile, branches in head-office counties outside head-office cities went from 23 percent to almost 28 percent between 1945 and 1986, while contiguous county branches went from 12 percent to 10 percent. Branches in noncontiguous counties, around one-sixth of all branches in the 1950s and 1960s, were almost one-fourth of the 1986 total.

The tidal wave of branching is as striking when measured by deposit volume as when measured by the number of offices. Unit banks had 47 percent of the dollars on deposit by 1939, and 48 percent a decade later. By mid-1972, however, less than one-fourth of commercial bank deposits were in unit banks, and the downtrend continued.

Bank of America, with 500 branches in 1946, had over 1,000 in every California county by 1976, twice as many as its closest rival, Security Pacific. Branch closings in the mid-1980s to cut costs brought its total down to 862 by 1988. First Interstate Bancorporation, a multibank holding company, had over 1,100 offices spread over eleven states and the District of Columbia.

Single-office banks tended to disappear in states that permitted branching. As recently as 1962 the seventeen jurisdictions where statewide branching prevailed still had more unit than branch banks. Nationally, unit banks declined by over 46 percent from the end of 1945 to the end of 1987.

Branch liberalization legislation, dormant in the 1940s and 1950s, picked up after 1962. New York and New Jersey moved to statewide branching in 1975 and 1973, respectively. Florida went from unit banking to countywide branching in 1977, and then to statewide branching by merger just three years later.

In contrast, Illinois, with over 1,000 unit banks by the late 1960s, has held out against full-service branches. In 1982 multiple-bank holding companies were allowed to own banks in one of the five regions into which Illinois was divided, as well as in a contiguous region.

Chicago-based bank holding companies could therefore operate in six counties, eighty-four years after Wall Street banks were permitted branches in the five counties of New York City. Under unit banking, Chicago had 34,000 people per bank in 1976, while New York City had 9,000.

As recently as mid-1982 there were still nine unit banking states. Over the next five years Kansas moved to statewide branching, while Texas, Missouri, Nebraska, and Oklahoma authorized limited branching. Illinois, Colorado, Montana, and Wyoming continued to forbid full-service branches but did allow multiple-bank holding companies. The latter are still forbidden in Mississippi (which does permit branching).

Cost-containment pressures are likely to slow the growth of branching, but the total continued to increase in the late 1980s. Rivalry in offering convenient locations is likely to continue until computerization and automated teller machines (ATMs) make many branches obsolete.

☐ ATMs and POS Systems

Automated teller machines (ATMs), which first appeared in the late 1960s, serve as adjuncts to or substitutes for branches. In 1973 fewer than 2,000 were in place; in 1980 there were 20,000; in 1984, 40,000; and in 1988, 67,000. ATMs can perform an increasing variety of banking services around the clock every day of the year, although cash withdrawals have been their main use to date. Several dozen networks are shared: New York Cash Exchange (NYCE), the largest, has almost 6,000 ATMs. Some are exclusive while others operate interstate. About 20 percent are not attached to branches.

Point-of-sale (POS) arrangements began to be made in the 1970s. Terminals located in retail establishments enable customers to obtain banking services, including a direct debit to a bank account to pay the retailer.

☐ Chain Banking

Especially in unit banking states, one or more individuals might own or control a chain of several banks. Nebraska, with no branches or multiple-bank holding companies in 1978, had fifty-five chains, thirty-nine of which held two or three banks. Chains controlled 40 percent of the banks in Nebraska, and 44 percent of deposits. When permitted by state law, chains tend to be replaced by branch banks or to develop into holding companies.

☐ Franchise Banks

In 1982 First Interstate Bancorporation announced a new option for banks wishing to extend their service possibilities while remaining independent. A franchised bank is renamed "First Interstate Bank of ———" and draws on the know-how of an industry giant, while continuing under existing ownership and management. The First National Bank in Golden, Colorado, was the first to join in April 1982. By 1988, forty-four banks with 143 offices in eleven states and the District of Columbia carried the "First Interstate" logo as licensees.

☐ Bank Holding Company Expansion

Bank holding company legitimacy was confirmed at the federal level in 1956. Since then, organizations with 25 percent control of at least two banks have had to register with the Board of Governors of the Federal Reserve System. Multi-bank holding company-owned banks amounted to just over 3 percent of all commercial banks and held some 8 percent of deposits from 1956 to 1965. A sharp rise began in 1966 after the Bank Holding Company Act was amended. The 121 registered multiple-bank holding companies at the end of 1970 (sixty-eight more than in 1965) owned 6.5 percent of all banks and had 16.2 percent of all deposits.

In 1955 there were 117 known cases of a nonfinancial corporation owning a single bank; that number grew to 550 by 1965, but their share of all commercial bank deposits dropped from 6.3 percent to 4.5 percent. These one-bank holding companies were not regulated by the Board of Governors.

Many giant banks sought to escape from legal and regulatory challenges to their diversification efforts by turning into one-bank holding companies, following the example set by First National City Bank of New York in October 1968. Over 1,350 banks, holding 38 percent of all deposits, were affiliated with one-bank holding companies by the end of 1970. At this point, Congress brought one-bank holding companies under the Board of Governors' jurisdiction. Their activities became subject to the same restrictions applied to multiple-bank holding companies.

Large organizations found the holding company convenient for product-line expansion, and especially for geographic expansion, as subsidiaries may conduct nonbanking activities anywhere. Almost all of the 300 largest banks are now subsidiaries of holding companies. At the end of 1987, 4,919 one-bank holding companies had 21 percent of total bank assets, and 985 multiple-bank holding companies controlled some 4,300 banks and 70 percent of all bank assets. In less than two decades, the holding company became the dominant form of banking organization.

☐ Interstate Banking

States have prohibited branching by out-of-state banks. The federally chartered First and Second Banks of the United States were the only major institutions with offices outside their headquarters state. In 1956 bank holding companies were limited to one state unless state law explicitly invited out-of-state institutions to acquire bank subsidiaries.

Maine was the first, in 1975, to offer out-of-state holding companies the opportunity to acquire Maine banks, provided the home state did the same for Maine-headquartered institutions. The reciprocity requirement was dropped in 1984. In 1982 Massachusetts invited bank holding companies from other New England states on a reciprocal basis, while New York adopted a nationwide reciprocity policy. So far, most states have limited interstate banking to neighboring states or to a somewhat broader region. California, Illinois, Ohio, Michigan, New Jersey, and Pennsylvania have provided for nationwide reciprocal banking via holding company subsidiaries by 1991.

States were notably rapid in lowering barriers to outside institutions after 1982. Among the forces at work were the anticipation of spurs to economic development, the need to bail out troubled banks, and the desire of local shareholders to receive higher prices for their shares. South Dakota aimed to attract banking jobs in 1980 by removing all interest rate limitations on consumer loans. Citicorp's subsidiary, with over 3,400 employees, is now the largest bank in the state. Delaware's Financial Center Development Act of 1981 attracted major institutions from New York City and nearby states whose subsidiaries engage in wholesale banking as well as consumer lending.

Except for local deposit-gathering facilities, nationwide banking was already under way by the late 1960s. Nonbank subsidiaries of holding companies could locate anywhere. Loan production offices were active in major cities all over the United States. Edge Act corporations engaging in international finance could also ignore state boundaries. By 1990 a majority of states had authorized out-of-state banking organizations to acquire deposit-taking subsidiaries.

☐ Local Concentration

In every large American city by the early 1930s, two or three banking organizations controlled 60–80 percent of resources. American concentration levels may have been higher than in Western Europe or Canada.[1] Between 1939 and 1959 asset concentration at the Census Bureau's Standard Metropolitan Statistical Area (SMSA) level tended to decline as the market share of the top five banks fell in thirty-five reserve city locations; in ten others the share rose from three to twelve percentage points. By mid-1972 concentration was lower in thirty-eight of these forty-five centers than in 1939. The three-bank concentration ratio in all metropolitan areas averaged 75.1 percent in 1966, 71.5 percent in 1970, 66.4 percent in 1980, and 67.5 percent in 1986. Some deconcentration thus appeared to be taking place in most metropolitan areas in the 1980s.

Whatever market power American-owned institutions may have enjoyed diminished significantly with the actual and potential entry of foreign institutions. Republic National Bank, a notable success, opened in the crowded Manhattan market in January 1966. It became one of the top fifty in less than a dozen years. By 1981 Republic was number twenty-nine, and in 1988 it was twentieth among American banks. Calling it "the outstanding bank built since World War II in the United States," George Moore, former head of Citibank, credited Republic's success to founder Edmond Safra, a fifth-generation member of a Middle Eastern banking family.[2]

☐ Size Patterns

Because of long-standing restraints on multiple offices, banking organizations have not fully reflected America's penchant for size. The top 100 had 39 percent of U.S. commercial bank deposits in 1928, 59 percent in 1940, 50 percent in 1960, and 61 percent in 1987. The fifty largest banks in the non-Communist world included twenty-five from the United States in 1956, six in 1980, and four in 1988. While the United States had ten of the world's top thirty industrial giants in 1988, it had only one of the thirty largest banks.

The list of American banking giants has changed over time as a result of management effectiveness, market conditions, and mergers. Ranking has also been subject to change. After being first for a generation, Bank America dropped to third in 1987. In 1988 Citicorp was more than twice the size of the California holding company.

☐ New York's Position

Despite the growing prosperity of other regions and the westward shift of population, New York has remained the financial center of North America and headquarters for many of the largest banking giants. The Wall Street district and Park Avenue (made fashionable by Citibank when it moved there in 1961) were addresses for seven of the top ten banking organizations in 1988. Among the top fifty, Chicago and Los Angeles had three each, Boston, San Francisco, Pittsburgh, Charlotte, Atlanta, Minneapolis, Detroit, and Cleveland had two each, and New York had nine. When Bank of America took first place in October 1945, for the first time in over a century the largest bank was not in New York City. When the California giant faltered, Citibank regained the lead in 1986.

All of the Houston and Dallas giants lost their independence when the Texas economy collapsed in the 1980s. In the glory days of 1981, Texas Commerce opened a 75-story tower in Houston, the tallest west of the Mississippi and said to be the tallest bank building in the world. It was Texas's answer to Chase Manhattan, whose 60-story headquarters near Wall Street had been completed twenty years earlier, and to Citicorp's 914-foot mid-Manhattan tower (whose top 130 feet are at a 45-degree angle), which opened in the fall of 1977. Now Texas Commerce is a subsidiary of Chemical.

As holding companies spread beyond state boundaries, the term *superregional bank* entered the vocabulary: It referred to a sizable institution with banks in two or more states and total assets of $20 billion. Because of their superior earnings performance in recent years, superregional banks represent a serious challenge to the largest multinational banks, whose worldwide interests have not done too well in the 1980s.

☐ Overseas Facilities of American Banks

Multinational banking is mainly a development of the 1960s and 1970s. Seven American banks operated seventy-two foreign branches in 1945, thirty-eight fewer than in 1939. Not until 1965 was the 181 foreign branch total of 1921 surpassed. In 1972, 107 member banks operated 627 branches in seventy-three foreign countries. Between 1967, when only fifteen banks had foreign branches, and 1972, the number of branches operated by 107 banks more than doubled.

Overseas banking facilities followed about a decade after American large-scale investment in foreign manufacturing plants began. Major American institutions feared the loss of business to a local foreign bank and/or to another American bank with offices capable of serving the nearby foreign subsidiary of a U.S. parent corporation. At first, overseas branches concentrated on U.S.-owned multinationals, but business with foreigners has grown in importance. To better serve the global financial requirements of the top 400 multinationals, Citicorp organized its World Corporation Group in 1974; half of these firms were headquartered outside the United States. By 1980 it had 2,500 multinational corporate customers.

Regulatory factors also stimulated foreign branching. From 1965 to 1974 controls on U.S. capital flows to foreigners—a special tax on overseas loans maturing in more than one year, and an aggregate ceiling on foreign credits—were in effect. American corporations had to finance overseas direct investments mainly from foreign sources. Offshore facilities offered a number of advantages over domestic offices. Foreign-located deposits were not subject to Regulation Q ceilings, reserve requirements, or FDIC insurance assessments. Foreign earnings received favorable income tax treatment.

No more than a few hundred U.S. institutions were in any way active in international banking in 1990. Initially, these banks had "foreign" departments, renamed "international" departments in the years after World War I. Many banks continue to confine their overseas activities to representative offices, which cannot accept deposits or make loans. The representative office links corporate customers with the bank's headquarters, where all transactions are directed.

The roster of American banks with foreign branches in 1956 included, in addition to Citibank (sixty-six branches), only Chase Manhattan (nineteen), First National Bank of Boston (fifteen), Bank of America (thirteen), Guaranty Trust (five), Hanover Bank (two), and Bankers Trust (one). A decade later Citibank still had more foreign branches than the dozen other U.S. participants combined. Today's major players also include Chemical Bank, First National of Chicago, Continental Illinois, Marine Midland, Security Pacific, and Wells Fargo. Citicorp expanded from sixty-three countries in 1967 to ninety-three by 1973. With direct representation in ninety countries on every continent, it remained preeminent in 1990. Citicorp is well on its way to achieving its goal of developing "a truly unique, global financial services business." Chase Manhattan under David Rockefeller expanded from eleven countries in 1960 to seventy-one by 1985.

The drive for foreign branches was strengthened when large banks came to use Eurodollars as a source of loanable funds. American banks increased their presence in London, the center of the Eurodollar market, from thirteen branches in 1968 to fifty-two by 1973. The British-owned Bahamas, with only two American branches in 1965, had ninety-one by 1973, while the tiny (British) Cayman Islands attracted thirty-two. Assets in foreign branches were only $9 billion as recently as 1965. Eight years later they soared to $122 billion, of which 20 percent was in the Bahamas and Caymans. At the peak in 1983, 166 banks operated over 900 overseas branches.

A majority of U.S. banks with overseas branches own but a single shell branch on a British Caribbean island. First authorized in 1969, these shells cannot have any contact with local business. Their Eurocurrency transactions are actually directed from American headquarters. Shells enable lesser institutions to conduct offshore banking with all the statutory privileges (including lower taxes) of full-scale facilities. Over 150 Caribbean branches held around 30 percent of all foreign branch assets in the late 1980s.

International banking facilities (IBFs) became available in December 1981 as an alternative to shell branches. IBFs require only a separate set of books. Like foreign branches, IBFs are exempt from reserve requirements, FDIC premiums, and state and local taxes. Only foreigners and other IBFs can become customers. Loans and deposits can be in foreign currencies as well as in U.S. dollars. By September 1982, there were some 400 IBFs. Most of their business represented shifts from existing entities or foreign offices rather than new business. A majority of the 532 IBFs in 1988 were located in New York, California, and Florida; total assets exceeded $300 billion.

Edge Act corporations (EACs) also engage in overseas activities. In 1959, forty years after EACs were authorized, there were only six, all but one of which had been formed after 1948. In 1988 there were 112, down from 142 in 1983; half of these EAC offices were in New York and Miami. EACs trade in foreign currencies, make foreign collections, and engage in foreign banking; they accept demand and time deposits related to identifiable international transactions from Americans as well as from foreigners. EACs (unlike banks) may make equity investments in foreign firms. Nonbanking EACs (down to forty-three from a peak of sixty-three in 1977) own foreign subsidiaries (usually in countries that forbid or discriminate against branches) and bank-affiliated companies. The International Banking Act of 1978 authorized EACs to finance production of U.S. goods intended for export and to offer a full range of banking services to U.S. firms with over two-thirds of their purchases and sales in international commerce.

☐ Foreign-Owned Banking Facilities in the United States

About a decade after American banks spread overseas on an extensive scale in the late 1970s, major foreign banks began a significant expansion of their U.S. presence. London, with 400, was still ahead of New York, which had over 350 foreign establishments in the late 1980s—but its lead was shrinking. On Park Avenue alone there are four times as many foreign bank offices as in Los Angeles, Chicago, San Francisco, Houston, Miami, Atlanta, Seattle, the District of Columbia, Dallas, and all other American locations. New York has become the largest money market in the world.

Foreign banks followed their clientele and were also interested in offering a variety of financial services to Latin American businesses and banks. U.S. facilities enabled foreign banks to engage in clearing the increasing amount of trade-generated dollar transactions, to manage their liquidity, and to profit from arbitrage opportunities in international money markets.

At first, U.S. offices of overseas banks offered foreign trade financing, particularly to customers of the parent bank. Later, they reached out to American customers. Three-fourths of U.S.-based multinationals do business with foreign banks. As the average number of U.S. banks used by major American corporations declined from 15.5 in 1984 to 9.7 in 1988, the average of foreign banks used rose from 3.2 to 5.6. Some major institutions, mainly British- and Japanese-owned, also expanded into retail banking in California and New York.

The share of all U.S. banking assets controlled by foreign banks jumped from 4 percent in 1972 to 14 percent in 1982; the number of branches rose from eighty-two owned by fifty-three banks, to 422 owned by 205 over the same period. At the end of 1988, 264 foreign banks operated 538 U.S. branches and agencies. Foreign banks also owned eighteen EACs, nine commercial lending companies, and at least a 25 percent interest in eighty-eight U.S. commercial banks—including such giants as Republic New York, Marine Midland, European-American, and Nat West USA. By these various arrangements, foreign banks controlled about 20 percent of U.S. banking assets at the end of 1988. Japanese banks in California, with under 11 percent in 1982, had over 24 percent of total assets in the state's banking institutions in 1988. With the acquisition of Union Bank in late 1988, the Japanese owned five of the ten largest California banks.

☐ Expanding Functions

Ambitious bankers were eager not only to add banks and/or branches to their organizations but also to expand the range of their financial service offerings. Comptroller of the Currency James J. Saxon (1961–66) took the position that banks should not be excluded from any financial market. Both he and his successor William Camp argued that solvency and liquidity were the only considerations that might restrain how banks perform a financial function. Saxon allowed national banks to engage in direct lease financing and service mortgages, to operate credit bureaus, and to extend credit through the use of credit cards. When he authorized banks to process data for bank customers on computers, commingle investments in a common trust fund, offer travel services, act as an insurance agent (writing insurance "incidental to banking transactions"), and underwrite revenue bonds of state and local governments, nonbank competitors challenged these rulings as improper extensions of "the business of banking" and often won in the courts. Banks hoping to escape harrassment adopted the one-bank holding company device in 1968–69.

In December 1970 amendments to the Bank Holding Company Act gave the Board of Governors the task of defining acceptable bank-related functions, with separation of banking and commerce as a guiding principle, as in the original act. In 1956 the Board of Governors could approve activities that were "[so] closely related to [the business of] banking or [of] managing or controlling banks as to be a proper incident thereto." (The expansive 1970 amendments omitted the words in brackets.) The list of permissible activities grew gradually over the years (Regulation Y).[3] Bank holding companies used subsidiaries (which could conduct approved activities anywhere) in a number of specialized fields, including mortgage banking, consumer finance, factoring, and equipment leasing. Despite significant growth of nonbank subsidiaries in the 1970s, their assets were below 4 percent of total consolidated bank holding company assets until 1981, and under 7 percent in the mid-1980s. Commercial banks continued to be the core of bank holding companies.

☐ What Is a Bank?

In legislating for holding companies, Congress struggled with the definition of a bank. The 1956 act included banks chartered by the federal and state governments, trust companies, and mutual savings banks. The 1966 amendments shifted from charter form to function: a bank was any institution that accepted demand deposit liabilities. A second criterion was added in 1970: a bank was an institution that also made commercial loans. Although the powers of savings and loan associations were greatly expanded in 1982, making them more like commercial banks, they remained exempt from the reach of the Bank Holding Company Act.

To close a loophole that had enabled commercial firms to acquire banks, the Competitive Equality Banking Act of 1987 provided an alternative definition: any institution insured by the FDIC. The fifty-seven existing limited service ("nonbank") banks, which usually did not make commercial loans, could not expand beyond the activities they were performing in March 1987 and could not grow in assets by more than 7 percent a year. Separation of banking and commerce, the Senate Banking Committee stated in 1987, "is a longstanding tradition" that serves "to preserve the equal availability of credit in the United States and minimize the concentration of financial and economic power."

Yet eagerness to stimulate American exports had led Congress to breach the principle in 1982. Bank holding companies could now establish export trading companies (ETCs). ETCs could buy and sell merchandise, investing no more than 5 percent of the holding company's capital and surplus in such ventures. Altogether forty-five ETCs had been approved by the Board of Governors by the end of 1988, some of which were not yet operational.

☐ Investment Banking Activities

Commercial banks were active in investment banking areas permitted by the Banking Act of 1933. Between 1953 and 1960 commercial banks were allotted almost 90 percent of all U.S. Treasury issues on cash offerings, 53 percent of those issued in exchange for existing securities, and over 65 percent of the $250 billion aggregate. Bank-managed syndicates increased their proportion of general obligation municipal bond underwritings from 23.3 percent in 1957 to 38.5 percent in 1965. But banks could not underwrite municipal revenue bonds (barely known in 1933) except, since 1968, for housing and higher education issues.

The 1933 law's barriers to underwriting corporate securities deprived banks of important business as various assets were increasingly securitized and lesser quality corporations turned to the "junk bond" market for financing. The Federal Reserve rather than Congress began to lower barriers, as the Board of Governors eventually came to recognize: "the entry of bank holding companies into securities underwriting would . . . reduce underwriting spreads and . . . lower financing costs. . . . In addition . . . dealing in currently ineligible securities is likely to enhance secondary market liquidity to the benefit of both issuers and investors."[4]

Meanwhile, Bankers Trust Company (which had shed its retail banking activities in the mid-1980s) came to see itself as a merchant bank. The holding company's 1987 annual report boasted "the on-balance-sheet capability and service breadth of a commercial bank with the intermediary skills and entrepreneurial spirit of an investment bank."

□ Toward Financial Service Organizations

By around 1960, First National City Bank of New York was no longer satisfied with being "merely a bank," President George Moore recalled. "We would seek to perform every useful financial service, anywhere in the world, which we were permitted by law to perform and which we believed we could perform at a profit."[5] A one-bank holding company, was set up in the fall of 1968 as the vehicle to turn the bank into a global financial services firm. Other important banks soon followed suit, such as Chase Manhattan in June 1969.

Among nonfinancial corporations, only Sears Roebuck and General Motors derived significant revenues from financial service activities in 1962. There were ten such nonbanking firms by 1972; their 1982 earnings from financial services were equal to the total for the seven largest bank holding companies. Law restricted the range of bank financial activities, but nonbank firms could offer almost every financial service. Bankers complained that while the balance sheet was being deregulated on the liabilities side (making deposit-gathering more expensive), on the asset side promising activities were still forbidden. As far as they were concerned, the "level playing field" that banks sought in the 1980 and 1982 legislation had still not been built at the end of the decade.

18

All-Purpose Lenders

As WORLD WAR II WAS ENDING, THE scope of bank activities was quite narrow. In mid-1945 U.S. Treasury securities were 57 percent of all bank assets, and loans as a percentage of earning assets had fallen to 16 percent—an all-time low. The bank share of net corporate long- and short-term debt, already down to 14 percent at the end of 1939, was 13.7 percent five years later.

After 1945 the loan spigot was opened wide. Banks became more determined and effective competitors with specialized financial institutions, such as home mortgage–oriented savings and loan associations and finance companies serving consumers and business.

□ Lending Revives

The resurgence of lending brought the share of loans in total assets to over 30 percent in 1953, and to 58 percent in the mid-1980s, matching the figure in 1929. By 1972 loans were twice the dollar total of investment, and in 1988 they were three and a half times as great. The volume of bank loans amounted to 11 percent of the GNP in 1945, 29 percent in 1972, and 35 percent (as in 1929) by the mid-1980s.

In the early 1950s the attitude was still one of caution: good borrowers would seek out good banks. As a new generation of loan officers replaced bankers traumatized by the early 1930s and the unpromising business scene before World War II, risk management took the place of risk avoidance. Aggressive loan promotion came into favor once again. Lenders sought out borrowers and devised financial arrangements that made loan approval possible.

Bank loans soared in the 1960s at a compounded annual rate of 9.5 percent. Slow growth occurred only in the recession year 1961 (4.6 percent) and in the minirecession of 1967 (6.7 percent). Even during the 1969 credit squeeze, total bank loans grew 11 percent. Total loans increased 4.7 percent during the 1970 recession, but rebounded with a 10 percent gain in 1971, and a further 19 percent gain in 1972. Commercial banks advanced directly, on average, just over 20 percent of the total funds raised in all credit markets each year from 1946 through 1956, and almost 36 percent from 1961 through 1968.

Banks financed on average 19 percent of the credit needs of the nonfinancial business sector during 1955–59, and 31 percent during 1965–68. Nonfinancial corporations borrowed from banks for short and intermediate needs an amount equal to one-seventh of their external financing and about two-thirds of the increase in their inventories from 1946 through 1965. Short-term bank loans had become "a marginal source of external funds," yet "indispensable" for needs arising out of seasonal and cyclical upswings.[1]

The severe 1973–75 recession dampened enthusiasm only temporarily. Total loans doubled within seven years from the end of 1975 and were 80 percent above the 1982 level by 1988. Banks remained eager to meet the credit needs of customers and the communities they were chartered to serve.

□ Term Loans

Term loans had become the largest single asset category in New York City banks by the mid-1960s, totaling almost 65 percent of their business loans at the end of 1969. Intermediate-term business loans expanded greatly during periods of heavy business investment outlays in the mid-1950s and a decade later. They were 14 percent of the total loans of all member banks in 1946 and 19 percent in 1957. At the end of 1972 term loans comprised over 38 percent of commercial and industrial loans made by large banks. After 1965 term loans, previously made on a fixed rate, were increasingly made on a floating rate basis and tied to the prime rate.

☐ Prime Rate Practices

The prime rate remained unchanged at 1.5 percent from its introduction in 1934 to December 1947. By August 1960 it had reached 4.5 percent, where it stayed until the end of 1965. For the rest of the 1960s, there were altogether a dozen changes, but then in 1971 alone there were another dozen movements. A 20 percent rate was quoted by April 1979, but it retreated to 14 percent in the next eight weeks. In 1980 the prime rate changed forty-seven times, reaching an all-time high of 21.5 percent between 19 December 1980 and 2 January 1981.

Since the mid-1970s the publicly announced prime rate was generally no longer the lowest rate for short-term business loans. Thus, over half of the dollar volume of business loans made by the forty-eight largest banks in February, May, and August of 1980 were below prime. In the fall of 1981 over 1,300 of the top 1,900 corporations were offered loans below prime. Very large firms with top-rated commercial paper and multinational corporations with easy access to international money markets were in an especially strong bargaining position.

By 1982 the practice of linking lending rates to marginal funding costs (measured by the federal funds rate or certificate of deposit [CD] rates) was well established. Business loans in the late 1980s were commonly offered with prime rate or open market reference rate options. The prime rate was still important for smaller loans and smaller banks.

☐ Equipment Leasing

Equipment leasing by banks became significant starting in the late 1950s. Involvement increased after the comptroller of the currency ruled in 1963 that national banks could own and lease personal property. Bank holding companies formed specialized lending subsidiaries that offered various leasing arrangements on equipment ranging in size from office machines to oil tankers. By 1975 equipment leases represented 0.9 percent of bank loans, and in 1980, 1.5 percent, where it remained for the next decade. Machinery, accounts receivable, and inventory can all serve as collateral. Banks and other lenders have broadened their secured lending since the pledging of assets ("asset-based lending") has lost its stigma.

☐ Lending Limits

For generations national banks chafed under the 10 percent limit on unsecured loans to a single borrower. In 1981, when Texaco borrowed

$5.5 billion and Mobil $5 billion, the limit for the top fifty U.S. banks combined was under $4 billion. To make $6 billion available to Gulf Oil for a week in the summer of 1981, Bankers Trust Company mobilized fifty-three banks—more than half from outside the United States—for the largest private credit ever arranged for a single corporation. Sears Roebuck, which kept accounts in 2,500 banks in the early 1980s, had 1,300 lines of credit aggregating some $3.5 billion.

As of March 1983 the limit was raised to 15 percent of capital and surplus. Even so, major corporations had a "primary relationship" with an average of five and a half banks in the mid-1980s, using them normally for financial services.

☐ Loans to Smaller Business

In the mid-1950s bank loans represented almost 80 percent of borrowings (exclusive of trade credit) of established small and intermediate-sized firms and 70 percent of credit needs of new business. Major banks opened special departments to serve the needs of smaller firms. Without ready access to the commercial paper or bond markets, they had a greater proportion of short-term to total debt, and of debt to equity, than large firms. Businesses with no more than $5–10 million in sales and $2.5–5 million in total assets obtained about three-fourths of their total bank loans from institutions with under $1 billion in assets; some 230 banks with over $1 billion provided the rest, a 1981 survey found. Alternatives expanded markedly after 1960 to include lease financing, equity participation, franchising, credit card loans, and high-yield "junk bonds" (for the larger ones).

Diminished profitability on loans to top-rated companies stimulated bank interest in lesser firms. In 1975 banks provided 37 percent of funds borrowed by manufacturing enterprises with less than $1 billion in assets; in 1986 the bank share was over one-half. With the acquisition of Texas Commerce in 1987, Chemical Bank, already the leader in middle-market and small-business banking in the New York area, became number one in the United States in serving the middle market (firms with sales of $10–250 million).

The adverse effects on lesser businesses of periods of tight money have been a matter of continued concern and debate since 1945. In June 1985, however, the Board of Governors assured the House Small Business Committee that, in the recent past, the cost of credit had declined for small business and its access to credit had expanded. In September 1988 the Board of Governors reported that "banks have maintained their predominant position in . . . small business lending . . . by a wide margin."[2] Banks have predominated in various Small Business Administration (SBA) programs but are no longer the sole lenders.

☐ SBA Loans

When the Reconstruction Finance Corporation was terminated in 1953, its business lending was continued by the SBA. The American Bankers Association dropped its opposition when the SBA was confined to lending only to firms that did not meet commercial bank standards. The SBA makes loans to firms unable to obtain bank credit in amounts under $350,000 for up to fifteen years at modest interest rates. The SBA also lends in partnership with private financial institutions and guarantees up to 90 percent of bank loans to small businesses. Long-term funds and equity capital are channeled through the Small Business Investment Corporation.

☐ Special Loan Programs

In the 1960s and 1970s, even before the enactment of federal legislation, a number of major banks began special loan programs for depressed neighborhoods. Inner-city small businesses with greater risk exposure were granted credit on more generous terms than a bank's general loan policy permitted. In 1970 the ABA set a five-year $1 billion target for loans to minority businesses under easy credit terms.

Since 1970 banking organizations have been authorized to invest in community development corporations. Citibank's Economic Development Center aims to stimulate small business development in New York City. This special lending unit seeks to accommodate minority entrepreneurs, businesses creating new jobs, and nonprofit groups that help the environment. The center often lends to previously rejected applicants or to those ineligible under normal credit criteria. Such loan activities are several steps removed from corporate philanthropic donations.

☐ Commercial Paper

After languishing for several decades, commercial paper, the oldest short-term money-market instrument in the United States (found elsewhere only in Canada), showed renewed vigor. Dealer-placed paper grew at an annual rate of 57 percent from mid-1966 to mid-1970, compared with 15 percent annually in the preceding decade. Paper of all kinds (including directly placed as well as dealer-placed paper) was under $1 billion in 1950 but rose to $4.5 billion in 1960, to $33 billion at the end of 1970, and to over $500 billion in 1989.

The number of nonbank firms issuing commercial paper increased from 335 in 1965 to 1,300 in the mid-1980s. Tight money episodes in 1966 contributed to its popularity. For a time following the Penn Central default in June, 1970, only the strongest firms could look to this source; others still turned to bank loans.

The main buyers of commercial paper traditionally had been banks, especially those in rural areas and small cities. By the end of the 1950s, however, banks held less than half; a decade later they held under one-fifth, and in 1986 they held under 5 percent of the greatly expanded total.

Instead, after 1969 banking organizations became important borrowers in the commercial paper market. Around $45 billion of their issues were outstanding in the mid-1980s. Bank holding companies follow the pattern of finance companies: major ones offer their paper directly; lesser institutions and intermittent borrowers use a dealer for that purpose.

□ Bankers' Acceptances

Less than $400 million in bankers' acceptances were outstanding in 1950; by 1960 the $1.6 billion in 1929 had been exceeded, and the total was over $7 billion in 1970. Around 100 U.S. banks important in international trade participated in acceptance financing in the 1960s; more recently, about 300 have become involved.

Accepting banks hold a larger proportion of their own acceptances in periods when they are not under pressure from the Federal Reserve. Thus, in 1964 they held 49 percent of outstanding acceptances, but in 1969 only 29 percent. In earlier decades most acceptances were related to U.S. exports and imports; starting in the 1960s these declined to less than half of the total of dollar acceptances. During the 1970s the share related to financing the movement of goods between two foreign countries rose from 45 percent to 53 percent of the total market. In the mid-1980s over 20 percent of U.S. foreign trade and over 10 percent of third-country (especially Asian) shipments were being financed with U.S. dollar acceptances. Domestic business accounted for only 4 percent of the 1982 total.

The Federal Reserve Act of 1913 had aimed to encourage development of an acceptance market in the United States. Accordingly, the

Federal Reserve Bank of New York's open market desk bought and sold bankers' acceptances. Finally, in March 1977, this function was no longer deemed necessary. Strong market growth rate in the 1970s brought many of the largest accepting banks to the statutory maximum. In 1982 Congress doubled the maximum to 200 percent of capital. A record $82 billion in bankers' acceptances were outstanding in June 1984; this figure was down to $63 billion five years later as other borrowing arrangements became more attractive.

☐ Challenges to Bank Lending

Domestic banks fear a loss of market position in lending activities. All banks located in the United States had a 29 percent share of total credit market claims against all sectors of the economy during the period 1965–75, but only 25 percent over the following decade. Banks supplied 88 percent of short- and intermediate-term credit of domestic nonfinancial corporations in 1966, but only 70 percent in 1986. Commercial paper supplied 5.2 percent of all short-term business loans in 1973, and 13.2 percent by 1984. Foreign-owned banks with U.S. offices lent 7.6 percent of the total in 1973, and 17.8 percent in 1984. Domestic banks, with an 87 percent share in 1973, were down to 69 percent by 1984. As U.S. branches of foreign banks made further inroads, their share of domestic commercial loans was as high as one-fourth in 1987.

　　Another challenge came from the junk bond market. High-yield, long-term debt of corporations below traditional investment-grade quality soared from $8 billion outstanding in 1978 to $164 billion in 1987. As banks refused during the 1980s to lend long-term at fixed interest rates, borrowers increasingly turned to the bond market. Almost 1,000 firms raised $136 billion by selling publicly traded bonds.

☐ Uncle Sam: Lender and Guarantor

The federal government is the largest financial institution in the United States. Direct loans—204 separate federal programs were in effect in 1981—are made by federal agencies, as well as by federally sponsored credit agencies now privately owned. Direct loans of the federal government, only $3 billion in 1951, peaked at $53 billion in 1985. Guaranteed loan commitments were under $9 billion in 1951, but ranged from $56 billion to $159 billion in the decade ending in 1987. Loan subsidies in fiscal 1989 came to $885 million for direct loan obligations, and to $8.7 billion for guaranteed loan commitments, the Office of Management and Budget estimated. Federal participation in domestic credit markets (direct, guaranteed loans, as well as government-sponsored enterprise loans) ranged from a low of 15.4 percent in 1978 to a high of 23.2 percent in 1987.

Special Washington-guaranteed loans to Lockheed (1971), Chrysler (1980), and the City of New York (1975 and 1978) were all repaid, but they raised difficult issues of principle and may have set a precedent. Of course, the banks directly involved were pleased.

☐ Federally Sponsored Agricultural Credit

Agricultural credit has received special federal attention since 1916. Congress, persuaded that family farmers faced problems of high interest rates, unavailability of credit of suitable maturities, and insufficient credit in terms of need, erected the Farm Credit System (FCS), which was restructured in 1988 to include eleven farm credit banks, a national bank for cooperatives, and ninety-four production credit associations. Launched with Treasury funds, the FCS today is entirely owned by farm members. The Federal Agricultural Mortgage Corporation was established in 1988 to create a secondary market for rural and farm housing mortgages: this will enable banks to offer mortgages without having to hold them in their portfolios.

The Farmers Home Administration, established in 1935, has been particularly active since 1970. Most of its funds are related to insured or guaranteed private loans. It makes credit available for acquiring and operating farms (when farmers are unable to obtain loans elsewhere), to cover losses caused by natural disaster, and to further rural home ownership, low-income rental housing, essential community facilities (water and waste disposal systems, for example), and rural development. The Farmers Home Administration alone had 15 percent of all institutionally held farm debt; this agency, together with the Commodity Credit Corporation and the SBA, had over 30 percent of all non–real estate farm debt in the mid-1980s—twice the 1971 share. With dependable production credit and real estate loans of appropriate maturity readily available to farmers at reduced cost from the FCS, banks faced intense competition, especially during the 1970s and early 1980s.

☐ Bank Loans to Agriculture

Despite the vigorous lending activities of federally sponsored farm credit programs, commercial banks remain significant sources of agricultural finance. A majority of the nation's banks are still in localities where agriculture is a major activity. In the 1980s one-third of all banks had an above-average ratio (15.5 percent in 1987) of agricultural loans in their loan portfolios.

Reflecting World War I expansion, farm loans (other than on real estate) by banks were almost $4 billion in 1921, a total not seen again until 1958. These loans (which do not include the Commodity Credit Corporation's guaranteed crop support operations) exceeded $29 billion in 1987. At 1.6 percent of total bank loans, that share is well below the 1935 figure, reflecting in part agriculture's declining importance. Banks have supplied about two-fifths of farm operating credit since 1945.

Bank farm mortgage holdings in 1945 were at their lowest level since the early 1900s, only 10.4 percent of the total outstanding. Although banks held 12.8 percent of the total from 1972 to 1986, they never regained the position they lost to life insurance companies in the early 1920s.

In many banks, farm departments headed by men trained in agriculture not only lend funds but also counsel farmers about their operations and finances. Banks serving agriculture today have more nonfarm deposits to draw on than in the past, as well as better correspondent arrangements for loans too large for them to handle.

The bank share of total agricultural credits was 30 percent in 1913 and 28 percent in 1960, after dropping as low as 15 percent in 1940. Thousands of rural banks still serve as "farm credit service stations,"[3] though government and the FCS held more than their 23 percent share of total farm debt in 1986.

Agricultural banks prospered in the 1970s only to suffer acute distress after a break in the generation-long trend of rising land values and crop prices. From 1981 through 1986 the value of farm land dropped by one-third. To ease the pressure on borrowers, regulatory authorities stretched bank capital requirements and loan evaluation standards. Nonmember banks (the great majority of farm-sector banks) have been eligible to borrow from the Federal Reserve banks since 1980 to meet seasonal loan requirements. The program was enlarged in March 1985 to accommodate unforeseen liquidity strains threatening the flow of credit to farmers.

☐ Consumer Loans

By 1955 favorable rates of return attracted all but 3 percent of commercial banks to consumer installment loans. Consumer credit rose from

under 1 percent of total bank assets in 1945 to 8.6 percent in 1971, and
to 11.6 percent in 1988.

Sales finance companies and consumer finance companies—the
pioneers—had around 40 percent of all consumer installment credit in the
early 1940s. By 1987, having lost ground to banks and credit unions, their
share was under 23 percent. One indication of the ready availability of
credit to lower income families is the decline of pawnshops. New York
City had 140 in 1946, 100 in 1965, 46 in 1978, and only 20 by 1980.

In financing consumer durables, banks tended to lend to somewhat
better risks, often for shorter terms, and required a larger down payment
than other sources. Banks lent directly to households and indirectly by
purchasing dealer paper from retailers (such as furniture stores) and
sellers of services (e.g., hospitals) and by lending to finance companies.

Bank participation in automobile credit (the largest single category
of consumer credit) was 40–45 percent of the total from 1945 to 1960,
soaring to 57 percent by 1972. In the 1970s bank lending averaged 60
percent of total auto paper, of which 26 percent was direct. Increasingly
after 1950, banks bought paper from dealers: the bank share rose from
34 percent in the 1970s to 40 percent in the mid-1980s. Also notewor-
thy was the trend toward longer maturities. In 1970 a thirty-six–month
auto loan was considered generous; by the early 1980s some banks
offered sixty-month loans.

A similar trend occurred in lending on mobile homes, an important
form of shelter for lower-income families. Loans on factory-built homes
used to be for sixty months. By the early 1980s, 120 months and more
were common, and banks were making about one-third of all mobile
home loans.

Citicorp stands out in consumer loans, as its loans to individuals
(other than real estate) rose from 12 percent of its total net loans outstanding worldwide in 1976 to over 19 percent by 1980. Some are loans
made by Citicorp's small loan company, its credit card subsidiary, or its
overseas finance companies. In 1987 one out of five American families
was doing business with Citicorp; it had become the largest bank credit
card issuer and the leading originator of residential mortgages. John
Reed, chosen to succeed Walter Wriston as chief executive in 1984, came
from the consumer banking division, which he had convinced the directors to expand in November 1974.

☐ Bank Credit Cards

Bank credit cards were a major consumer banking service developed
after 1945. Charge account banking began in September 1950 when

John C. Biggins, vice president of Paterson Savings and Trust Company in New Jersey, launched "Charge-It." Six months earlier the (nonbank) Diners Club had offered the first travel and entertainment card (limited at first to restaurant meals). Long Island merchants who competed with department stores offering charge accounts encouraged Arthur Roth, head of Franklin National Bank, to introduce a credit card in 1951.

At first, progress was very slow. Some seventy banks offered charge account plans in mid-1953. The Charge Account Bankers Association was founded in 1954; at year-end, forty-one banks reported fewer than 500,000 cardholders. By the end of 1955 only twenty-seven of the 100 plans initiated from 1951 to 1955 were still active. Some large banks introduced credit cards in the late 1950s, but entry on a large scale started only in 1966.

Bank of America, the first to expand credit card use beyond the immediate locality, introduced a California-wide operation in 1959. "Bank-Americard" went national in 1966 and was renamed "Visa" in 1977. In 1966, fourteen New York banks organized "Interbank Card" as a regional program. They merged with a Western group in 1967 to form "Master Charge," (later "Mastercard"). Banks offering BankAmericard were also permitted to offer Master Charge in 1976. By the late 1970s Visa overtook Mastercard; it had 165 million cards in 1987, to its rival's 145 million.

In 1984 over 40 percent of American families had at least one bank credit card. About 3,000 depository institutions offered their own credit cards by the mid-1980s; thousands of others acted as local agents of large issuers. Over two million merchants here and abroad accepted bank credit cards.

Revolving credit was introduced in 1958. Outstanding bank credit card balances did not reach $1 billion until August 1968. Bank cards represented 6 percent of all installment debt outstanding in 1975, but 14 percent a decade later. Pretax earnings on bank cards from 1972 to 1985 averaged 1.9 percent, 0.5 percent less than on consumer installment debt. Fraud has always been a serious problem; in 1982 losses were $128 million, compared with $47 million from bank robberies. American Express (which entered the travel and entertainment card field in October 1958) introduced the Optima Card in 1987. This is its first revolving credit card product, on which it charges lower interest rates than most banks.

☐   Real Estate Loans

Housing credit, another area of consumer concern, has long been favored by Congress. Millions of families have joined the ranks of homeowners over the years, thanks to readily available mortgage loans.

Real estate loans of all types were under 4 percent of total bank assets in 1946. By 1955 that share had recovered to the 10 percent level of the late 1920s, then climbed to almost 19 percent of assets by 1987. Loans secured by all types of real estate had overtaken commercial and industrial loans by mid-1987. In the post-1945 era the bank share of all mortgage debt was around 17 percent, and by 1987, over 20 percent.

The bank share of government-supported home mortgages (FHA-insured and Veterans Administration-guaranteed) declined sharply, from 37 percent of the total in 1946 to 12.5 percent in 1965, and to less than 3 percent in 1985. Under 6 percent of nonfarm residential mortgages held by banks at the end of 1987 were backed by the FHA or the VA.

The role of commercial banks in home financing goes well beyond ownership and origination of mortgages. Extensive loans are made to the construction industry. Banks also offer interim financing to other institutional mortgage holders (savings and loans, insurance companies). Mortgage companies depend on banks for carrying their financial inventory. In the 1980s around one-sixth of all mortgages originated by banks were sold to other investors.

In 1963 Congress authorized twenty-five–year conventional mortgages based on 80 percent of market value, bringing national banks up to par with the powers of savings and loans. Subsequently, the limit was raised to thirty years and 90 percent. In 1974 national banks were permitted to hold mortgages equal to their time and savings deposits.

The substantial increase in market value of residential property after 1970 encouraged homeowners to borrow on their increased equity. First and second (junior) mortgages were used for household spending. Financial institutions promoted home equity loans, especially after the 1986 tax reform act permitted deductibility of interest on such loans while discontinuing interest deductions for regular consumer loans. By mid-1988 home equity loans had been taken out by 11 percent of homeowners and were 6 percent of total commercial bank real estate loans.[4]

☐ The REIT Debacle

In 1960 Congress exempted real estate investment trusts (REITs) from corporate income taxes, but as late as 1968 their total assets were still only $1 billion. In 1974 REITs peaked at $21 billion. Major banks already involved in short-term construction lending and real estate development financing were interested in REITs. Of the 216 REITs operating in 1975, thirty-seven with 30 percent of all REIT assets, were advised by banks. The largest—Chase Manhattan Mortgage and Realty Trust (CMART)—was sponsored by the Wall Street bank. Some Chase officers became associated with the REIT. The bank served as adviser and sold real estate investments from Chase's portfolio to the REIT.

As severe recession gripped the economy, real estate suffered the worst downturn since the early 1930s. In 1974 REITs could not refinance paper maturing in the open market. Banks called upon to honor prior commitments made loans to REITs that came to $11.1 billion in late 1974 equal to 55 percent of REIT assets and 2 percent of total bank loans. Recession, spiraling construction and interest costs, and overbuilding in many areas wiped out REIT profits. By the spring of 1978 banks (most of them very large) had charged off over $1 billion of the $11.4 billion in loans previously made to REITs.

In February 1979 CMART filed for Chapter XI bankruptcy. Its relationship with Chase ended (the holding company had never owned CMART stock) in May 1980, and the name was changed to the Triton Group. Chase charged off over $600 million in real estate loans of all types from 1975 through 1979, representing over 60 percent of all its loan charge-offs during these five years.

☐ Securitization of Loans

Securitization, the packaging of loans by financial institutions and their sale in the secondary market, began with government-guaranteed home mortgages in the 1960s. More recently, banks have assembled from their loan portfolios—auto loans, credit card receivables, computer leases, equipment, airplane and vehicle leases—and sold the packages to investors. The selling bank earns fees for servicing the loans and record-keeping. The volume is expected to grow in the 1990s as large banks rearrange assets to meet regulatory capital requirements.

In a related development, business loans to low-risk nonfinancial firms are being sold in their entirety (rather than in a number of participations), most of them immediately after the bank makes the loan. At the twenty largest banks, loans sold increased from 1.5 percent of total assets in the spring of 1983 to over 9 percent just four years later. Buyers have included regional banks seeking to diversify, as well as foreign banks. Loan sales generate fee income. Chase Manhattan began to sell loans in 1984 when it found that lending to the highest grade borrowers was no longer profitable. Bankers Trust sells numerous short-term loans that it generates in its merchant banking role.

□ Off–Balance Sheet Activities

Very large banks have increasingly moved into a growing variety of fee-producing activities that do not appear as assets on the balance sheet—and (until recently) did not require additional capital. Standby letters of credit (SLCs) obligate the bank when the customer cannot meet the terms of an agreement with a third party. Bank-guaranteed commercial paper, for example, grew in importance following Penn Central Railroad's default in June 1970. Used also to back tax-exempt industrial revenue bonds, to guarantee construction performance, and lately in mergers and acquisitions, SLCs, altogether $10 billion in 1976, climbed to $47 billion in 1980, and to $175 billion in 1985. As a share of bank capital, they increased from 60 percent in 1981 to 95 percent in 1987.

Formalized loan commitments provide bank customers with assured access to a specified total at prearranged rates. Unused lines of credit under formal commitments rose from 8.5 percent of total credit market debt of nonfinancial corporations in 1975 to 16 percent a decade later. Almost half of all commercial and industrial loans in 1985 were made under prior commitments. As interest rates became more volatile in the 1970s and 1980s, customers became more willing to pay a fee for protection against run-ups. Loan commitments grew from $432 billion at the end of 1983 to $586 billion in mid-1987.

Altogether, off–balance sheet activities (loan commitments, SLCs, foreign exchange trading, interest rate swaps, and a variety of other financial commitments) grew in amount from 67 percent of all bank assets at the end of 1985, to 108 percent in mid-1987; in giant banks (with $10 billion or more of assets) they increased from 159 percent to 260 percent.

□ Lending to Foreigners

The claims of U.S.-chartered banks on foreigners soared from 0.9 percent of total assets in 1945 to 17.4 percent in 1975. The Federal Reserve expressed concern about "the enlarged risk exposure of our banks," particularly the rapid increase in loans to non–oil-producing less developed countries (LDCs), in March 1977. Chairman Arthur Burns urged banks to manage their international loans with "a heightened sense of caution."[5] However, claims of American banks on foreign borrowers doubled between 1976 and 1983, when they peaked at $441 billion; foreign loans went from 17.4 percent of total assets in 1975 to 24.5

percent in 1981. Indeed, in 1983 David Rockefeller hailed "the explosion of international bank lending" after 1958 as one of the century's "truly remarkable achievements."

The huge accumulations of the Organization of Petroleum Exporting Countries (OPEC) following the upsurge in oil prices after October 1973 took the form largely of Eurodollar deposits. Massive lending by multinational banks recycled these funds. Higher income developing countries grew much more rapidly than industrialized nations in the 1970s. Banks lent at interest rates that were under 1 percent when adjusted for current inflation. At first the lending spree involved only the largest American banks, but after the mid-1970s regional banks joined increasing numbers of foreign banks in lending abroad.

Soon after the second great oil price rise in 1979, lending rose sharply. Fed Chairman Paul Volcker urged restraint, but as with Burns earlier, bankers paid no attention. Citing his very low loan-loss ratio, Wriston boasted that his international loans were the best on Citicorp's books. "Sovereign nations don't go broke," he often stated. Wriston led other bankers up the primrose path, Volcker is reported to have told friends.[6] By the time Mexico announced in August 1982 its inability to meet its debt obligations, American banks had lent over $100 billion to LDCs.

Comprehensive analyses of country risk, developed and refined by banks in the 1970s, embraced political, societal, and economic factors. These appraisals did not, however, save bankers from serious losses in the 1980s. As Third World nations defaulted, rescheduling became increasingly necessary. Recession in the United States in 1981–82, disinflation of commodity prices, high real interest rates, and sharp dollar appreciation in the first half of the 1980s—all added to the LDCs' woes.

Outstanding loans to LDCs fell by over one-fifth from 1983 to the end of 1986, when American banks had 25 percent of all bank claims on LDCs and Eastern Europe. Some reassurance was found in the decline in the ratio of LDC loans from 288 percent of total capital of the nine leading American banks at the end of 1982 to 154 percent four years later.

In May 1987, Citibank, by far the largest lender, added $3 billion to its reserve for bad debts soon after Brazil suspended interest payments on its debts to banks. Other very large banks followed, providing $18 billion for loan losses.

Claims on all foreign countries by American banks declined from a peak of $359 billion in 1983 to $259 billion at the end of 1988. U.S. banks' share of all international bank assets (as measured by the Bank for International Settlements) declined from 26.4 percent in 1984 to 14.7 percent at the end of 1988, while Japanese banks moved into first place.

International activities of American banks averaged twice the annual increase in domestic assets from 1952 to 1986, almost double the rate of growth of international trade in goods and services. Major American banks are likely to remain inextricably bound up with the world economy, but a period of consolidation and retrenchment appears to be at hand in the wake of enormous actual and potential losses.

In 1970 Citicorp was the only American banking organization deriving as much as 40 percent of earnings from international activities. Around 1980 the ten largest banks active in international operations had about 45 percent of all their loans and over half of their deposits overseas. International earnings were 42 percent or more of their net earnings. Net income attributable to the international business of the 190 U.S. banks with foreign offices in 1981 represented 35 percent of their after-tax net.

Foreign activities subsequently declined in relative importance. For fifteen major banks, average foreign office loans were 40 percent of total loans in 1983–84, but 31 percent in 1986–87; foreign office deposits were 44 percent and 39 percent, respectively. International losses of $12 billion in 1987 (reflecting huge provisions for bad debts) wiped out international gains reported from 1979 through 1986.

Earnings of leading bank lenders are likely to be adversely affected for years to come. The International Monetary Fund, the World Bank, and governments of the major industrial economies will all be involved with the multinational banks in efforts to restore the credit worthiness of the heavily indebted LDCs. Meanwhile, securitization of international debt quadrupled between 1982 and 1988. By mid-1988 almost one-third of international lending was through the bond markets rather than direct bank loans.

☐ Credit Policy

As lending became more varied and voluminous, formalization of policies became necessary. Citibank appointed a vice president to supervise credit policy in 1951; he was responsible for setting loan standards and maintaining portfolio balance. A weekly meeting of senior lending officers reviewed proposed major credits. Chase Manhattan's department of credit and loan standards in 1965 issued a manual of policies for loan officers to follow.

As in earlier episodes of lending enthusiasm, the rescheduling of foreign loans and the domestic energy lending fiasco made lenders more sober. Tightening of standards in the wake of large losses has been a recurring pattern, followed by easing after the passage of time.

□ Loan Losses

Realized loan losses less recoveries (net loan losses) were under 0.1 percent a year of total loans outstanding for twenty years after 1939, and less than 0.2 percent for the decade ending in 1959. Beginning in 1970 net losses climbed sharply, reaching 1 percent of loans in 1986.

Bank America referred proudly to "our tradition of careful . . . risk management, our well-established system of quality controls" in its annual report for 1975. A surge of lending in 1978, 1979, and 1980 accounted for the bulk of its loans that later went bad. Losses were over $1 billion in 1984.

As the volume of troubled loans grew, some banks shed them by placing them in a "problem loan bank," which was spun off to shareholders. In 1986 Britain's Midland Bank removed $3.5 billion in bad loans from Crocker Bank before selling this subsidiary to Wells Fargo.

□ Treasury and Agency Securities

Banks usually prefer to act as lenders rather than security-holders. For want of better alternatives, securities came to total over 60 percent of bank assets by 1945. Postwar opportunities made it possible for loans to exceed securities in bank portfolios by 1956, for the first time since 1934. In 1960 securities were 32 percent of total assets; the downtrend continued (though more slowly), leveling at around 17 percent of total assets in the 1980s. When loan demand slackened (as in 1971), security holdings moved up. Securities were 19 percent of total assets in 1988, compared with 22 percent in 1928.

The investment portfolio from 1933 to 1966 consisted mainly of U.S. Treasury obligations. The proportion was 83 percent in 1950, despite a $29 billion decline over the previous five years. In 1970 the $62 billion of U.S. government holdings matched the holdings for 1950 but represented only 42 percent of total investments. U.S. government obligations were over 45 percent of total assets in 1947 but dropped to 25 percent a decade later, and to 14 percent in 1967. By 1974 the share was under 6 percent, the lowest since 1917. In the mid-1980s around 4 percent of bank assets consisted of U.S. Treasury securities. Banks held about one-third of the federal debt in 1945, one-fifth in 1960, one-sixth in 1970, and less than one-ninth of the 1988 total.

After the March 1951 Treasury–Federal Reserve accord, holders were no longer assured that federal debt would sell for at least par value. Bonds maturing in five years or less were only 46 percent of banks' federal portfolio in 1946. A decade later their share was 72 percent, rising by 1971 to 87 percent, and to 91 percent in 1982. Federal obligations represented a source of liquidity for smaller banks. Many institutions owned federal securities in order to satisfy the pledging requirements for federal, state, and local government deposits.

In addition to owning Treasury obligations, seventeen major bank organizations were among the forty primary dealers in these securities that the Federal Reserve Bank of New York dealt with in executing open market operations in 1986. Other banks were also active as dealers in Treasury obligations.

Increasingly, banks turned to the higher yielding issues of federally sponsored credit agencies. Although not formally guaranteed by the Treasury, some federal government backing of these agencies is implied. Bank holdings climbed from $1 billion in 1946 to almost $14 billion in 1970, or 32 percent of total agency issues outstanding. By 1986 their share was 42 percent of a greatly expanded total. Agency securities went from a fraction of 1 percent of total bank assets in 1946 to 2.4 percent in 1970, and to 5.4 percent in 1986.

☐ Municipal Bonds

Obligations of state and local government units were only 2.5 percent of bank assets in 1945. Not until 1952 was the 5.3 percent share in 1939 matched. Unlike with their Treasury obligations, banks increased their state and local government bond holdings year after year until 1986. The 1969 total exceeded Treasury bonds for the first time ever. The 12.8 percent of total bank assets in municipals was a peak ratio in 1971. Banks held one-fourth of all municipals outstanding in 1945, and half of the total in 1971.

Enthusiasm waned in the 1970s. In 1987 municipals represented less than 7 percent of total bank assets. Once again in the 1980s (as in the 1950s), individuals held more than banks; banks owned some 24 percent of total municipals outstanding in 1987, down from 42 percent in 1980.

Sharp fluctuations in interest rates diminished the attractiveness of long-term municipal bonds. Some of the decline in bank demand was related to the growing importance of other sources of tax-favored income in major institutions. There was, however, a surge in letters of credit—which serve as backing for municipals—issued for a fee by the largest banks.

□   Other Securities

Various corporate and foreign securities totaled over 11 percent of total bank assets in the late 1920s. There was a marked shift to less risky securities issued by various domestic units of governments in the 1930s. Corporate issues were less than 2 percent of bank assets in 1945, and a fraction of 1 percent in 1971, as banks lent directly to business. In the 1980s securities that represented participations in pools of private assets (most of them guaranteed by the U.S. government) rose to one-sixth of total security holdings, and to over 2.5 percent of their total assets.

The vigor with which banks financed the private sector, devising new arrangements as needs arose, was a major feature of the post-1945 American economy. Loans to households overtook the total of commercial and industrial loans in 1988. As a percent of total assets, all loans soared from 55.3 in 1980 to 60.6 in 1988. As the range of borrower types, industries, and sectors expanded, banks were pressed to devise new sources of funds.

19

Funding a Vigorous Banking System

To FUND THEIR GROWING LOAN VOLUME
and expanded range of activities, banks had to move beyond traditional
deposit arrangements. Their use of nondeposit sources of funding has
increased—as has bank capital, although at a generally slower rate than
assets since 1945.

☐ Demand Deposits Fade

For almost two centuries commercial banks were the only depository
institutions that offered deposits payable on demand and withdrawable
by writing a check. Thrifts began to receive such authority in 1976, but
thus far have garnered only a small market share. Nevertheless, demand
deposits as a percentage of total bank assets tumbled from 74.7 in 1945
to 40.2 in 1972, and to 15.4 in 1987. Demand deposits were at least half
of total bank deposits up to 1971; by 1989 they were 27 percent of all
deposits.

In the 1930s large corporations kept substantial demand balances.
Until the founder's death in 1947, the Ford Motor Company had $50
million on deposit with First National Bank of New York. Rising interest
rates after 1945 made this policy increasingly costly. Corporate treasur-
ers shifted idle funds into Treasury bills and other income-yielding
money-market investments. Nonfinancial corporations' cash holdings

declined from a high of $33.6 billion in 1958 to $28.8 billion in 1968. The greater part of business demand deposits eventually consisted of compensating balances. At the end of 1986 nonfinancial business held almost 56 percent of total demand deposits; interbank demand deposits have remained around 12 percent. The household share went from 27.5 percent in 1947 to 32 percent in 1971, where it stayed for the decade.

Checking accounts became nearly universal by the 1980s, increasing from 34 percent of all households in 1946 to 50 percent in 1956, to 75 percent in 1970, and to 84 percent in 1984. Over 90 percent of households had a checking account and/or savings account relationship with a commercial bank by the mid-1980s. Once again (as in the late 1920s), banks found that many checking accounts were unprofitable. Minimum balance requirements were raised and special fees assessed. For low-income customers, a majority of banks offered a "no-frills" account in 1988.

□   Checks and Par Clearance

From under four billion checks in 1941 and five billion in 1945, volume rose to some twenty-eight billion in 1971. To handle this rising flood of paper expeditiously and economically, the American Bankers Association developed the check routing symbol (the denominator of the fraction printed in the upper right-hand corner of checks) in 1945 and later encouraged magnetic ink encoding to enable electronic handling. By the mid-1960s nearly 90 percent of all checks were electronically sorted. Starting in 1967 Federal Reserve banks handled only checks that could be processed on high-speed electronic equipment.

Nonpar banks continued to complicate the check-clearing process, however. One out of seven banks did not remit the face value of checks drawn on it in the 1950s, half a century after the Federal Reserve mandated par clearance for member banks. In 1966 over 1,400 nonmembers did not remit at par. As late as 1971, 501 banks—3.7 percent of all banks—were still following the practice. By 1980 all banks remitted at par, for the first time in U.S. history.

□   Computerization

Within two years after the United States installed the first commercial computer in the Bureau of the Census in 1953, Bank of America acquired one. Chase Manhattan installed a fully automated check-processing and demand deposit accounting computer system in 1961. Industrial National

Bank of Rhode Island opened the first bank computer center twelve miles from its Providence headquarters in 1963.[1]

Electronic data processing (EDP) was initially applied to demand deposit operations. Subsequently, pressure to reduce clerical costs brought computerization to various other operations, such as savings deposits, installment loans, and mortgage loans. Banks with their own computer installations offered computer time for sale—payroll-handling, account reconciliation, and on-line teller arrangements, among other services, usually on a fee basis. By the end of 1967 banks holding three-quarters of the nation's deposits were using computers. In 1968 banks were the largest users of commercial EDP on-line computer services and employed 20 percent of all programmers and systems analysts in the United States.

In 1970 banks belonging to the New York Clearing House developed the Clearing House Interbank Payments System (CHIPS), the first fully automated funds transfer network. Other banks could become associate members; about 1,000 use CHIPS for international transfers. Automated clearinghouses (ACHs) employ magnetic tapes for credit and debit payments instead of paper checks. The first ACHs opened in San Francisco and Los Angeles in 1972; by the end of 1977, thirty-two were in operation. In 1987, twenty-eight ACHs served 24,000 depository institutions. An interregional network enables the exchange of electronic payments between ACHs.

ACHs, teller machines, point-of-sale systems, and wire transfers represent under 2 percent of the total number of noncash payments. Average daily transfers on the Fed's payment system ("Fedwire") soared from $30 billion in 1970 to $530 billion in 1987, and CHIPS volume jumped from $3 billion to $520 billion in the same period.

Despite electronic funds transfer and growing credit card volume, the number of checks written reached fifty billion in the late 1980s. Forecasts of a checkless society proved premature. Meanwhile, despite rapidly growing check usage, the currency and coin component of transactions balances increased from 20 percent in 1960 to 26 percent in 1988. Cash is preferred in the underground economy. Since 1970 the Currency and Foreign Transactions Reporting Act requires depository institutions to identify customers who deposit over $10,000 in cash.

☐ Cash Management and Deposit Turnover

Lockbox arrangements facilitate customers' efforts to maximize interest earnings. Bill payments are sent directly to a post office box emptied by the bank, which credits the depositor's account. In 1947 RCA made the first such arrangement with Bankers Trust Company in New York and First National Bank in Chicago.

Cash management systems speed deposit turnover. In 1973 demand deposits turned over about 100 times a year at all insured commercial banks, and 250 times at leading New York City banks (which handle substantial financial transactions). Turnover rates were 641 for all banks and 2,903 for New York City banks in 1988.

☐ Correspondent Bank Balances

Transactions balances kept by American commercial banks with other domestic institutions represented 5.7 percent of total transactions accounts in 1987, down sharply from 10.5 percent in 1946. Fees rather than deposits have been increasingly used to compensate banks rendering various correspondent services.

The Depository Institutions Deregulation and Monetary Control Act of 1980 gave nonmembers access to the Fed, which now must charge *all* users fees based on long-term costs. Involved are payment services such as check clearing and collection, wire transfer of funds and securities, automated clearinghouse activities, settlements of financial institutions' debits and credits, safekeeping of securities, and transportation and insurance of currency and coin. Under the fee system in effect since August 1981, the Fed lost some business to leading correspondent commercial banks, but it has retained over 50 percent of potential volume. Bankers have complained that the Fed was not competing fairly.

☐ U.S. Treasury Deposits

War loan depositories, used in 1917–18, became important once again in 1943. War loan accounts with commercial banks, renamed "Treasury tax and loan accounts" in 1950, held income and retirement taxes as well as bond receipts. What had been originally a war emergency measure thus developed into a permanent arrangement, the Treasury wishing to avoid a disruptive impact on money markets. Until November 1978 commercial banks paid no interest on Treasury tax and loan accounts. In exchange, they rendered a number of services without charge to the federal government, including the sale and redemption of bonds, cashing government checks, and handling "depository receipts" for the Internal Revenue taxes collected.

Some 90 percent of American banks served as depositories for the U.S. Treasury in 1988. Payroll, withholding, and business income tax payments are left on deposit with the taxpayer's bank, as are receipts from sales of savings bonds. Thrift institutions qualify as well, and the Treasury pays for services on a fee basis. Treasury balances held for more than one day are transferred to an open-end note account (technically, not a deposit account) payable on demand; depositories pay a market rate of interest (0.25 percent below the federal funds rate).

☐ Soaring Time Deposits

The bank share of time deposits owned by individuals and business firms in 1945 (53.5 percent) was the same as in 1930. By 1960, however, it was less than 40 percent. Bankers complained about the unequal competition: mutual thrift institutions paid much lower income taxes and enjoyed regulatory advantages, including the absence of a legal reserve requirement on their deposit-type obligations.

Regulation Q interest rate ceilings on time deposits were well above rates actually paid by commercial banks for some two decades. Some banks began to feel constrained already in the 1950s, though the prevailing average was below the 2.5 percent limit. In January 1957 ceiling rates were raised for the first time. Time deposits in banks rose 11 percent in 1957, and even more in 1958, a recession period. When the ceiling became increasingly restrictive, the Board of Governors raised it again in January 1962. The differential between the rate offered by commercial banks and thrift institutions on passbook savings narrowed and might have vanished, but in September 1966, to encourage housing finance, Congress mandated a ceiling 0.5 percent higher for thrifts than for banks. The differential, reduced to 0.25 in 1975, lasted until 1984.

Wall Street banks did not pay interest on the time deposits of businesses. Insignificant growth of total deposits after 1945 forced a change in 1961. Other large banks quickly followed First National City Bank's lead when the New York innovator introduced negotiable CDs in denominations of $100,000 and over in February 1961, after arranging with Discount Corporation of New York to make a market for CDs. Other dealers soon followed. A buyer could sell the negotiable CD at any time in the open market; the obligations of leading banks soon became a major trading instrument and attracted nonfinancial corporations to become large holders.

Large-denomination CDs soared to $18.6 billion by August 1966, only to decline by $3 billion over the next three months. For the first time, the Board of Governors refused to raise the ceiling rates at a time when investors could get a higher return in the open market. CDs shrank by 60 percent from November 1968 to December 1969—over $14 billion—because of the unfavorable differential between what banks were permitted to offer and the open market rates. In mid-1970 ceilings for large CDs maturing in less than ninety days were suspended, and for all other large CDs in May 1973. Banks could offer market-determined rates for CDs during tight money period of 1973–74. When loan demand slackened in 1975, banks voluntarily reduced the volume of large CDs for the first time since their introduction.

New York City banks issued almost 60 percent of large CDs in 1975, but their share was less than 33 percent by 1980 because increasing numbers of major banks nationwide were issuing them. The large-denomination CD offered a convenient alternative to nonbank money-market instruments. Shifting demand deposit balances to overnight repurchase agreements was another arrangement to earn interest.

Banks were authorized to offer savings deposits to local governments in November 1974, and to business corporations, up to $150,000, in November 1975. Telephone transfers from savings accounts to cover checks were sanctioned in April 1975. Preauthorized automatic transfer services (ATS)—moving funds from savings accounts to cover checks—have been permitted since November 1978. These various devices circumvented (however imperfectly) the 1933 ban on interest payments on demand deposits.

Non-negotiable CDs (not a new instrument) were promoted vigorously in the 1960s. As a result, noncertificate savings deposits declined from over 75 percent of total time deposits at the end of 1961 to some 45 percent a decade later.

Even small depositors learned to move funds out of depository institutions when market rates climbed above the Regulation Q ceiling ("disintermediation"). To assist financial institutions, the minimum denomination on Treasury bills was raised from $1,000 to $10,000.

Money-market mutual funds (MMMFs) offering a (noninsured) market return and check-like withdrawal privileges, first appeared in 1972. Initial purchases might be for $1,000 or less. Federal Reserve administration of Regulation Q prevented bank rates from rising in 1974 and early 1975, and again starting late in 1978. MMMFs soared from $4 billion in December 1977 to $45 billion in December 1979. The Depository Institutions Deregulation and Monetary Control Act stated:

> (1) limitations on the interest rates which are payable on deposits and accounts discourage persons from saving money, create inequities for depositors, impede the ability of depository institutions to compete for funds, and have not achieved their purpose of

> providing an even flow of funds for home mortgage lending; and
> (2) all depositors, and particularly those with modest savings, are
> entitled to receive a market rate of return on their savings as soon
> as it is economically feasible for depository institutions to pay
> such rate.[2]

Accordingly, the 31 March 1980 law directed a depository institutions deregulation committee to arrange an "orderly phaseout" of deposit interest ceilings over a six-year period.

Negotiable order of withdrawal (NOW) accounts paying interest had begun to appear in New England thrifts in 1973. Legally, NOW accounts were savings accounts, but withdrawals could be made by drafts resembling checks in appearance and function. After December 1980 all depository institutions could offer them.

The household share of all demand deposits declined from one-third in 1980 to one-fourth in 1987. Other checkable deposits (mainly NOW, but also ATS) comprised 6 percent of total checkable deposits in October 1979, but over 40 percent in 1988.

Meanwhile, MMMFs grew by $175 billion from 1979 to 1982. To help depository institutions meet this challenge, in October 1982 Congress authorized a new type of deposit arrangement competitive with MMMFs. Introduced in mid-December 1982, money-market deposit accounts attracted $300 billion in less than six months. In 1983 MMMFs declined, by $40 billion, for the first time ever. Growth resumed in 1984 and continued even after bankers were free to decide what rates to offer on savings and other time deposits; MMMFs exceeded $350 billion in 1989.

☐ Foreign Deposits

For a few giant banking organizations, foreign accounts were at least 47 percent of their total deposits at the end of 1987: Citicorp, Chase, Morgan Guaranty, Manufacturers Hanover, Bankers Trust, and Continental Illinois. These six, together with Bank America and Chemical, were also the major American participants in international lending. Deposit liabilities in foreign offices, around 16 percent of total consolidated assets of all American banks in the early 1980s, were under 11 percent in 1988.

☐ Liability Management

By the late 1950s, banks had liquidated their swollen bond portfolios. To fund further loan growth traditional deposit sources proved inadequate.

Aggressive lenders embarked on a course of liability management, actively bidding for funds in domestic and international money markets with newly devised credit instruments, or old ones used in new ways. Managed liabilities included large time deposits in domestic offices, subordinated notes, repurchase agreements (RPs), purchased federal funds, and various other borrowings. Major banks came to perceive day-to-day liquidity as the ability to roll over existing liabilities as they fell due and to expand total liabilities as needed. A large bank could sell a variety of negotiable instruments in the money market, some nondeposit in form. Previously, liquid assets would be sold to fund new loans.

The Board of Governors moved to discourage the use of these instruments when it aimed to restrain credit growth after 1965. Moreover, at a time of recession in the national economy, with soaring interest rates and soured loans, even some very large institutions found that the market had become unreceptive. By mid-1974 banks discovered that managed liabilities were vulnerable.

Liability management made "go-go" banking expansion possible. First Pennsylvania Bank funded over 90 percent of its increase in earning assets between 1967 and the end of 1979 with interst-sensitive borrowings; managed liabilities soared from 26 percent to 75 percent of net earning assets. In 1980 the Philadelphia organization needed to be rescued by the FDIC.

For all insured commercial banks, purchased funds were 10.6 percent of total assets in 1970, but 37.6 percent from 1976 through 1979; they peaked at almost 49 percent in 1980. At the top twenty-five banks, purchased funds peaked at 64 percent of total assets in 1981, but were down to 53 percent in 1986.

Liability management dominated bankers' thinking in the 1960s and early 1970s. Later in the decade, a funds approach that considered simultaneously asset and liability management came into favor. Heralding this newer approach, Edward Palmer revealed in February 1971 that Citicorp has set up an asset and liability committee to coordinate general strategies and policies. Asset-liability management focused on control of the volume and mix of rate-sensitive assets and liabilities and the gap between them.

☐ Deposit and Nondeposit Sources of Funds

As a share of total deposits, time deposits climbed from 20 percent in 1945 to 40 percent in 1963 (the same as in 1929), and to 75 percent by 1985. Time and savings deposits in banks exceeded those in thrifts in

1981. Although deposits have remained the major source of banks' funds, nondeposit liabilities have grown increasingly important, reaching $100 billion by 1979 and over $200 billion in 1988. Nondeposit funds (mainly federal funds bought, RPs, and other borrowings) are not subject to reserve requirements or FDIC insurance assessments.

☐ Federal Funds

Near the end of 1964 Morgan Guaranty announced it would borrow (buy) federal funds as a long-range resource instead of merely as a temporary device for reserve adjustments. Since then, the rate on federal funds has been above the Federal Reserve discount rate almost continuously. Average daily volume was less than $2 billion in 1955, but seven to nine times as great by the late 1960s, and up to $130 billion in 1985. As the federal funds rate became more attractive, increasing numbers of small banks became sellers. With computerization, large correspondent banks became willing to place lesser amounts for small banks. Most banks have come to view the sale of federal funds as an alternative to acquisition of other secondary reserves.

☐ Repurchase Agreements

The sale of Treasury and federal agency securities with the commitment to buy them back at a later date (often the next day) represents another source of immediately available funds. RPs, initially used by bond dealers to finance their inventories, developed into a common method for banks to manage their cash position in the 1960s. From the standpoint of the borrowing institution, federal funds and RPs are similar, except that slightly less is paid for the latter because they are secured loans. The two sources combined amounted to 1.1 percent of total assets in 1967, 7.5 percent in 1977, and around 8.5 percent ever since.

☐ Discount Window Borrowings

Since the twelve Federal Reserve banks opened in 1914, member banks have been borrowing from them. Other depository institutions became eligible in 1980. For decades, the greater part of borrowings was short-term adjustment credit. In 1973 banks with less than $250 million in deposits (mostly in farm or resort areas) were offered seasonal borrowing privileges for longer intervals than adjustment credit. Other extended-term credits can be granted to depository institutions with liquidity problems arising out of unforeseen events or serious management errors. Such credit has fluctuated widely—from nothing in 1978 to 77 percent of discount window borrowings in 1984, when Continental Illinois was in serious trouble.

☐ Melting Core Deposits

Banks must pay market rates of interest for purchased funds. Core deposits involve some kind of customer loyalty; they include various transactions accounts, savings accounts, and time deposits under $100,000. As managed liabilities soared, core deposits fell from 82 percent of all commercial bank deposits at the end of 1976 to 54 percent by 1987. Major banks developed an interest in core deposits from households by the early 1960s, opening branches and advertising for the purpose. In the 1980s they renewed their interest, hoping for more reliable and less expensive funds.

☐ Capital

Compared with deposit and nondeposit liabilities of banks, capital has been a minor source of funds. Over the years most of the increase in bank capital has come from retained earnings, around 55 percent of net profits on average. Sale of additional common stock by existing organizations has generally been less than one-tenth of total capital financing. Preferred stock, authorized for national banks since the early 1960s, has been offered only occasionally. New financing has mainly taken the form of capital notes and debentures, with the interest deductible in calculating income tax liability.

Long-dormant investor interest in bank stock began to revive in the mid-1960s. Chase National Bank, listed on the New York Stock Exchange since 1878, had itself removed in January 1928. At the time banks wished to avoid highlighting fluctuations in share prices. Only one—Corn Exchange Bank—remained continuously listed until it merged into Chemical in 1954. As of March 1965, Chase Manhattan was again traded on the Big Board. Many others followed in the 1970s.

☐ Profits

In 1987, for the first time since the early 1930s, banks withdrew $7 billion from prior years' earnings accumulations to pay dividends.

Banks earned a return on equity under 2 percent in 1987, but rebounded to 13.4 percent in 1988. At no time had returns been below 10 percent from 1970 through 1985. The rate of return averaged 9.6 percent in the 1960s, 12.4 percent in the 1970s, and 10.4 percent from 1980 through 1988, even including 1987's dismal performance. The peak of the post-1930 era was 13.9 percent in 1979. Inflation, however, exaggerated accounting profits; adjusted for price level increases, the average return of the 1970s was nearly identical with the 7.4 percent inflation-adjusted return for the 1960s.

Commercial banks succeeded in remaining the foremost depository institutions despite powerful challenges from thrifts and (starting in the late 1970s) MMMFs, the handicap of limited branching powers in most states, and (until April 1986) Regulation Q. Demand deposits increased slowly; by 1971 they were less than half of total deposits. As traditional deposit arrangements proved insufficient to fund loan demands, banks developed new financial instruments and new ways of using old ones. As a result, interest expense came to exceed employee compensation in the early 1960s, and soared thereafter. Liability management permitted major institutions to grow more rapidly, while increasing their vulnerability. Capital increased more slowly than assets after 1962, until the supervisory agencies called a halt in the early 1980s.

20

Supervision and Regulation

BANKS HAVE REMAINED CLOSELY SUPER-
vised even though the regulatory straitjacket into which the industry
was fitted during the 1930s eased considerably after 1960. Meanwhile,
new areas of regulation have appeared, reflecting present-day societal
concerns.

☐ Federal Bank Regulators

At the federal level, three agencies share responsibility for the comprehensive supervision of commercial banks. The Office of the Comptroller
of the Currency has regulated national banks since 1863. The Federal
Reserve System arrived on the scene in 1914 to regulate national and
state member banks. Since 1934 the FDIC has overseen all insured
commercial banks, particularly state-chartered nonmember banks.

Although nonmembers increased from 45 percent of all commercial banks in 1945 to 59 percent by 1988, the Federal Reserve, with
exclusive jurisdiction over bank holding companies, has become the
most significant federal regulator. After 1967 most important banks
were turned into subsidiaries of bank holding companies. Today bank
subsidiaries hold over 90 percent of all bank assets. In addition to the
three agencies, the Justice Department's Antitrust Division has inter-
vened in bank combinations since 1960, while the Securities and Ex-

change Commission has set disclosure standards for larger banking organizations since 1974.

Fed Chairman Arthur Burns in 1974 described bank regulation as "a jurisdictional tangle that boggles the mind." Existing arrangements were "conducive to subtle competition among regulatory authorities sometimes to relax constraints, sometimes to delay corrective measures."[1] His predecessor, Eugene Meyer, had remarked similarly forty-four years earlier.

The Federal Financial Institutions Examination Council, a step in the direction of coordination, consists of representatives of the three federal banking agencies as well as the Office of Thrift Supervision and the National Credit Union Administration. Congress ordered the council, established in 1979, to work for uniformity in the examination and supervision of financial institutions.

All proposals for federal agency reorganization have been successfully opposed by bankers. Consolidation of the three federal agencies into a "superagency" would represent "a concentration and centralization of financial power unparalleled in our financial history," according to the American Bankers Association.[2] Critics fear that a single agency would be more likely to limit entry into banking and to unduly restrict the range of financial activities. States have been concerned that their supervisory role and the dual banking system would come to an end.

□ Dual Banking System

A century and a quarter after its unplanned appearance, the dual banking system is still alive. Two out of three banks operate under a state charter, including about half of all new ones in recent years.

In September 1965 Chase Manhattan, then the largest state bank, gave up its historic 1799 charter, citing the new services and greater flexibility it could enjoy as a national bank.[3] In 1968 the largest state bank in the Southeast (Wachovia) and the largest outside New York City (Wells Fargo) converted. Marine Midland converted in 1980 after a fifteen-month debate with the New York State Banking Department over a proposed takeover by the Hong Kong and Shanghai Banking Corporation. Despite these defections, state banks had over 45 percent of total deposits at the end of 1980, an increase of six percentage points since 1945.

From the outset, higher reserve requirements deterred state banks from joining the Fed. From 1950 to 1980, 665 state members fled while over 400 national banks converted to state charters in order to escape

Fed jurisdiction. As interest rates rose in the 1970s hundreds of member banks left. The Fed became alarmed. Member bank deposits, 86 percent of the total for all commercial banks in 1945, were down to 72 percent in 1979.

The Depository Institutions Deregulation and Monetary Control Act of 1980 phased in uniform reserve requirements for *all* depository institutions (including thrifts), regardless of chartering agency. Since September 1987 all have had to meet identical reserve requirements on checkable deposits, on time deposits placed for less than eighteen months and owned by other than natural persons, and on all types of Eurocurrency liabilities. One motive for conversions was eliminated. From 1981 through 1988, 161 national banks became state banks, while 291 state banks became national banks. The continued vitality of dual banking reflects banker insistence on the availability of options aided by the National Association of Supervisors of State Banks seeking "to assure equality and protection of the rights of all institutions," as stated in the 1958 amendment to its constitution.

□ Supervisory Examinations

Following the failure of Franklin National Bank in October 1974, the federal agencies developed improved methods of surveillance of banks under their supervision, emphasizing bank policies and internal controls: managerial review of bank practices, board of directors' review of management, and audit procedures. Reports supplement comprehensive on-site examinations. Since 1985 the comptroller of the currency has used a supervisory monitoring system that incorporates up-to-date information on each national bank.

Examination findings are the basis for supervisory agency ratings of banks from 1 (best) to 5 (worst). Ratings consider capital adequacy, asset quality, management and administration, earnings, and liquidity. Banks rated 4 and 5 are considered problem banks and receive close supervision.

□ Problem Banks

A severe recession starting in November 1973 launched a roller-coaster decade for the American economy. Double-digit inflation in the late 1970s was followed by dislocating disinflation in the early 1980s in the aftermath of a recession even more severe than that of 1973–74, the worst since 1937–38. Volatile interest rates reflected price trends with a lag but remained high in the 1980s in real terms as the federal budget showed exceptionally high deficits in years of economic expansion. Banks had to contend with a fluctuating economy and increased competition unleashed by market forces and government deregulation.

From 1970 through 1981 there was an average of 262 problem banks (including for the first time some with over $1 billion in deposits) each year, representing under 2 percent of all insured commercial banks. In the 1980s the proportion of problem banks climbed: 2.5 percent of insured commercial banks in 1982, 5.7 percent in 1984, and 11 percent in 1987. At the peak in mid-1987 there were 1,624 problem banks; over 95 percent had under $300 million in total assets, but twenty-four had over $1 billion. Agriculture, real estate, and oil loans accounted for most of the trouble. Many problem banks improved; some failed. In May 1988 the FDIC chairman reassured the Senate Banking Committee that "despite increased competition from all sectors of the financial community, severe economic problems in parts of our country, and an unprecedented pace of change in the industry, the banking system as a whole is sound and is getting sounder."[4]

☐ A New Era of Big Bank Failures

Only small banks failed during the forty years after the Bank Holiday of 1933. From the FDIC's beginning in 1934 through 1972, 632 commercial banks (including 134 noninsured institutions) had to close because of financial difficulties. That aggregate was no more than the number of failures in a single year in the late 1920s; losses in the FDIC fund averaged $2 million a year.

Failures averaged less than four a year from 1945 through 1972. The forty-three insured bank failures during the 1960s had altogether under $300 million in deposits. In 1962, for the first and only time since 1934, there was not a single failure. At the dedication of the FDIC headquarters in 1963, House Banking Committee Chairman Wright Patman expressed the view that "we have gone too far in the direction of bank safety."

A few months later the era of negligible failures ended.

In October 1973 the United States National Bank of San Diego was forced to close, a victim of massive fraud by its president. The $1.3 billion institution—fourteen times the asset size of the previous record-holder for insured bank failure—was acquired by Crocker National with financial assistance from the FDIC. Depositors lost nothing.

Less than a year later, Franklin National Bank set a new bank failure record. Opened in 1926 in Franklin Square, New York, it became the outstanding commercial bank on Long Island in the first two decades after World War II, expanding very successfully in fast-growing Nassau and Suffolk counties. In May 1964 it opened its first three New York City branches. By 1970 Franklin derived the bulk of its deposits from national and international sources. A Nassau (Bahamas) facility was added in 1969, and a London branch was opened in 1972. Michele Sindona, an Italian financier, paid Loew's Inc. $40 million for one million shares (21.6 percent of the total outstanding) in July 1972.

Franklin's return on equity averaged 14.5 percent from 1960 through 1969, compared with Chase Manhattan's 10 percent and First National City's 8.7 percent. Subsequently, the rate of return on equity declined ominously from 17.7 percent in 1970 to 12.6 percent in 1971, 9.1 percent in 1972, and 8.7 percent in 1973. Management attributed the continuing slide to Franklin's transition to a "major worldwide financial service institution and a leading money center banking operation."

Franklin's long-standing liberal lending policy was well known. The 1959 annual report boasted that a majority of its loans would not have been made by other New York City banks. The move into New York City had been accompanied by loans to large borrowers of lesser quality than those accommodated by Franklin's competitors, and interest rates were too low for the risk involved. Almost 6 percent of the loan portfolio at the end of 1973 was of doubtful quality. The comptroller of the currency ordered $12 million in loans written off as a loss.

The earnings slide after 1970 prompted management to reach for quick profits. Franklin's investments, especially its municipals, had long average maturities: the proportion falling due in more than five years went from 58 percent in December 1972 to 82 percent in May 1974. The (unrealized) decline in market value of these investments by May 1974 represented 44 percent of total capital funds.

Between December 1972 and November 1973 total assets swelled by 29 percent, though demand and savings deposits actually declined by 5.5 percent. Half of Franklin's liabilities came to consist of highly volatile federal funds, CDs, and time deposits bought by other banks. The holding company, with assets of $5 billion on New Year's Day 1974, had grown 67 percent in the previous three years. Only nineteen U.S. banks had more deposits. Franklin's 104 domestic offices included one-third of all Nassau commercial banking offices, one-fourth of the Suffolk total, as well as thirty-one branches in New York City. Over 30 percent of total deposits were in its foreign branches.

In April 1974 Franklin reported first-quarter earnings of 2¢ a share, compared with 68¢ a year earlier. On 1 May the Board of Governors rejected Franklin's application to acquire Talcott (a leading business finance and factoring firm then controlled by Sindona), noting publicly the bank's below-average earnings in the 1970s and the recent substantial shift in its management policies.

On 12 May Sindona agreed to turn over his voting rights to David Kennedy, respected former secretary of the Treasury. The next day the president of the bank and the head of the foreign exchange department were fired. On 14 May foreign exchange trading losses amounting to $12 million (which turned out to be $47 million) were announced.

Once Franklin's problems became known, the private sector became unwilling to advance funds. Large CDs could not be renewed at maturity. Franklin's managed liabilities and London branch deposits stood at $2.24 billion on 3 May. By 28 June, $1.23 billion of these funds had been withdrawn, replaced by borrowings, which peaked at $1.77 billion on 2 October, from the Federal Reserve Bank of New York. The Fed granted this unprecedented volume of discounts in order to avoid "the severe deterioration of confidence at home and abroad that would have resulted from an abrupt failure."[5] The funds outflow reached $2.8 billion by 8 October, the day the comptroller of the currency declared Franklin insolvent. The next morning all its offices opened as branches of European-American Bank and Trust Company (owned by six major European banks). All deposits—foreign as well as domestic—were paid in full.

Less than three months later, in January 1975, Franklin's major rival on Long Island, Security National Bank (the forty-fourth largest bank in 1972), was involved in an emergency merger. Chemical Bank bought Security without any FDIC assistance.

For the balance of the 1970s, however, bank failures did not make the front page. In the spring of 1980, First Pennsylvania, the largest in Philadelphia, and number twenty-three nationally, had to be rescued by the FDIC. Failures climbed to 120 in 1985 (breaking the previous high of 84 in 1937), to 138 in 1986, to 184 in 1987, and to 221 in 1988.

☐ Energy Bank Failures

Many of the closed banks had been heavily involved in energy lending. The most notorious, Penn Square National Bank, opened in 1960 in an Oklahoma City shopping center. When bought by Beep Jennings in February 1975, it had $35 million in assets. Involved at first in real estate loans, Jennings turned to making oil and gas loans on a massive scale. Assets reached $100 million in 1978.

Rig operations dropped 40 percent between December 1981 and July 1982, but Penn Square's loans soared from $239 million to $421 million. Participations sold to other banks grew to $2.1 *billion*. By July 1982 Continental Illinois had acquired $1.13 billion, and Seattle First National $378 million. Chase Manhattan (long renowned as an oil lender) had $275 million, 58 percent of which was charged off by 1985. Michigan National Bank lost almost half of its $199 million in Penn Square loans. Among these gullible lenders, only Chase Manhattan survived intact.

Until mid-1982 deposits of every sizable failed bank had been turned over to a sound bank, so depositors lost not one cent. When Penn Square (the fourth largest insured bank failure up to then) was closed, depositors holding balances in excess of $100,000 faced losses of one-third of the uninsured balance, depending on the course of liquidation of $519 million in assets. Banks, credit unions, and savings and loan associations held 80 percent of the uninsured funds. Faced with unknown loss exposure on $3 billion in off–balance sheet claims, the FDIC chose to make a payoff rather than arrange a merger. This worried Board of Governors Chairman Paul Volcker, who feared a "substantial chance of financial chaos." The payoff policy for large banks was soon abandoned.

Another aggressive energy lender, Abilene National Bank, went under on 6 August 1982. On 3 October 1982 Oklahoma National Bank had to be merged into First National Bank in Oklahoma City. In October 1983 First National Bank of Midland, Texas ($1.4 billion in assets) became the second largest failure since 1934. In July 1986 there was a new claimant for the title, First National Bank of Oklahoma City ($1.9 billion in assets).

Oil had soared from a few dollars a barrel in 1973 to a record $42 in 1982. OPEC cut the price to $28.50 early in 1983; by 1986 the price was half as much. The collapse of oil prices eroded the quality of loan portfolios and seriously depressed bank earnings. Of the top ten Texas banking organizations only San Antonio-based Cullen/Frost survived intact. Seven of the ten were merged into other organizations (all but one out of state) with $8.2 billion in FDIC assistance. Despite notable profits of almost 20 percent on equity from 1980 to 1983, subsequent heavy losses compelled Texas Commerce to agree to be taken over by Chemical New York Corporation in May 1987. Another Houston giant, Allied Bancshares, became part of Los Angeles–based First Interstate in January 1988. Republicbank and Interfirst combined to form First Republicbank Corporation in June 1987. It hoped to survive as a Texas-controlled entity but had to be taken over by NCNB of Charlotte in July 1988 with $4 billion of FDIC assistance. First City Bancorp required a

$1.5 billion bailout in April 1988. In mid-1989 MCorp's twenty banks were acquired by Banc One of Ohio, with about $2 billion in FDIC aid.

Penn Square was the first of many bank closings in the seven energy belt states: fifty-two in 1985, eighty-four in 1986, and 120 in 1987. Texas alone had 36 percent of the failed banks from 1986 through 1988. Oil was turning into water.

☐ Continental Illinois Collapse

The greatest of all FDIC rescue operations until 1989 involved the Midwest's largest banking organization. Half a century earlier, Continental Illinois had to sell $50 million of preferred stock to the RFC to survive a write-off of $128 million in loan losses. For decades thereafter the chastened bank pursued a conservative policy.

By 1960 Continental Illinois, like other important institutions, had begun to move forward. Roger Anderson (who became head in 1973) aimed to create a world-class bank. Continental was the nation's eighth largest in 1974, and sixth largest in 1981. Anderson's bank had become the largest lender to American industry by 1982, moving ahead of its main rival, First National Bank of Chicago. A handsome brochure celebrating the bank's 125th anniversary in 1982 began with a quotation from the *New York Times* describing Continental as "an acknowledged member of the nation's banking elite."

The severe recession of 1981–82 hurt many of Continental's borrowers, among them such giants as International Harvester, Massey-Ferguson, Nucorp Energy, and Dome Petroleum. In mid-1982 nonperforming loans were about double the ratio for other major banks.

Energy loans were a specialty. By the end of 1980, altogether $167 million had been bought from Penn Square. The inexperienced midcontinent division of the oil and gas group nearly doubled its loans in 1981, at a time of falling oil prices. By the spring of 1982 Penn Square had unloaded $1.1 billion—an amount that represented 17 percent of Continental's total oil and gas loans, and 3 percent of all its loans. Losses from these loans came to $800 million—$500 million alone from 1982 to 1984.

In the first quarter of 1984 nonperforming loans were 7.7 percent of Continental's total loans, and $500 million more than its total capital. In May 1984 a run on the bank began in Hong Kong, then moved to London. The comptroller of the currency officially denied rumors of insolvency. Foreign depositors continued their withdrawals even after sixteen major American banks led by Morgan Guaranty arranged a $4.5

billion line of credit on 16 May. On the seventeenth, the three federal banking agencies and twenty-four leading banks joined in a "comprehensive financial assistance program." Despite the FDIC's unprecedented assurance that all general creditors would be fully protected, the greatest bank run in history continued. Deposits shrank by more than one half by 19 July.

A week later, a permanent assistance program was put in place. Continental Illinois sold $4.5 billion of poor loans to the FDIC, receiving $3.5 billion cash. The FDIC also bought $1 billion of nonvoting preferred stock, thereby gaining 80 percent ownership of the bank holding company. Major banks loaned $5.5 billion, and the Federal Reserve Bank of Chicago continued to provide for extraordinary liquidity requirements, averaging $4.9 billion in the second half of 1984. The Fed deemed this necessary "to keep the financial system from exploding on us."

The FDIC also wished to avoid "worldwide chaos." Moreover, Continental held over 2,000 correspondent accounts; for 179 smaller banks these deposits represented over half of their capital. Nine institutions, including Bank of America, First National of Chicago, and Manufacturers Hanover, "would have been in the soup" if Continental had not been "handled," according to the head of the FDIC. The FDIC expects to lose $1.7 billion on this rescue operation. Owners of Continental Illinois Corporation's bonds, notes, and even preferred stock, with a par value of $1.5 billion, and all depositors were protected from loss. The Fed, concerned about the ability of other holding companies to fund nonbank operations, insisted on this arrangement.

The FDIC's apparent willingness to protect creditors of the holding company turned out not to be the case two years later. Creditors of First Oklahoma Bancorporation suffered significant losses when First National of Oklahoma City went under in July 1986. Beginning in August 1986, in a case involving the Bank of Oklahoma, the FDIC insisted that holding company creditors agree to concessions when it came to the aid of banks to enable them to remain open.

□   FDIC Handling of Failures

From 1934 through 1988 the FDIC paid off depositors in 470 insured failed banks; some loss occurred on the uninsured portion. Most banks treated as deposit payoff cases were quite small: only nine had assets of more than $50 million. Penn Square National Bank was the notable exception.

Depositors in the 705 closed banks that were taken over by the best bidders lost nothing. In the case of larger institutions, the FDIC was "almost forced" into this purchase and assumption arrangement, the chairman of the FDIC acknowledged in 1984, "to prevent disruptive consequences to financial markets." As the FDIC explained with regard to the near failure of Continental Illinois in *Mandate for Change* (October 1987): "The U.S. government cannot permit a large bank failure to be handled in a way that would result in losses to depositors . . . . The chance of a deposit run on other large banks if uninsured funding sources lose confidence probably is too great to effect a modified payoff or similar transaction in this type of situation."

In 1971 the FDIC began to make advances to enable an institution to remain open and to prevent its failure. This authority (granted in 1950) was used in sixty-eight cases through 1988, mostly since 1981. The Texas-size bailout of First Republicbank Corporation in the summer of 1988 is expected to cost the FDIC more than the $1.7 billion final bill for Continental. In assistance cases, the FDIC changes management and virtually wipes out shareholders. The agency denies that large banks receive preferential treatment. Its goal has been to use the most cost-effective option, while minimizing depositor losses and community disruption.

Of the 1,389 instances since 1934 when the FDIC had to make disbursements, 795 occurred from 1982 through 1988 (including thirteen of the sixteen mutual savings bank cases). Public anxiety mounted in the late 1980s as the number of large troubled banks rose sharply. The deposit insurance fund—little more than 1 percent of insured deposits—did not offer reassurance.

Meanwhile, Congress passed a concurrent resolution in March 1982, confirming that "deposits up to the statutorily prescribed amount, in federally insured depository institutions, are backed by the full faith and credit of the United States." In August 1987 the Competitive Equality Banking Act reiterated this statement verbatim after declaring that "(1) since the 1930's, the American people have relied upon Federal deposit insurance to ensure the safety and security of their funds in federally insured depository institutions; and (2) the safety and security of such funds is an essential element of the American financial system."

Depository institutions face continued federal supervision and regulation as long as government insurance and Federal Reserve advances are made available. The large number of problem banks and the failure of substantial banks and thrift institutions in the 1980s resulted in a slowdown of deregulation. Bank capital supervision tightened significantly.

☐ Bank Capital Regulation

Capital adequacy has been a source of regulatory concern, especially since the early 1930s. Equity capital rose from 6.8 percent of total bank assets in 1950 to 8.1 percent in 1960, only to decline to 5.6 percent by 1974. In 1979 (when the ratio was 6.7 percent) the FDIC asserted that the declining trend after 1960 had "not imperilled the safety and soundness of banks." By 1981 the decline had reached the point where the Board of Governors resisted further shrinkage in the capital ratios of large banking organizations. Those with assets over $5 billion had a ratio of equity capital to total assets of 4.12 percent in 1980, down from 5.34 percent in 1970. Recognizing that for the many banks whose shares were selling below book value the sale of new equity was not attractive, the Federal Reserve suggested a slower growth policy that would "tend to dissuade banks from extending credit to more marginal borrowers at questionable spreads." Bank capital generally was "at an uncomfortably low level," the Fed stated in May 1982.

Regulatory agencies made individual bank evaluations of adequacy until December 1981, when it was specified that primary capital (equity plus loan loss reserves, perpetual preferred stock, and convertible bonds) should be at least equal to 6 percent of assets for banks with less than $1 billion, and 5 percent for larger ones. The November 1983 International Lending Supervision Act empowered the federal agencies to enforce minimum capital standards. All three federal agencies set a uniform minimum for all banks in June 1985: primary capital was to equal 5.5 percent of total assets. By then, the ratio of equity to total assets averaged over 6 percent.

A more sophisticated measure, which adjusts the requirement for apparent riskiness of the asset portfolio, was devised in conjunction with the Bank of England (a first in international cooperation) and adopted at the end of 1988. Ten major industrial nations and Luxembourg agreed to require an 8 percent capital ratio, of which at least 4 percent would be common equity as of 1992.

☐ International Supervision

In recognition of growing problems, the 1983 act instructed the three federal banking agencies to develop a more comprehensive system for supervising foreign lending. In December 1983 they strengthened the uniform system devised in 1979 to examine country risk exposure. In 1975 a dozen leading nations had established guidelines dealing with foreign operations of branches, subsidiary banks, and joint ventures. The Basle Concordat was updated in 1983 to ensure adequate supervision on a consolidated basis by both host and parent authorities.

Yet there remained ample cause for concern. Financial shocks might be transmitted worldwide with "alarming speed," given the "intricate financial connections among widespread institutions" and banking's globalization, as Arthur Burns insisted shortly before his death in 1987. The former Fed chairman noted the absence of an "international counterpart to the national safety nets."[6]

☐ The Regulatory Burden

Most of the nation's banks are not directly involved in international banking and lending. All are concerned, however, about government regulation. Bankers complain that the federal bureaucracy has sharply curtailed management prerogatives.

The banking section of the Code of Federal Regulations grew from 397 pages in 1963 to 2,425 pages by 1980. To administer truth in lending, the Board of Governors had ninety-two printed pages of regulations, in addition to 1,506 court decisions and letters interpreting the law (a pile of papers almost two feet high). In recognition of this problem, the 1980 Regulatory Flexibility Act required each federal financial regulatory agency to review regulations that bear heavily on small institutions and to make sure that regulations are as simple and clearly written as possible, and no more burdensome than necessary. The 1989 edition of the code was 642 pages longer than 1980's.

Government began to interfere in new areas, even as longstanding restraints (such as Regulation Q, and product-line and branching limitations) were being loosened. Bank dealings with consumers of financial services, borrowers, and employees were increasingly governed by laws and regulations mandating certain performance. Whether their purpose was to provide information for customer decision-making or fair treatment of customers and employees, these regulations carried substantial compliance costs of record-keeping, agency monitoring, and enforcement. Federal regulators now conduct compliance examinations to check on bank performance.

☐ Consumer Protection Legislation

The Consumer Credit Protection Act of 1968 was the first of a long series of laws intended to safeguard the interests of the nonbusiness public. The truth-in-lending section requires clear statements of finance charges, usually in the form of an average percentage rate (APR), to facilitate comparison of various credit offers. Another 1968 law, the Fair Housing Act, forbade real estate credit denial because of race, color, religion, sex, or national origin. Significant consumer-oriented laws added in the 1970s included the Fair Credit Reporting Act (1970), the Fair Credit Billing Act (1974), the Equal Credit Opportunity Act (1974), the Consumer Leasing Act (1976), the Fair Debt Collection Act (1977), the Electronic Fund Transfer Act (1978), and the Right to Financial Privacy Act (1978).

☐   Community Reinvestment

A notable effort to influence bank lending policy, the Community Reinvestment Act of 1977 required federal supervisory agencies to assess the performance of all financial institutions in meeting the credit needs of their communities. Regulated financial institutions have a "continuing and affirmative obligation to help meet the credit needs of the local communities in which they are chartered" with housing finance, loans to small businesses and small farms, purchase of municipal securities, and bank participation in student loan programs, for example. The act called upon the regulatory authorities to prod bankers to respond sensitively to the needs of the local market, on the basis of their solid knowledge of the local economy and reasonable prospects for profit.

Since November 1978 (when the Community Reinvestment Act went into effect) regulatory agencies have conducted thousands of examinations to measure performance. Fewer than 2 percent of banks received less than a satisfactory rating from 1984 through 1986. Performance is also reviewed when banks apply for branches, change of location, mergers, and charters.

In the first nine years, community groups won some $5 billion in concessions, $1 billion in 1986 alone. Wells Fargo committed $41 million of low-cost financing for community projects when it received approval to acquire Crocker in 1986. Fleet Financial promised to advertise that it had earmarked $50 million for low- and moderate-income housing.

☐   Equal Employment Opportunity

Bankers responded to societal pressures partly out of personal conviction. The Community Reinvestment Act and the Treasury's affirmative action enforcement program were also influential. In lending, financial institutions face pressures for "equal access." In the personnel area, businesses are now expected to offer equal access to desirable positions based on job qualifications.

Women, long a majority of bank employees, occupied mainly routine clerical positions until recently. The National Association of Bank Women (limited to bank officers) was started in 1921. A quarter of a century later, there were 6,000 women officers (not even one for every two banks); by the early 1970s there were 25,000. As bank officers increased by two-thirds overall, the proportion of women officials and managers rose from 15 percent in 1970 to 33 percent in 1978. During these years, minorities (blacks, Asians, American Indians, and Hispanics) increased their presence by five percentage points, up to 12.4 percent of these upper-level positions. In the top fifty banks, women were 47 percent of officials and managers in 1988, and minorities were 16 percent. Every institution that acts as a federal depository or paying agent for U.S. savings bonds must have an affirmative action program.

□ Social Responsibility

In February 1971 Vietnam War protesters set ablaze Bank of America's Isla Vista branch. David Rockefeller told friends a few months later that in the current environment banks could not ignore the growing demands for more socially responsible behavior. Chase Manhattan, which set up a corporate responsibility committee in 1962, increased its contributions to charitable, scientific, and educational organizations, and made loans available for community economic development and small business and minority enterprises. To Rockefeller, business involvement in community problems was an economic as well as moral imperative. Bank of America's social policy committee has dealt with issues such as corporate disclosure, redlining, and environmental concerns, as well as the bank's collection practices and complaint-handling procedures.

In the 1970s large institutions formulated formal codes of conduct for employees. Among the areas covered by ethics codes are situations involving possible conflicts of interest, taking or giving gifts, loans to insiders, and confidentiality of information. Bankers have realized that the only alternative to an insistence on high standards of conduct is more government regulation of what the public perceives as abuses.

□ Lobbying

Given the scope and growth of government regulation and pressure, financial institutions have felt the need to lobby through their organizations. In 1971 the American Bankers Association moved from New York to Washington to be closer to the scene of major battle. The ABA supports a professional staff and registered lobbyists. The 12,000 banks that belong to the ABA divide on many issues because of their diverse interests. The Association of Reserve City Bankers (150 large banks) and the Independent Bankers Association of America (for 6,600 smaller, usually nonbranch banks) are among the other nationwide commercial banking organizations speaking out on behalf of their members' interests. In addition, various associations operate in the states and localities.

Many restrictive laws and regulations have been adopted at the federal and state levels, despite banker protests. No industry has been regulated longer, and possibly more comprehensively, than banking.

21

Some Perspectives and Prospects

COMMERCIAL BANKING IS ONE OF AMER-
ica's oldest industries. As other financial institutions were established—
insurance companies, mutual savings banks, savings and loan associations, credit unions, investment companies, finance companies, and small
loan companies—banks were destined to diminish in relative importance.
The bank share of assets of all private financial intermediaries was 66.7
percent in 1860, 64.1 percent in 1912, 53.6 percent in 1929, and 48.5
percent in 1933; it made a sharp recovery to 63 percent by 1945, but
dropped over the next four decades to less than 30 percent. Despite
increased competition, banks have retained their primacy among financial institutions because of their adaptability; they have increased the
variety of loans, debt obligations, and transactions services offered.

☐ Banks as Lenders

At first exclusive organizations for well-connected seaport merchants,
banks became more accessible to a widening range of aspiring businessmen, rural as well as urban, as growing numbers of competitors entered
the field. State-chartered institutions were better suited than national
banks to meet rural requirements after the Civil War. State banks'
inability to issue bank notes after 1866, however, was a handicap until
the farm sector became habituated to writing checks.

Retail banking came to be increasingly prominent in the 1920s. Households were encouraged to become depositors and borrowers, even of small sums. Expanding "department stores of finance" sought out new opportunities. Investment banking activities shrank and security flotations declined after Wall Street crashed and the government forced separation.

Swelling excess reserves and persistent low earnings after 1933 pressured banks into modifying their lending practices and extending new types of accommodations—most notably, the term loan. As banks extended the scope and nature of their lending activities, they found themselves increasingly in competition with other financial institutions. By the late 1930s lending directly to consumers, as well as indirectly through advances to consumer and commercial finance companies, had become significant.

Retail banking blossomed only after 1945. Traditionally lenders to business, banks now increasingly financed the household sector of the economy. By 1960 there were few exclusively wholesale banks dealing only with large business customers. The combined total of loans to individuals and residential real estate loans exceeded commercial and industrial loans year after year starting in 1954, and by a widening margin.

By the early 1980s substantial corporations with high credit ratings increasingly turned to commercial paper financing, while lower rated firms could more readily sell bonds. Banks continue as significant lenders to business as most firms are too small or too little known to have access to the open market. Well-run banks will assess credit risks and diversify loans, funding them by selling loan packages and offering a growing variety of deposit instruments.

☐ Deposits

Banks have supplied the greater part of the means of payment ever since the early 1800s, at first mainly with bank notes. After 1850 deposits subject to check came to the fore. National bank notes were all safe, unlike the multifarious issues of state banks. Seventy years later, deposits came under federal guaranty.

Commercial bank checking accounts were "so distinctive that they are entirely free of effective competition from . . . other financial institutions," the Supreme Court stated in 1963. By the early 1980s, however, thrifts had acquired the power to offer checkable deposits, and banks funded most of their loans from other sources.

For generations bankers (particularly in large cities) looked askance at the practice of paying interest for deposit accounts, yet by the mid-1980s, three-fourths of total bank deposits paid interest. With the development of liability management in the 1970s, a significant and growing fraction of bank deposits became interest-sensitive. Money-market liabilities climbed until they were over 40 percent of total bank assets in 1981–82; they retreated to around 35 percent in the years that followed.

The 1933 ban on the payment of interest on demand deposits has yet to be repealed. Meanwhile, banks continue to process ever more checks. The "checkless society," predicted decades ago, has not arrived, but a "less-check" society is likely to evolve by the end of the century.

□   Failure and Deposit Insurance

From 1865 through 1929 annual total depositor losses averaged 0.08 percent of deposits in all operating banks. From 1930 through 1933 losses were over thirty-three times that—2.7 percent of all deposits, enough to call forth the FDIC. The years since have been panic-free.

□   Structural Developments

The unit banking heritage has left the United States with 13,800 separately chartered institutions. For over three-quarters of a century after the start of the branch banking movement, a majority of the nation's banks were without a single branch. In 1988, 78 percent of U.S. banking offices were branches, compared with 27 percent as recently as 1952. Although only half the states allowed state-wide branching in the 1980s, nationwide banking was under debate.

The House Banking and Currency Committee was still rhapsodizing over "home-owned and home-managed banks . . . responsive to the needs of the people of their area" in 1956. Since then, the popularity of bank holding companies, especially after 1970, swept all but a tiny fraction of the nation's deposits into subsidiary banks, while their non-bank subsidiaries operated all over the United States.

Giants did develop, despite this country's traditional fear of bigness in financial activities. National City Bank, in 1897 the first to attain $100 million in assets (equivalent to $1.7 billion in 1988 dollars), had $1 billion ($7.7 billion in 1989 dollars) by 1924. At the end of 1989, sixty-seven banking organizations had at least $7.4 billion in assets.

Between 1900 and 1949 the deposit share of the ten largest banks almost doubled—to 19.7 percent of the U.S. total, with the 100 largest growing from 35.3 percent to 45.5 percent. Long-standing, deep-seated suspicion of Wall Street reflected concern over the concentration of economic power, as did unit banking legislation, prohibition of inter-state banking, limits on multiple-bank holding company expansion (1956), limits on growth by merger (1960), and regulation of one-bank holding company movement into other industries (1970).

Insofar as bank survival relates to scale economies, recent studies indicate there is room for thousands of small local banks offering more personal service. By 2000 extensive interstate banking through holding company subsidiaries will be a reality, as nationwide branching looms. Public anxiety over the specter of concentrated economic power may slow growth by acquisition. Well-run institutions a fraction the size of the top ten are likely to grow relative to supergiants: banking organizations in Florida, North Carolina, Ohio, and elsewhere are acquiring banks in neighboring states.

In 1900 the great banks of New York (and to a much lesser extent of Chicago and San Francisco) were the focal points of American banking. These money-center banks diminished in importance as the Federal Reserve banks went into operation. A generation later, they continued to decline relatively as other sections of the country prospered. New York City, already the financial center of the United States by the 1830s, retains a special position despite significant slippage in its share of the nation's deposits: from 25.4 percent in 1939 to 18.4 percent in 1949, and to less than 9 percent in 1987. Although important regional financial centers developed elsewhere, national and international corporations continue to use the services perfected by Wall Street and Park Avenue banks. Moreover, hundreds of foreign institutions located in Manhattan after 1960.

Foreign banks interested in the American market have acquired branches and subsidiaries—mainly in New York, but in other trade centers as well. By 1988 foreign banks had 20 percent of U.S. banking assets.

☐ Globalization of American Banking

Large-scale internationalization of business in the 1970s brought leading American banks to distant shores. Nine American giants were prominent as global financial supermarkets, with 144 others also represented over-seas. Overseas deposits soared from 8 percent of total deposits in U.S. banks in 1970 to 25 percent in 1980. The number of foreign branches peaked at 967 in 1985 and dipped to 854 three years later. Branch assets,

$421 billion in 1988, had grown but $30 billion since 1981. The Third World debt crisis has triggered retrenchment, at least for now. Increasing integration of financial markets worldwide also places greater competitive pressures on American banking organizations.

☐ Regulation and Supervision

Accretion rather than design accounts for the present dispersal of banking regulation among three separate federal agencies. The comptroller of the currency was alone from 1863 until the Federal Reserve appeared on the scene fifty-one years later. Neither welcomed the organization of the FDIC in 1934. Insured state nonmember banks, still the majority of all U.S. banks, have vigorously supported the FDIC over the years. Bankers strongly oppose unification of the banking agencies, as well as proposals to merge them with thrift institution regulators (Office of Thrift Supervision, Savings Association Insurance Fund, National Credit Union Association).

The dual banking system, enshrined in banker ideology when the tax on state bank notes did not eliminate state banks, may nevertheless be threatened. States began to specify minimum reserve ratios for their banks in the mid–nineteenth century. Eventually, all but Illinois did so. Beginning in 1980, however, uniform requirements were also applied to state-chartered banks and thrifts to achieve more effective Fed control over monetary policy. Although state chartering authority remains intact, over time states are likely to play a diminished role as regulators and supervisors of the institutions they have chartered.

Notwithstanding the mass of statutory restrictions from an early period, the government actually interfered little with banking practices until the collapse of the early 1930s. Outside the national banking system, examination was generally perfunctory. Even the comptroller of the currency refrained from undue meddling, lest national banks switch allegiance. Expanded regulation and more careful supervision of banks followed the collapse in the early 1930s. Through FDIC insurance, all but the tiny proportion of noninsured banks came under federal jurisdiction.

Regulatory authorities, anxious to ensure bank solvency, dampened banking enterprise from the 1930s through the 1950s. Policies reflected the view that before the collapse, "there were too many banks engaged in unregulated and unrestricted competition," as the FDIC chairman told a congressional committee in 1957. Comptroller James Saxon (1961–66) encouraged reinvigoration. His October 1966 farewell address before the American Bankers Association rightly hailed "a new spirit . . . confident in its outlook, aggressive in its conduct, and optimistic of the future."[1]

Increased emphasis on competition and less on regulation was a pronounced trend under way in the 1960s. The Supreme Court upheld the Justice Department's opposition to certain acquisitions previously approved by the banking agencies, where anticompetitive consequences were foreseen. Prohibited from growing by combining with other local institutions, larger banks opened new branch offices and sought out distant partners where permitted. Management channeled its energies into devising new ways of better serving customers.

Notwithstanding significant changes in the regulatory climate in all jurisdictions, President Richard Nixon's Commission on Financial Structure and Regulation had good reason for finding in 1971 that "the existing regulatory system is, on balance, too restrictive." Growing awareness of the social costs of regulation inspired the deregulation movement in banking in the late 1970s. Elimination of interest rate ceilings on time deposits was the most notable consequence. Governmental oversight came to emphasize improved supervisory techniques rather than ever more complex rules.

Despite increasing reliance on market forces, federal regulation and supervision of financial institutions offering insured deposits is likely to continue. Efforts at international coordination will grow, lest multinational banks shift activities to less-regulated centers.

☐ Public Ownership

Government-owned banks are found in some countries with a mixed capitalist economic system. In the United States, one by one, states sold bank shares previously acquired, or closed the institutions they had sponsored, especially after the panic of 1837. North Dakota opened a state-owned bank in 1919 to encourage and promote the state's agriculture, commerce, and industry; it does not make loans for nonagricultural business purposes. No other state followed this example, though there was some talk of doing so in the late 1970s.

The federal government, owner of one-fifth of the First and Second Banks of the United States, sold its shares in the Second Bank in 1836. Roosevelt did not nationalize the banks after the acute crisis of March 1933 (much to the regret of advocates of government ownership). Instead, the federal government became a temporary investor, coming to the assistance of faltering banks. As soon as banks could, they retired the shares bought by the RFC. In the 1980s shares acquired by the FDIC when advancing capital funds to rescue failing institutions were sold to private investors at an opportune time.

American tradition has always placed ultimate responsibility for sound operation with bank management selected by the board of directors and the shareholders. Banking agency regulation and supervision set limits, and over the years 1880 to 1914 examinations had developed to the point where the comptroller's examiners advised management. The system of privately owned banks under government oversight has so far satisfied the electorate. Nevertheless, a vast array of credit programs developed under federal auspices.

□ Federal Government Credit

Federally-sponsored credit first became available in 1916. Federal loans, loan insurance, and guarantees continued to grow, even after the Great Depression. As a percentage of GNP, the total was 2.2 percent in 1945, 3.8 percent in 1953, and 5.8 percent in 1962. Assets of goverment lending agencies grew considerably more rapidly than commercial bank assets between 1955 and 1965 and represented 4.1 percent of the assets of all main types of financial intermediaries in 1965. Although housing and agriculture loans predominated after 1965, the focus has been increasingly directed toward stimulation of exports, community development, small business, and higher education. Funds advanced under federal auspices were usually around 14 percent of total credit flows in the 1970s, and as much as 23 percent in 1987.

□ Toward a Financial Services Industry

The industry adopted the slogan, "a full-service bank," in the 1960s to signal commercial banks' ambition to perform an ever-widening range of activities as regulatory and statutory constraints were eased. At the time, thrifts had a highly specialized, mainly consumer focus. Since then (especially after the legislation of 1980 and 1982), thrifts "have become, or at least have the potential to become, major competitors of commercial banks not only in the provision of consumer banking services but also in . . . commercial lending services," the Board of Governors noted in March 1983.[2]

Meanwhile, as the cost of information processing and telecommunications declined dramatically, borrowers and nonbank lenders could bypass all depository intermediaries and deal directly with each other.

Since the early 1970s less regulated (or unregulated) outsiders—including retailers, computer companies, insurance companies, and investment banks—have increasingly engaged in activities traditionally performed by depository institutions. Merrill Lynch exemplified the nonbank financial services company for household and business customers. Sears aimed to become "the largest consumer-oriented financial service entity" (1980).

In amending the Bank Holding Company Act in 1970, Congress defined a commercial bank as an institution whose balance sheet combines business lending on the asset side with demand deposit liabilities—two areas in relative decline over the past seventy-five years. Growth-minded bankers eager to push into new fields have felt frustration at being excluded from many activities while their nonbank rivals expand financial services. Major institutions have been pressing for new powers and the elimination of long-standing restrictions in areas such as real estate brokerage, insurance brokerage, general data processing, travel agencies, equity holdings, and especially the underwriting of all types of corporate and municipal revenue securities. Banks expanding their product lines appear to enjoy economies of scope.

Already in the early 1960s outside consultants persuaded Citibank that it wanted to be a financial service institution, an information business.[3] Chase Manhattan defined its general mission in 1978 as being "a broad-based international banking institution which provides a wide range of *selective* banking and bank-related services and products to quality customers in *selected* markets throughout the world."[4] Chase would not follow Citibank all the way in offering all services to all customers. Bank America, after staggering reverses, decided to become "much more focused," providing "premier retail and wholesale banking services in the western United States," A. W. Clausen told shareholders in May 1987.[5] Even if authorized to perform all types of financial services, all but a very few banks would be likely to remain selective.

Lawmakers and regulators face serious unresolved issues affecting the future of the financial services industry. Among the more important are: interstate banking, interest on demand deposits, federal lending to the private sector and loan guarantees, restructuring the federal agencies regulating financial institutions, the role of market discipline, deposit insurance coverage and risk-related premiums, chartering policy, societal demands, consumer protection, international banking, further enlargement of financial institutions' asset powers, and the extent to which banking and commerce remain separate. Federal and state policymakers face the challenge of allowing greater competition and innovation to proceed, without endangering the stability of our financial system and the economy.

In 1984, *American Banker,* "The Only Daily Banking Newspaper" for almost sixty years, proclaimed itself "The Daily Financial Services Newspaper." Are we then witnessing "the twilight of the banks," as Martin Mayer's *Money Bazaars* concluded in 1984? The evolving commercial banking industry may yet surprise those ready to write it off. As on several earlier occasions, renewal may enhance the effectiveness and importance of commercial banks in their venerable role as a source of credit and third-party payment services to the business sector of the American economy, and in their newer major role in accommodating consumers.

APPENDIX

Independent Treasury Subtreasury Cities, and Financial Centers under the National Bank Act and under the Federal Reserve Act, 1914–72

Central Reserve Cities

New York City[1,3,4,5]
Chicago[1,3,4,5]
St. Louis[1,3,4,6]

Reserve Cities

Albany (1929)[4]
Atlanta[1,7]
Baltimore[2,3,4]
Birmingham (1914–)[2]
Boston[1,3,4]
Brooklyn
Buffalo (1918–)[2]
Cedar Rapids (1957)
Charleston, S.C. (1914–1923)[3]
Charlotte (1927–)[2]
Chattanooga (1915–1922)
Cincinnati[2,3,4]
Cleveland[1,4]

Dubuque (1954)
El Paso (1918–)[2]
Fort Worth
Galveston (1951)
Grand Rapids (1918–1948)
Helena (1921–)[2]
Houston[2]
Indianapolis
Jacksonville, Fla. (1918–)[2]
Kansas City, Mo.[1]
Kansas City, Kan. (1962)
Leavenworth, Kan. (1864–1872)[4]
Lincoln (1954)

249

Columbus, Ohio
Dallas[1]
Denver[2]
Des Moines
Detroit[2,4]
Milwaukee[4]
Minneapolis[1]
Muskogee, Okla. (1930)
Nashville (1915–   )[2]
National City, Ill. (1948–   )
New Orleans[2,3,4]
Oakland (1918–1940)
Ogden (1917–1948)
Oklahoma City[2]
Omaha[2]
Peoria (1918–1951)
Philadelphia[1,3,4]
Pittsburgh[2,4]
Portland, Ore.[2]
Pueblo, Colo. (1965)
Richmond[1,7]
St. Joseph (1954)

Little Rock (1919–   )[2]
Los Angeles[2]
Louisville[2,4]
Memphis (1918–   )[2]
Miami (1958–   )[2]
St. Paul
Salt Lake City[2]
San Antonio[2]
San Francisco[1,3,4]
Savannah (1945)[2]
Seattle[2]
Sioux City (1957)
South Omaha (1915)
Spokane (1948)[2]
Tacoma (1923)
Toledo (1918–1965)
Topeka (1962)
Tulsa (1917–   )
Waco (1951)
Washington, D.C.[4]
Wichita (1962)

Source: Federal Reserve System, Board of Governors, *Supplement to Banking and Monetary Statistics*, sect. 10, pp. 63–64, for reserve city designations, updated in *Federal Reserve Bulletin*; U.S. Senate Committee on Banking and Currency, *Member Bank Reserve Requirements*, Hearings, 86th Cong., 1st sess. (1959), pp. 134–137.

Note: Year in parentheses is year reserve city ceased to be one. A dash following a date indicates the year the city was designated a reserve city, remaining one until 1972. Two dates in parentheses show the years the city was a reserve city.

1. Federal Reserve bank headquarters

2. Federal Reserve bank branch

3. Subtreasury city under Independent Treasury System

4. Redemption city under 1863 National-Bank Act

5. Changed to reserve city 28 July 1962

6. Changed to reserve city 1 July 1922

7. Not a reserve city under 1863 National-Bank Act

CHRONOLOGY

1781   Bank of North America chartered by Continental Congress 31 December. Opens one week later in Philadelphia.

1784   Bank of Massachusetts, first state-chartered institution, is incorporated 7 February and opens 5 July.

1784   Bank of New York opens 9 June (charter enacted 12 March 1791).

1791   Federal Congress charters First Bank of the United States 25 February (charter expires 4 March 1811).

1816   Second Bank of the United States chartered 10 April (charter expires 1 March 1836; continues as United States Bank of Pennsylvania until failure 4 February 1841).

1825   Suffolk Bank in Boston establishes collection system 16 June to redeem country bank notes at par.

1829   New York passes Safety Fund Act (insurance of creditor's claims) on 2 April.

1838   Free Banking Act is passed in New York 18 April.

1840   Independent Treasury Act is passed 4 July (repealed 13 August 1841); reinstated 6 August 1846.

1842   Louisiana banking law passed 5 February is first to require specie reserves against deposit liabilities.

1853   New York Clearing House Association opens 11 October.

1860   Clearinghouse loan certificate for use in emergencies first created 21 November in New York under George S. Coe, president of American Exchange Bank.

1863   National Currency Act passed 25 February (amended 3 June 1864; later renamed National-Bank Act).

1865   10 percent tax on state bank notes passed 3 March (effective 1 July 1866).

1875   20–22 July Saratoga Springs convention lays plans for permanent nationwide organization (American Bankers Association established 1876).

1899   Corn Exchange Bank, for decades thereafter the leader in branching in New York City, opens two acquired Manhattan banks as branches on 20 March.

1900   Gold Standard Act, authorizing capital of $25,000 for national banks in places with under 3,000 inhabitants, is signed 14 March.

1903   First Trust and Savings Bank organized 28 December by James B. Forgan's First National Bank of Chicago (First National Bank of New York follows in 1908; security affiliates become popular in the 1920s).

1904   A. P. Giannini opens Bank of Italy in San Francisco 17 October.

1908   Aldrich-Vreeland Act, authorizing emergency issues of asset-secured bank notes and establishing National Monetary Commission, the forerunner of federal reserve legislation, is enacted 30 May.

1909   California bank act, authorizing statewide branching as of 1 July, is enacted 1 March.

1913   Federal Reserve Act signed 23 December by Woodrow Wilson.

1914   Twelve district Federal Reserve banks open for business 16 November.

1916   Federal Farm Loan Act, establishing twelve federal farm land banks to extend long-term credit passes 17 July (stock initially owned by federal government).

1927	McFadden Act, authorizing home-town branches for national banks, is enacted 25 February.
1930	Chase National Bank (New York) becomes world's largest bank 1 June after merger with Equitable Trust Company and Interstate Trust Company.
1930	Bank of America, National Trust and Savings Association formed 3 November by merger of two Giannini-controlled banks: Bank of Italy and Bank of America of California.
1932	Reconstruction Finance Corporation Act, creating major federal lender to troubled banks, is signed 2 February.
1933	Emergency Banking Act, providing for reopening banks after Bank Holiday, is approved 9 March.
1933	Banking Act of 1933 (Glass-Steagall Act) enacted 16 June. It provides for deposit insurance, orders separation of corporate securities underwriting and commercial banking, and allows national banks to branch statewide in states where permitted for state-charted banks.
1934	FDIC insurance in effect 1 January.
1935	Banking Act of 1935, providing for permanent deposit insurance plan and greatly enhancing powers of Board of Governors of the Federal Reserve System over Federal Reserve banks, is enacted 23 August.
1956	Bank Holding Company Act, regulating expansion and activities of corporations owning two or more banks, is signed 9 May.
1961	First National City Bank of New York offers negotiable certificates of deposit 20 February after persuading Discount Corporation of New York (a large securities dealer) to make a secondary market for CDs.
1962	The only year when not even one FDIC-insured bank failed.
1965	Chase Manhattan Bank, largest state bank, converts to national bank status 23 September, relinquishing 1799 charter of Bank of the Manhattan Company.

1966   Bank of America announces 25 May plan to license "BankAmericard" nationwide (renamed "Visa" in 1977).

1968   First National City Corporation organized 31 October to own First National City Bank and serve as vehicle for expanding financial services business. Holding company renamed Citicorp 28 March 1974.

1970   One-bank holding company expansion brought under 1956 act 31 December.

1974   Franklin National Bank fails 8 October—largest insured bank to close since 1934.

1978   International Banking Act, providing for federal regulation of foreign banks' U.S. operations, is approved 17 September.

1980   Depository Institutions Deregulation and Monetary Control Act, providing for universal reserve requirements, interest rate deregulation, and NOW accounts, is approved 31 March.

1982   Garn–St. Germain Depository Institutions Act, authorizing money market deposit accounts and expanding lending activities for thrift institutions, is approved 15 October.

1984   Continental Illinois, seventh largest banking organization in United States, receives comprehensive financial assistance 17 May, but deposit shrinkage continues (permanent assistance package 26 July, including $1 billion capital infusion, from FDIC).

1986   Interest rate ceilings on time and savings deposits (Regulation Q) ended 31 March.

1987   Expedited Funds Availability Act, establishing specific funds' availability schedules and requiring the Fed to improve the payments system, is signed 10 August.

1989   Financial Institutions Reform, Recovery, and Enforcement Act reorganizing thrifts deposit insurance and disposal of insolvent thrifts, and strengthening regulation of depository institutions, is approved 9 August.

NOTES AND REFERENCES

Chapter 1

1. Theodore Thayer, "The Land-Bank System in the American Colonies," *Journal of Economic History* 13 (1953): 148.

2. H. F. Williamson, ed., *The Growth of the American Economy* (New York: Prentice-Hall, 1951), 232.

3. Quoted in Adolph O. Eliason, *The Rise of Commercial Banking Institutions in the United States* (Minneapolis: University of Minnesota Press, 1901), 23.

4. *Maryland Journal*, 19 November 1784.

5. Quoted in Howard Kemble Stokes, *Chartered Banking in Rhode Island* (Providence: Preston & Rounds, 1902), 2.

6. "Petition of Merchants of Alexandria, 1792," *William and Mary Quarterly*, 2d series, 3 (1923): 206.

7. Norman S. B. Gras, *Massachusetts First National Bank of Boston* (Cambridge, Mass.: Harvard University Press, 1937), 37.

8. Quoted in Frank Weston, *The Passing Years* (Providence: Industrial National Bank of Rhode Island, 1966), 19.

9. "To the Honorable The Legislature of Virginia: The Petition of sundry inhabitants of the City of Richmond, Town of Manchester and their vicinities" (Broadside, 18 December 1811), in Virginia State Library.

10. John Gurley and Edward Shaw, "Money," in *American Economic History*, ed. Seymour E. Harris (New York: McGraw-Hill, 1961), 109.

11. Quoted in Earl S. Sparks, *History and Theory of Agricultural Credit in the United States* (New York: Crowell, 1932), 228.

12. Quoted in Leonard Helderman, *National and State Banks* (Boston: Houghton Mifflin, 1931), 39.

13. Timothy Pitkin, *Statistical View of the Commerce of the*

United States of America, 2d ed. (New Haven, Conn.: Durrie & Peck, 1835), 433.

14. George Tucker, *Theory of Money and Banks Investigated* (Boston: Little, Brown, 1839), 259.

15. Lorenzo Sabine of Framingham, Mass., "Suggestions to Young Cashiers on the Duties of Their Profession," *Bankers Magazine* (January 1852) 514. Reprinted in Isaac S. Homans, *The Banker's Commonplace Book* (New York: Banker's Magazine, 1870), 163.

16. Mark Twain, *Autobiography,* ed. Charles Neider (New York: Harper & Row, 1959), 90. See also Mildred McClary Tymeson, *Worcester Bank Book: from Country Barter to County Bank* (Worcester, Mass.: Worcester County National Bank, 1966), 9.

17. "Autobiography of Col. William Few of Georgia," *Magazine of American History* 7 (1881): 356.

18. James de Peyster Ogden, *Remarks on the Currency of the United States* (New York: Wiley & Putnam, 1840), 300.

19. Bray Hammond, "Free Banks and Corporations: The New York Free Banking Act of 1838," *Journal of Political Economy* 44 (1936): 184.

20. William M. Gouge, *A Short History of Paper Money and Banking in the United States,* 2d ed. (New York: Collins, 1835), 75.

21. "Wildcat banking, a name given, especially in the western United States, to the operations of organizations or individuals who, under the loose State banking-laws which prevailed before the passage of the National Bank Act of 1863, issued large amounts of bank-notes though possessing little or no capital" (*The Century Dictionary* [1891], 435).

22. Quoted in Donald R. Adams, Jr., *Finance and Enterprise in Early America: A Study of Stephen Girard's Bank 1812–1831* (Philadelphia: University of Pennsylvania Press, 1978), 23.

23. Richard E. Sylla, *The American Capital Market, 1846–1914* (New York: Arno Press, 1975); "Forgotten Men of Money: Private Bankers in Early U.S. History," *Journal of Economic History* 36 (1976): 185.

24. Gouge, 64.

Chapter 2

1. Quoted in Bray Hammond, *Banks and Politics in America from the Revolution to the Civil War* (Princeton, N.J.: Princeton University Press, 1957), 189.

2. *New York American,* 31 December 1841. Quoted in Sheridan Logan, *George F. Baker and His Bank* ([s.l.], The Author, c.1981), 287.

3. Albert Gallatin, *Suggestions on the Banks and Currency*

of the Several United States (New York: Wiley and Putnam, 1841), in *Writings of Albert Gallatin*, vol. 3, ed. Henry Adams (Philadelphia: Lippincott, 1879), 384.

    4. Ibid., 384.

    5. Fred Merritt, *Early History of Banking in Iowa* (Iowa City: University of Iowa Press, 1900), 137.

    6. Howard H. Preston, *History of Banking in Iowa* (Iowa City: State Historical Society of Iowa, 1922), 59–60. On the eve of the Civil War, bonds of Southern states were the backing for two-thirds of the notes of Illinois banks, and for an even greater proportion of Wisconsin's free banks. Missouri state bonds were selling at 80 percent of par in July 1860; by December they were at 61 percent. All but seventeen of the 104 banks in Illinois were insolvent by the summer of 1861. See William Gerald Shade, *Banks or No Banks: The Money Issue in Western Politics 1832–1865* (Detroit: Wayne State University Press, 1972), 205–6.

    7. "Money," *Encyclopedia Britannica* (Boston: Little, Brown, 1856–57), 494.

    8. Carter H. Golembe, *State Banks and the Economic Development of the West 1830–1844* (New York: Arno Press, 1978), 63–64.

    9. Condy Raguet, *Treatise on Currency and Banking*, 2d ed. (Philadelphia: Grigg & Elliot, 1840), 101.

    10. Michel Chevalier's letter of 1 September 1835, *Society, Manners, and Politics in the United States*, ed. John W. Ward (Garden City: Doubleday, 1961), 338.

    11. Hugh McCulloch, *Men and Measures of Half a Century* (New York: Scribner's, 1888), 126.

    12. Entry dated 24 November 1841 from *Gouge's Journal of Banking* (Philadelphia: J. Van Court, 1842), 168.

    13. Federal Deposit Insurance Corporation, "Insurance of Bank Obligations Prior to Federal Deposit Insurance," *Annual Report 1952*, 59–72; Charles W. Calomiris, "Deposit Insurance: Lessons from the Record," in Federal Reserve Bank of Chicago, *Economic Perspectives* (May–June 1989): 10–30.

    14. *The Letters of Lowndes [pseud.] Addressed to Hon. John C. Calhoun* (New York: D. Appleton, 1843), 60–61.

    15. John A. Ferris, *The Financial Economy of the United States* . . . (San Francisco: A. Roman, 1867), 231. The 1859 annual report of the New York superintendent of banks made the same twentyfold estimate.

    16. *American State Papers*, vol. 8 (Washington: Gates & Seaton, 1832), 351.

    17. Samuel Hooper, *An Examination of the Theory and the Effects of Law Regulating the Amount of Specie in Banks* (Boston, 1860), 16.

18.   Gallatin, *Suggestions on the Banks and Currency*, 369.

19.   Elbert J. Benton, *A Century of Progress: Being a History of the National City Bank of Cleveland from 1845 to 1945* (Cleveland: National City Bank of Cleveland, 1945), 15.

20.   George David Rappaport, "The First Description of the Bank of North America," *William and Mary Quarterly* 33 (1976): 666.

21.   Adams, *Finance and Enterprise*, 104.

22.   Amasa Walker, *The Nature and Uses of Money and Mixed Currency* (Boston: Crosby, Nichols, 1857), 47.

23.   Edward J. Stevens, "Composition of the Money Stock Prior to the Civil War," *Journal of Money, Credit, and Banking* 3 (1971): 100. For the pre-1867 period, various estimates are found in Milton Friedman and Anna J. Schwartz, *Monetary Statistics of the United States* (New York: National Bureau of Economic Research, 1970), 214–59.

Chapter 3

1.   Albert Gallatin, *Suggestions on the Banks and Currency*, 370.

2.   Washington Trust Co., *One Hundred Years of Banking in Westerly* (Westerly, R.I., 1908).

3.   *An Address to the People of Maryland on the Necessity of Establishing a Bank for the Benefit of Agriculturalists* (Annapolis, 1817), 9–10.

4.   McCulloch, *Men and Measures*, 117.

5.   Ibid., 116.

6.   Quoted in John T. Holdsworth, *Financing an Empire: History of Banking in Pennsylvania*, vol. 1 (Chicago: S. J. Clarke, 1928), 261.

7.   Edwin Freedley, *Philadelphia and its Manufactures* (Philadelphia: E. Young, 1859), 128.

8.   Quoted in Frederick A. Cleveland and Fred W. Powell, *Railroad Promotion and Capitalization* (New York: Longmans, Green, 1909), 171.

9.   Joseph Hedges, *Commercial Banking and the Stock Market before 1863* (Baltimore: Johns Hopkins University Press, 1938), 76.

10.   Quoted in Frank R. Diffenderfer, *A History of the Farmers Trust Company of Lancaster* (Lancaster, Penn.: Farmers Trust Co., 1910), 107.

11.   Jacob N. Cardozo, *Reminiscences of Charleston* (Charleston: J. Walker, 1866), 78.

12.   H. Parker Willis, "Banking in the United States," in Herman T. Warshow, ed., *Representative Industries in the United States* (New York: Holt, 1928), 120.

13.   Bray Hammond, "Long- and Short-Term Credit in Early American Banking," *Quarterly Journal of Economics* 49 (1934): 100.

14.   Edmund Ruffin (editor), *Farmer's Register* 10 (30 April 1842): 181. Ruffin's war against banking and currency extravagances lost this outstanding agricultural journal many subscribers, forcing it to suspend publication in its tenth year. See Avery Craven, *Edmund Ruffin, Southerner: A Study in Secession* (New York: Appleton-Century-Crofts, 1932), 61ff.

15.   "Autobiography of Col. William Few," 357.

16.   Naomi R. Lamoreaux, "Banks, Kinship, and Economic Development, the New England Case," *Journal of Economic History* 46 (1986): 659.

17.   George D. Green, "Banking in Antebellum Louisiana," *Journal of Economic History* 26 (1966): 581.

Chapter 4

1.   Larry Schweikart, *Banking in the American South from the Age of Jackson to Reconstruction* (Baton Rouge: Louisiana State University Press, 1987), 157.

2.   Quoted in F. Mauldin Lesesne, *The Bank of the State of South Carolina* (Columbia: University of South Carolina Press, 1970), 65.

3.   Guy S. Callender, "The Early Transportation and Banking Enterprises of the States in Relation to the Growth of Corporations," *Quarterly Journal of Economics* 17 (1902): 111–62.

4.   Oscar and Mary F. Handlin, *Commonwealth: A Study of the Role of Government in the American Economy: Massachusetts 1774–1861*, rev. ed. (Cambridge, Mass.: Harvard University Press, 1969), 121.

5.   George W. Dowrie, *The Development of Banking in Illinois, 1817–1863* (Urbana: University of Illinois Press, 1913), 130.

6.   Lee Benson, *Concept of Jacksonian Democracy* (Princeton, N.J.: Princeton University Press, 1961), 93.

7.   *Curtis et al. v. Leavitt*, 15 N.Y. Rpts. 78 (1857).

8.   Quoted in Ben Ames Williams, Jr., *Bank of Boston 200* (Boston: Houghton Mifflin, 1984), 43.

9.   Hugh T. Rockoff, "Varieties of Banking and Regional Economic Development in the United States, 1840–1860," *Journal of Economic History* 35 (1975): 171.

10.   Quoted in Hammond, *Banks and Politics*, 213.

11.   [David Henshaw]. "A Merchant," *Remarks upon the Bank of the United States* (Boston: Irve & Greene, 1831), 35. Henshaw's Commonwealth Bank went bankrupt in 1837.

12. William M. Gouge, *An Inquiry into the Expediency of Dispensing with Bank Agency and Bank Paper in the Fiscal Concerns of the United States* (Philadelphia: William Stavely, 1837), 15.

13. Richard H. Timberlake, Jr., *The Origins of Central Banking in the United States* (Cambridge, Mass.: Harvard University Press, 1978), 85.

Chapter 5

1. Amasa Walker, *The National Currency and the Money Problem* (New York: Holt, 1876), 18.

2. James Richardson, ed., *A Compilation of the Messages and Papers of the Presidents 1789–1897*, (Published by Authority of Congress, 1898), vol. 5, 441.

3. Burke A. Parsons, *British Trade Cycles and American Bank Credit: Some Aspects of Economic Fluctuations in the United States 1815–1840* (New York: Arno Press, 1977), 340.

4. Henry C. Carey, *The Credit System of France, Great Britain, and the United States* (Philadelphia: Carey, Lea, and Blanchard, 1838), 37.

5. John R. McCulloch, *A Dictionary of Practical, Theoretical and Personal Commerce and Commercial Navigation*, new ed. (London: Longman, Orme, Brown, Green & Longmans, 1840) Supplement, 21.

6. Francis A. Walker, *Money in Its Relations to Trade and Industry* (New York: Holt, 1879), 316.

7. *Hunt's Merchants Magazine* (February 1862): 121, quoted in Davis R. Dewey, *State Banking before the Civil War* (Washington, D.C.: U.S. Government Printing Office, 1910), 16.

8. Hugh Rockoff, "Money, Prices and Banks in the Jacksonian Era," in Robert W. Fogel and Stanley Engerman, eds., *The Reinterpretation of American Economic History* (New York: Harper & Row, 1971), 454.

9. Ronald E. Seavoy, "Borrowed Laws to Speed Development: Michigan, 1835–1863," *Michigan History* 59 (1975): 68.

10. Arthur J. Rolnick and Warren E. Weber, "Free Banking, Wildcat Banking, and Shinplasters," *Quarterly Review* (Federal Reserve Bank of Minneapolis) (Fall 1982): 18–19; "Banking Instability and Regulation in the U.S. Free Banking Era," *Quarterly Review* (Federal Reserve Bank of Minneapolis) (Summer 1985): 4–9; "The Causes of Free Bank Failures," *Journal of Monetary Economics* 14 (1984): 283, 290.

11. Quoted in Harry E. Miller, *Banking Theories in the United States before 1860* (Cambridge, Mass.: Harvard University Press, 1927), 20.

12. Quoted in Joseph M. Grant, "Analysis of Evolution of the State Banking System of Texas" (Ph.D. diss., University of Texas, 1970), 4.

13. James R. Sharp, *The Jacksonians Versus the Banks* (New York: Columbia University Press, 1970), 328.

14. Chevalier, *Society, Manners, and Politics,* 36.

15. Franz Anton Ritter von Gerstner, *Berichte aus den Verein-igten Staaten* (Leipzig: Melzer, 1839), 30.

16. Thomas H. Sill, *Speech . . . on Corporations, Banks and Currency* (Philadelphia: Kay, 1838), 14.

17. Albert Gallatin, *Writings,* vol. 2, 512, 513.

18. *Documents of the 36th Ohio General Assembly 1837–38,* quoted in Golembe, *State Banks and Economic Development,* 196.

19. Carey, *The Credit System in France, Great Britain, and the United States,* 86.

20. Golembe, *State Banks and Economic Development,* 239.

21. George D. Green, *Finance and Economic Development in the Old South* (Stanford, Cal.: Stanford University Press, 1972), 62.

22. Schweikart, *Banking in the American South,* 261.

23. Fritz Redlich, *The Molding of American Banking,* vol. 1 (New York: Hafner, 1947), 66.

24. Rondo Cameron, *Banking in the Early Stages of Industrial-ization* (New York: Oxford University Press, 1967), 304.

25. Norman Walker Smith, "History of Commercial Banking in New Hampshire, 1792–1843" (Ph.D. diss., University of Wisconsin, 1967), 107.

26. "Junius," *The Currency,* Junius Tracts #2 (New York: Greely & McElrath, 1844). Colton was professor of political economy at Trinity College from 1852 to 1857.

27. Walker, *Money in Its Relations,* 270.

28. Stanley Engerman, "A Note on the Economic Conse-quences of the Second Bank of the United States," *Journal of Political Economy* 78 (1970): 727.

29. John S. Hittell, *The Resources of California* (San Fran-cisco, 1863), 338.

Chapter 6

1. Bray Hammond, *Sovereignty and an Empty Purse* (Prince-ton, N.J.: Princeton University Press, 1970), 226.

2. John C. Schwab, *The Confederate States of America* (New Haven, Conn.: Yale University Press, 1913), 160.

3. Quoted in Richard C. Todd, *Confederate Finance* (Athens: University of Georgia Press, 1954), 21.

4.   *Keith* v. *Clark*, 97 U.S. 454, 457 (1878).
5.   36 Cong., 2d Sess., House of Representatives Executive
Document 77 (1861), 195.

Chapter 7

1.   Comptroller of the Currency *1864 Annual Report*, 38
Cong., 2d Sess. (1864), House of Representatives Executive Document 3,
49.
2.   Jay Cooke, *Questions and Answers; or What the People
Ought to Know About the National Banks.* (Sandusky, Ohio Daily Register, 1867), 10.
3.   McCulloch, *Men and Measures*, 169.
4.   Hugh McCulloch letter to Stevens, 2 July 1864, in the John
Austen Stevens Papers (New York Historical Society), quoted in David M.
Gische, "The New York City Banks and the Development of the National
Banking System 1860–1870," *American Journal of Legal History* 23 (1979):
56.
5.   H. Parker Willis, "The Demand for Centralized Banking,"
Sound Currency 8 (March 1902): 23–24.
6.   John A. James, "Cost Functions of Postbellum National
Banks," *Explorations in Economic History* 15 (1978): 194.
7.   Quoted in Bascom N. Timmons, *Portrait of an American:
Charles G. Dawes* (New York: Holt, 1953), 110. Dawes's Kansas speech
quoted in Frederick A. Cleveland, *The Bank and the Treasury* (New York:
Longmans, Green, 1905), 46.
8.   Benjamin J. Klebaner, "Commercial Bank Branching in
New York City, 1898–1933," *International Review of the History of Banking* 30–31 (1985): 128.
9.   Founded in 1830, the New York Life Insurance and Trust
Company merged with the Bank of New York in 1933. The Buffalo Trust
Company opened for business in 1855 but lasted only eight years.
10.   H. Peers Brewer, *The Emergence of the Trust Company in
New York City* (New York: Garland, 1986), 2.
11.   Howard M. Jefferson, *Banking Practice and Foreign Exchange* (Chicago and New York: DeBower-Elliott Co., 1910), 7.
12.   Knickerbocker Trust Co., *Trust Companies and their Functions* (New York, 1901), 11.

Chapter 8

1.   A. Barton Hepburn, *A History of Currency in the United
States* (New York: Macmillan, 1915), 339.

2. Secretary of the Treasury, *Annual Report 1890.* Quoted in *Report of the Monetary Commission of the Indianapolis Convention* (Chicago: University of Chicago Press, 1898), 322.

3. Walker, *Money in Its Relations,* 405.

4. Amasa Walker, *The Science of Wealth* (Boston: Little, Brown, 1866), 152.

5. H. Parker Willis, *American Banking* (Chicago: La Salle Extension University, 1917), 16.

6. Clark Williams, *The Story of a Grateful Citizen: An Autobiography,* vol. 1 (New York: privately printed, 1934), 183.

7. In 1874 the Treasurer of the United States was given the redemption responsibility. Redemption centers came to be called "reserve cities."

8. See Benjamin J. Klebaner, "The Money Trust Investigation in Retrospect," *National Banking Review* 3 (1966): 393–403, and Vincent P. Carosso, *Investment Banking in America: A History* (Cambridge, Mass.: Harvard University Press, 1970), 137–55.

9. J. Laurence Laughlin, *The Federal Reserve Act: Its Origins and Problems* (New York: Macmillan, 1933), 146–47.

10. R. M. Breckenridge, "Discount Rates in the United States," *Political Science Quarterly* 13 (1898): 138.

Chapter 9

1. Lloyd Mints, *A History of Banking Theory* (Chicago: University of Chicago Press, 1945), especially 206–207. This is sometimes called the "real bills doctrine."

2. Charles A. Conant, *Wall Street and the Country* (New York: G. P. Putnam's Sons, 1904), 221.

3. Harold G. Moulton, "Commercial Banking and Capital Formation," *Journal of Political Economy* 26 (1918): 644, 729.

4. Thomas P. Kane, *The Romance and Tragedy of Banking* (New York: Bankers Publishing Co., 1922), 270.

5. Quoted in Donald L. Kemmerer, *The Life of John E. Rovensky, Banker and Industrialist* (Champaign, Ill.: Stipes Publishing Co., 1977), 27.

6. James B. Forgan, *Recollections of a Busy Life* (New York: Bankers Publishing Co., 1924), 139.

Chapter 10

1. Charles Dunbar, *Economic Essays* (New York: Macmillan, 1904), 182.

2.   For dates of the formation of state bankers' associations, see Fritz Redlich, *The Molding of American Banking: Men and Ideas*, vol. 2 (New York: Hafner, 1968), 301–302, n. 268.

3.   Wesley C. Mitchell, *Business Cycles and Their Causes*, part III (1913; reprint, Berkeley: University of California Press, 1941), 127–28.

4.   O. M. W. Sprague, *History of Crises under the National Banking System* (Washington, D.C.: U.S. Government Printing Office, 1910), 319.

5.   A. Piatt Andrew, "Substitutes for Cash in the Panic of 1907," *Quarterly Journal of Economics* 22 (1908): 515.

6.   Comptroller of the Currency (William Ridgeley) *Annual Report 1907*, 79.

7.   Calomiris, "Deposit Insurance," 18–24.

8.   Quoted in George L. Anderson, *Essays on the History of Banking* (Lawrence, Kan.: Coronado Press, 1972), 201.

Chapter 11

1.   Quoted in Robert G. Cleland and Frank B. Putnam, *Isias W. Hellman and the Farmers and Merchants Bank* (San Marino, Cal.: Huntington Library, 1965), 67.

2.   Comptroller of the Currency (Henry Cannon), *Annual Report 1884*, 49.

3.   National Monetary Commission, *Publications*, no. 19 (Washington, D.C.: U.S. Government Printing Office, 1911), 281.

4.   Raymond Moley, *The First New Deal* (New York: Harcourt, Brace & World, 1966), 129.

5.   William Rhawn, quoted in Belden L. Daniels, *Pennsylvania—Birthplace of Banking in America* (Harrisburg: Pennsylvania Bankers Association, 1976), 278.

6.   William S. Gray, *The Hanover Bank* (New York: Newcomen Society, 1951), 12.

7.   Woodrow Wilson, *The Papers* (Princeton: Princeton University Press, 1974) 18, 428.

8.   Frank W. Nye, *Knowledge Is Power: The Life Story of Percy H. Johnston, Banker* (New York: Random House, 1956), 64–65.

9.   Quoted in John A. James, "The Development of a National Money Market," *Journal of Economic History* 36 (1976): 891.

10.   Quoted in John K. Winkler, *The First Billion: The Stillmans and the National City Bank* (New York: Vanguard Press, 1934), 198–99.

11.   Sereno Pratt, "New York's Financial Institutions," *Indepen-*

dent (22 December 1904): 1435; William J. Boies, *American Monthly Review of Reviews* (October 1904): 429.

    12. Mitchell, *Business Cycles and their Causes*, 126.

Chapter 12

    1. "The Banking and Currency Act of 1913," *Journal of Political Economy* 22 (1914): 421.

    2. Quoted in Fred R. Niehaus, *Seventy Years of Progress: A History of Banking in Colorado 1876–1946* (FDIC, 1948), 45.

    3. Quoted in Harold G. Moulton, *Principles of Money and Banking* (Chicago: University of Chicago Press, 1916), 330.

    4. H. Parker Willis, "The Federal Reserve Act," *American Economic Review* 4 (1914): 19. Willis headed the division of research at the Federal Reserve Board from 1915 to 1922. He launched the *Federal Reserve Bulletin*.

    5. J. Laurence Laughlin, "The Banking and Currency Act of 1913," *Journal of Political Economy* 22 (1914): 424.

    6. Emmanuel A. Goldenweiser, *American Monetary Policy* (New York: McGraw-Hill, 1951), 296. Goldenweiser served as chief economist to the Federal Reserve Board for many years.

    7. *Congressional Record*, vol. 79 (24 July 1935), pt. 11, p. 11,777.

    8. Quoted in Timberlake, *Origins of Central Banking*, 205.

    9. Quoted in Roger T. Johnson, *Historical Beginnings . . . The Federal Reserve* (Boston: Federal Reserve Bank of Boston, 1977), 26.

    10. Benjamin H. Beckhart, *The Federal Reserve System* (New York: Columbia University Press, 1972), 111.

    11. E. D. Hulbert, "Trust Companies and the Federal Reserve System," *Trust Companies* 27 (1918): 325.

    12. Benjamin M. Anderson, *Effects of the War on Money, Credit and Banking in France and the United States* (New York: Oxford University Press, 1919), 171–72.

Chapter 13

    1. Jesse R. Sprague, *The Romance of Credit* (New York: Appleton-Century, 1943), 13.

    2. Edwin R. A. Seligman,*The Economics of Instalment Selling* (New York: Harper & Bros, 1927) vol. 1, 337.

    3. H. Parker Willis, in Charles A. Beard, ed., *A Century of Progress* (Chicago: Harper & Bros., 1933), 197.

    4. An antecedent was the Boston clearinghouse's unique ar-

rangement from 1880 to 1910. Balances would be borrowed and lent at the morning exchanges and settled the same day by orders of the clearinghouse.

     5.   George W. Dowrie, *American Monetary and Banking Policies* (New York: Longmans, Green, 1930), 25.

     6.   Willis, "The Federal Reserve Act," 21.

     7.   Mitchell, in Conference on Unemployment, Committee on Recent Economic Changes, *Recent Economic Changes in the United States* (New York: McGraw-Hill, 1929), 899.

     8.   Alexander D. Noyes, *The War Period of American Finance, 1908–1925* (New York: G. P. Putnam's, 1926), 407.

     9.   Dowrie, *American Monetary and Banking Policies*, 69.

     10.   Comptroller of the Currency, (Joseph McIntosh), *Annual Report 1927*, 13–14.

     11.   As recently as mid-1963, fifty-five private banks operated in Georgia; twenty-two of these had been organized since 1949. A 1966 law ordered the incorporation of all private banks by the start of 1968. See William Sherard Rawson, "Entry, Exit, and Structural Evolution of Markets: A Case Study of Georgia Banking, 1900 to 1964" (Ph.D. diss., Duke University, 1967), 178–80.

     12.   Dowrie, *American Monetary and Banking Policies*, 117.

     13.   Leverett S. Lyon, et al., *Government and Economic Life*, vol. 1 (Washington, D.C.: The Brookings Institute, 1940), 163.

     14.   Arndt E. Dahl, *Banker Dahl of South Dakota: An Autobiography* (Rapid City, S.D.: Fenske, 1965), 31.

Chapter 14

     1.   Although its assets (a large proportion in real estate loans) were liquidated during the poor market of the 1930s, depositors and other creditors got back 83 percent of the amount due them, all but 2 percent within eight years. A background article appeared in *Fortune* (March 1933): 62–65. See also Joseph L. Lucia, "The Failure of the Bank of United States: A Reappraisal," *Explorations in Economic History* 22 (1985): 402–16, and Milton Friedman and Anna J. Schwartz, "The Failure of the Bank of United States: A Reappraisal, A Reply," *Explorations in Economic History* 23 (1986): 199–204.

     2.   Lauchlin Currie, *The Supply and Control of Money in the United States* (Cambridge, Mass.: Harvard University Press, 1934), 124.

     3.   Goldenweiser, *American Monetary Policy*, 161.

     4.   *Ibid.*, 160.

     5.   Clark Warburton, *Depression, Inflation, and Monetary Policy* (Baltimore: John Hopkins University Press, 1966), 340.

     6.   To meet the banking needs of the fourth largest city in the United States, General Motors sponsored the National Bank of Detroit. It

took over the assets of the First Wayne and the Guardian National banks and opened on 24 March 1933. In August 1933 Ford opened the Manufacturers National Bank. Neither automaker intended to remain in banking.

7. Quoted in Milton Friedman and Anna J. Schwartz, *A Monetary History of the United States, 1867–1960* (Princeton, N.J.: Princeton University Press, 1963), 350, n. 60. Both devaluation and currency expansion did occur.

8. Quoted in Marion E. Cross, *Pioneer Harvest* (Minneapolis: Farmers and Mechanics Savings Bank of Minneapolis, 1949), 145.

9. *Texas Bankers Record* (January 1933), quoted in Joseph M. Grant and Lawrence L. Crum, *The Development of State-Chartered Banking in Texas* (Austin: Bureau of Business Research, University of Texas, 1978), 231.

10. Speech by the president of Teague National Bank, reprinted in *Congressional Record,* vol. 77 (19 May 1933), pt. 4, p. 4,172.

11. *Congressional Record,* vol. 77 (19 May 1933), pt. 4, p. 3729.

12. 73 Cong., 1st Sess., Senate Banking Committee Hearings, *Stock Exchange Practices* (1933), 3978. Printed separately as Winthrop W. Aldrich, *Suggestions for Improving the Banking System* (New York: Chase National Bank, 1933), 6–7.

13. George W. Edwards, "Control of the Security-Investment System," *Harvard Business Review* 12 (1933): 9.

14. Elmus R. Wicker, *Federal Reserve Monetary Policy, 1917–1933* (New York: Random House, 1966), 195.

15. 84 Cong., 1st Sess., House Judiciary Committee, *Current Antitrust Problems Hearings . . . 1955*, pt. 3, p. 2188.

Chapter 15

1. Charles O. Hardy and Jacob Viner, *Report on the Availability of Bank Credit in the Seventh Federal Reserve District* (Washington: Government Printing Office, 1935), 17.

2. Ben S. Bernanke, "Nonmonetary Effects of the Financial Crisis in the Propagation of the Great Depression," *American Economic Review* 73 (1986), 257–76.

3. Neil H. Jacoby and Raymond J. Saulnier, *Business Finance and Banking* (New York: National Bureau of Economic Research, 1947), 139.

4. George S. Moore, *The Banker's Life* (New York: W. W. Norton & Co., 1987), 151.

5. In its first twenty years, the Export-Import Bank lent $4.6 billion, mostly during 1945–53.

6. *The Index* 19 (Winter 1939): 67.

7.   *Federal Reserve Bulletin* 74 (1988): 454.

8.   H. Parker Willis, *The Federal Reserve System* (New York: Columbia University Press, 1923), 1523.

9.   American Bankers Association Bank Management Commission, *City Clearinghouse Associations* (New York: ABA, 1931), 5.

10.   Quoted in Gerald C. Fischer, *American Banking Structure* (New York: Columbia University Press, 1967), 208.

11.   Ross M. Robertson, *The Comptroller and Bank Supervision* (Washington, D.C.: Office of the Comptroller of the Currency, 1968), 129.

12.   American Bankers Association, *The Commercial Banking Industry* (Englewood Cliffs, N.J.: Prentice-Hall, 1962), 51.

13.   The original FDIC legislation (not an administration measure) provided for compulsory membership for all insured banks after 1 July 1936. Banks with deposits under $1 million, however, were exempted in 1935. In June 1939 the membership requirement was eliminated before it was to go into effect.

14.   Arndt E. Dahl, *Banker Dahl of South Dakota*, 214.

15.   Marriner Eccles, *Beckoning Frontiers* (New York: Knopf, 1966), 276.

16.   Quoted in Larry Schweikart, *A History of Banking in Arizona* (Tuscon: University of Arizona Press, 1982), 86.

17.   A. L. M. Wiggins, president of the Bank of Hartsville (South Carolina), testimony before Senate Committee on Banking and Currency, 76th Cong., 3d sess., Hearings on S. 2998 *Business Loans by Federal Reserve Banks* (Washington, D.C.: U.S. Government Printing Office, 1940), 38.

Chapter 16

1.   Ray B. Westerfield, *Money, Credit, and Banking* (New York: Ronald Press, 1938), 297.

2.   A. R. Ammons, "The Making of a Writer," *New York Times Book Review* (17 January 1982): 13.

3.   H. Parker Willis, "The Future in Banking," *Yale Review* 23 (Winter 1934): 247.

4.   Edward L. Bernays, *Public Opinion and the Banks* (Chicago: Financial Advisors Association, 1936), 8.

5.   Congressman Henry Steagall, speech before the National Association of Supervisors of State Banks, *Proceedings, Thirty-fifth Annual Convention* (1936), 75.

6.   Comptroller of the Currency (Preston Delano), *Annual Report 1944*, 4.

7.   James J. Saxon, "Public Regulation of Private Financial

Resources," in *Financial Policies in Transition,* ed. Thomas O. Depperschmidt (Memphis: Memphis State University Press, 1966), 26.

Chapter 17

 1. Raimund W. Goldschmidt (Raymond Goldsmith), *The Changing Structure of American Banking* (London: Routledge, 1933), 177–78.
 2. George E. Moore, *The Banker's Life* (New York: W. W. Norton, 1987), 302.
 3. Arthur F. Burns, *The Ongoing Revolution in Commercial Banking* (Washington, D.C.: American Enterprise Institute, 1988), 69–72.
 4. Alan Greenspan, statement to Senate Committee on Banking and Currency (1 December 1987), reprinted in *Federal Reserve Bulletin* 74 (1988): 92.
 5. Moore, *The Banker's Life,* 231, 249.

Chapter 18

 1. Raymond W. Goldsmith, *Financial Institutions* (New York: Random House, 1968), 135.
 2. Federal Reserve, Board of Governors, statement of 9 September 1988, reprinted in *Federal Reserve Bulletin* 74 (1988): 736.
 3. Aaron Nelson and William Murray, *Agricultural Finance,* 5th ed. (Iowa City: University of Iowa Press, 1967), 320.
 4. "Home Equity Lending," *Federal Reserve Bulletin* 75 (1989): 333–43.
 5. Arthur F. Burns, *Reflections of an Economic Policy-maker* (Washington: American Enterprise Institute, 1978), 411–12.
 6. William R. Neikirk, *Volcker: Portrait of the Money Man* (New York: Congdon & Weed, 1987), 176, 162.

Chapter 19

 1. Frank Weston, *The Passing Years 1791 to 1966,* 144.
 2. 94 Stat. 142, sec. 202 (1980).

Chapter 20

 1. Speech of 21 October 1974, "Maintaining the Soundness of Our Banking System," reprinted in Burns, *Reflections of an Economic Policy Maker,* 364–65.
 2. A. A. Milligan, ABA president, 23 August 1978 testimony

before Senate Committee on Governmental Affairs and Committee on Banking joint hearings on *Consolidated Banking Regulation Act of 1978,* 95th Cong., 2d sess. (Washington, D.C.: U.S. Government Printing Office, 1978), 66.

　　　3.　John D. Wilson, *The Chase* (Boston: Harvard Business School Press, 1986), 145.

　　　4.　100th Cong., 2nd Sess., Senate Banking Committee Hearings, *Oversight on the Condition of the Financial Services Industry* (Washington: Government Printing Office, 1988), 251.

　　　5.　Federal Reserve Bank of New York, *Annual Report 1974* (New York: The Bank, 1975), 23.

　　　6.　Burns, *The Ongoing Revolution,* 42.

Chapter 21

　　　1.　Speech before the National Bank Division, 24 October 1966, in Comptroller of the Currency (James Saxon), *Annual Report 1965– 1966,* 215.

　　　2.　*Federal Reserve Bulletin* 69 (1983): 299.

　　　3.　Moore, *The Banker's Life,* 249.

　　　4.　Wilson, *The Chase,* 338.

　　　5.　Gary Hector, *Breaking the Bank: The Decline of Bank America* (Boston: Little, Brown, 1988), 339.

SELECTED
BIBLIOGRAPHY

General

Adams, Donald R., Jr. *Finance and Enterprise in Early America: A Study of Stephen Girard's Bank 1812–1831.* Philadelphia: University of Pennsylvania Press, 1978.

Adams, Henry, ed. *Writings of Albert Gallatin,* vol. 3. Philadelphia: J. B. Lippincott, 1879.

American Bankers Association. *The Commercial Banking Industry.* A monograph prepared for the Commission on Money and Credit. Englewood Cliffs, N.J.: Prentice-Hall, 1962.

Andersen, Theodore. *A Century of Banking in Wisconsin.* Madison: State Historical Society of Wisconsin, 1954.

Anderson, George L. *Essays on the History of Banking.* Lawrence, Kan.: Coronado Press, 1972.

Aspinwall, Richard C., and Eisenbeis, Robert A. *Handbook for Banking Strategy.* New York: John Wiley & Sons, 1985.

Barnett, George E. *State Banks and Trust Companies Since the Passage of the National-Bank Act.* Washington, D.C.: U.S. Government Printing Office, 1911.

Baughn, William H., ed. *Bankers Handbook,* 3d ed. Homewood, Ill.: Dow Jones–Irwin, 1988.

Beckhart, Benjamin H. *The Federal Reserve System.* New York: Columbia University Press, 1972.

Buenger, Walter L., and Pratt, Joseph A. *But Also Good Business: Texas Commerce Banks and the Financing of Houston and Texas, 1886–1986.* College Station: Texas A&M University, 1986.

Burns, Helen M. *The American Banking Community and New Deal Banking Reforms, 1933–1935.* Westport, Conn.: Greenwood Press, 1974.

Burr, Anna R. *Portrait of a Banker: James Stillman, 1850–1918.* New York: Duffield & Co., 1927.

Cable, John R. *Bank of the State of Missouri.* New York: Columbia University Press, 1923.

Caldwell, Stephen. *Banking History of Louisiana.* Baton Rouge: Louisiana State University Press, 1935.

Chadbourne, Walter W. *A History of Banking in Maine, 1799–1930.* Orono: University of Maine Press, 1936.

Clain-Stefanelli, Elvira, and Clain-Stefanelli, Vladimir. *Two Centuries of American Banking.* Washington, D.C.: Acropolis Books, 1975.

Cleveland, Harold Van B., and Thomas F. Huertas. *Citibank, 1812–1970.* Cambridge, Mass.: Harvard University Press, 1985.

Cole, David M. *The Development of Banking in the District of Columbia.* New York: William-Frederick Press, 1959.

Colwell, Stephen. *The Ways and Means of Payment.* Philadelphia: J. B. Lippincott, 1859.

Compton, Eric N. *The New World of Commercial Banking.* Lexington, Mass.: Lexington Books, 1987.

Dale, Richard. *The Regulation of International Banking.* Englewood Cliffs, N.J.: Prentice-Hall, 1986.

Dana, Julian. *A. P. Giannini, Giant in the West.* New York: Prentice-Hall, 1947.

Dewey, Davis R. *Financial History of the United States,* 12th ed. New York: Longmans, Green & Co., 1939.

————. *State Banking before the Civil War.* Washington, D.C.: U.S. Government Printing Office, 1910.

Dillistin, William H. *Bank Note Reporters and Counterfeit Detectors, 1826–1866. With a Discourse on Wildcat Banks and Wildcat Bank Notes.* New York: American Numismatic Society, 1949.

Dowrie, George W. *The Development of Banking in Illinois, 1817–1863.* Urbana: University of Illinois Press, 1913.

Eccles, Marriner. *Beckoning Frontiers: Public and Personal Recollections.* New York: Knopf, 1951.

Federal Deposit Insurance Corporation. *Federal Deposit Insurance Corporation: The First Fifty Years.* Washington, D.C.: FDIC, 1984.

Federal Reserve System, Board of Governors. *Banking Studies.* Baltimore: Waverly Press, 1941.

Fenstermaker, J. Van. *The Development of American Commercial Banking: 1782–1837.* Kent, Ohio: Bureau of Economic and Business Research, Kent State University, 1965.

Fischer, Gerald C. *American Banking Structure: Its Evolution and Regulation.* New York: Columbia University Press, 1967.

Forgan, James B. *Recollections of a Busy Life.* New York: Bankers Publishing Co., 1924.

Friedberg, Robert. *Paper Money of the United States.* New York: Coin and Currency Institute, 1975.

Friedman, Milton, and Schwartz, Anna J. *A Monetary History of the United States, 1867–1960.* Princeton, N.J.: Princeton University Press, 1963.

Gallatin, Albert. *Considerations on the Currency and Banking System of the United States.* Philadelphia: Carey and Lea, 1831.

Goldsmith, Raymond W. *Financial Intermediaries in the American Economy Since 1900.* Princeton, N.J.: Princeton University Press, 1958.

Golembe, Carter H. *State Banks and the Economic Development of the West 1830–1844.* New York: Arno Press, 1978.

Gouge, William M., ed. *The Journal of Banking from July 1841 to July 1842.* Philadelphia: J. Van Court, 1842.

Govan, Thomas. *Banking and the Credit System in Georgia, 1810–1860.* New York: Arno Press, 1978.

Grant, Joseph M., and Crum, Lawrence L. *The Development of State-Chartered Banking in Texas.* Austin: Bureau of Business Research, University of Texas, 1978.

Gras, Norman S. B. *Massachusetts First National Bank of Boston.* Cambridge, Mass.: Harvard University Press, 1937.

Green, George D. *Finance and Economic Development in the Old South.* Stanford, Cal.: Stanford University Press, 1972.

Gruchy, Allan G. *Supervision and Control of Virginia State Banks.* New York: D. Appleton-Century, 1937.

Hales, Charles A. *The Baltimore Clearing House.* Baltimore: Johns Hopkins University Press, 1940.

Hammond, Bray. *Banks and Politics in America from the Revolution to the Civil War.* Princeton, N.J.: Princeton University Press, 1957.

———. *Sovereignty and an Empty Purse: Banks and Politics in the Civil War.* Princeton, N.J.: Princeton University Press, 1970.

Hector, Gary. *Breaking the Bank: The Decline of Bank America.* Boston: Little, Brown & Co., 1988.

Hedges, Joseph. *Commercial Banking and the Stock Market before 1863.* Baltimore: Johns Hopkins University Press, 1938.

Helderman, Leonard. *National and State Banks: A Study of Their Origins.* Boston: Houghton Mifflin, 1931.

Hepburn, A. Barton. *History of Currency in the United States,* rev. ed. New York: Macmillan, 1924.

Hoag, W. Gifford, *The Farm Credit System: A History of Financial Self-Help.* Danville, Ill.: Interstate Printers and Publishers, 1976.

Holdsworth, John Thom. *Financing an Empire: History of Banking in Pennsylvania.* Chicago: S. J. Clarke, 1928.

Hopkins, Ernest J. *Financing the Frontier: A Fifty-Year History of the Valley National Bank.* Phoenix, Ariz.: Arizona Printers, 1950.

Hubbard, Timothy W., and Davids, Lewis E. *Banking in Mid-America: A*

History of Missouri's Banks. Washington, D.C. Public Affairs Press, 1969.

Hyman, Sidney. *Challenge and Response: The First Security Corporation, First Fifty Years, 1928–1978.* Salt Lake City: Graduate School of Business, University of Utah, 1978.

———. *Marriner S. Eccles: Private Entrepreneur and Public Servant.* Stanford, Cal.: Graduate School of Business, Stanford University, 1976.

Jacoby, Neil H., and Saulnier, Raymond J. *Business Finance and Banking.* New York: National Bureau of Economic Research, 1947.

James, F. Cyril. *The Growth of Chicago Banks.* New York: Harper, 1938.

James, John A. *Money and Capital Markets in Postbellum America.* Princeton, N.J.: Princeton University Press, 1978.

James, Marquis. *Biography of a Bank: The Story of Bank of America.* New York: Harper, 1954.

Kane, Thomas P. *The Romance and Tragedy of Banking.* New York: Bankers Publishing Co., 1922.

Kennedy, Susan E. *The Banking Crisis of 1933.* Lexington: University Press of Kentucky, 1973.

Knowles, Asa S. *"Shawmut": 150 Years of Banking, 1836–1986.* Boston: Houghton Mifflin, 1986.

Knox, John J. *History of Banking in the United States.* New York: Bradford Rhodes, 1900.

Krooss, Herman E. *Documentary History of Banking in the United States.* New York: Chelsea House/McGraw-Hill, 1969.

Krooss, Herman E., and Blyn, Martin. *History of Financial Intermediaries.* New York: Random House, 1971.

Lesesne, F. Mauldin. *The Bank of the State of South Carolina: A General and Political History.* Columbia: University of South Carolina Press, 1970.

Mayer, Martin. *The Money Bazaars: Understanding the Banking Revolution Around Us.* New York: E. P. Dutton, 1984.

McCollom, James P. *The Continental Affair: The Rise and Fall of the Continental Illinois Bank.* New York: Dodd, Mead & Company, 1987.

Miller, Harry E. *Banking Theories in the United States Before 1860.* Cambridge, Mass.: Harvard University Press, 1927.

Mints, Lloyd W. *History of Banking Theory in Great Britain and the United States.* Chicago: University of Chicago Press, 1945.

Moore, George S. *The Banker's Life.* New York: W. W. Norton & Co., 1987.

Myers, Margaret. *The New York Money Market: Origins and Development,* vol. 1. New York: Columbia University Press, 1931.

Peach, William N. *Security Affiliates of National Banks.* Baltimore: Johns Hopkins University Press, 1938.

Popple, Charles S. *Development of Two Bank Groups in the Central Northwest.* Cambridge, Mass.: Harvard University Press, 1944.

Preston, Howard H. *History of Banking in Iowa.* Iowa City: State Historical Society of Iowa, 1922.

Prochnow, Herbert V., ed. *The Changing World of Banking.* New York: Harper & Row, 1973.

Raguet, Condy. *Treatise on Currency and Banking,* 2d ed. Philadelphia: Grigg & Elliot, 1840.

Redlich, Fritz. *The Molding of American Banking: Men and Ideas,* New York: Hafner, 1968.

Robertson, Ross M. *The Comptroller and Bank Supervision.* Washington, D.C.: Office of the Comptroller of the Currency, 1968.

Rockoff, Hugh. *The Free Banking Era.* New York: Arno Press, 1978.

Rodkey, Robert G. *Legal Reserves in American Banking.* Ann Arbor: University of Michigan Press, 1934.

Rose, Peter S. *The Changing Structure of American Banking.* New York: Columbia University Press, 1987.

Ross, Walter S. *People's Banker: The Story of Arthur T. Roth and the Franklin National Bank.* New Canaan, Conn.: Keats Publishing, 1988.

Schweikart, Larry. *Banking in the American South from the Age of Jackson to Reconstruction.* Baton Rouge: Louisiana State University Press, 1987.

Scroggs, William O. *A Century of Banking Progress.* New York: Doubleday, 1924.

Shade, William G. *Banks or No Banks: The Money Issue in Western Politics, 1832–1865.* Detroit: Wayne State University Press, 1972.

Sharp, James R. *The Jacksonians Versus the Banks: Politics in the States After the Panic of 1837.* New York: Columbia University Press, 1970.

Singer, Mark. *Funny Money.* New York: Knopf, 1985.

Smith, James G. *Development of Trust Companies in the United States.* New York: Holt, 1928.

Smith, Norman Walter. "History of Commercial Banking, New Hampshire 1792–1843." Ph.D. diss., University of Wisconsin, 1967.

Smith, Walter B. *Economic Aspects of the Second Bank of the United States.* Cambridge: Harvard University Press, 1953.

Sparks, Earl S. *History and Theory of Agricultural Credit in the United States.* New York: Crowell, 1932.

Spero, Joan E. *The Failure of the Franklin National Bank: Challenge to the International Banking System.* New York: Columbia University Press, 1980.

Sprague, Irvine H. *Bail Out: An Insider's Account of Bank Failures and Rescues*. New York: Basic Books, 1986.

Studenski, Paul, and Krooss, Herman E. *Financial History of the United States*. New York: McGraw-Hill, 1952.

Sumner, William G. *A History of Banking in the United States*. New York: Journal of Commerce and Commercial Bulletin, 1896.

Sylla, Richard E. *The American Capital Market 1846–1914*. New York: Arno Press, 1975.

Taus, Esther R. *Central Banking Functions of the United States Treasury, 1789–1941*. New York: Columbia University Press, 1943.

Timberlake, Richard H., Jr. *The Origins of Central Banking in the United States*. Cambridge, Mass.: Harvard University Press, 1978.

Trescott, Paul B. *Financing American Enterprise*. New York: Harper & Row, 1963.

Tucker, George. *Theory of Money and Banks Investigated*. Boston: Little, Brown & Co., 1839.

U.S. Senate Committee on Banking and Currency, *Federal Banking Laws and Reports: A Compilation of Major Federal Banking Documents*. Washington, D.C.: U.S. Government Printing Office, 1963.

Wainwright, Nicholas. *History of Philadelphia National Bank: A Century and a Half of Philadelphia Banking, 1803–1953*. Philadelphia: Historical Society of Pennsylvania, 1953.

Walton, Gerome. *A History of Nebraska Banking and Paper Money*. Lincoln, Neb.: Centennial, 1978.

Wessells, John H., Jr. *The Bank of Virginia: A History*. Charlottesville: The University Press of Virginia, 1973.

West, Robert C. *Banking Reform and the Federal Reserve, 1863–1923*. Ithaca, N.Y.: Cornell University Press, 1977.

White, Horace. *Money and Banking*, 5th ed. Boston: Ginn, 1914.

Williams, Ben Ames, Jr. *Bank of Boston 200: A History of New England's Leading Bank, 1784–1984*. Boston: Houghton Mifflin, 1984.

Willis, H. Parker, and Chapman, John M. *The Banking Situation*. New York: Columbia University Press, 1934.

Wilson, John D. *The Chase: The Chase Manhattan Bank, N.A., 1945–1985*. Boston: Harvard Business School Press, 1986.

Zweig, Phillip L. *Belly Up: The Collapse of the Penn Square Bank*. New York: Crown Publishers, 1985.

Recent Banking Developments

Abboud, A. Robert. *Money in the Bank*. Homewood, Ill.: Dow Jones–Irwin, 1988.

Ballarin, Eduard. *Commercial Banks Amid the Financial Revolution*. Cambridge, Mass.: Ballinger, 1986.

Baughn, William H., and Mandich, Donald R., eds. *International Banking Handbook*. Homewood, Ill.: Dow Jones–Irwin, 1983.

Benston, George, ed. *Financial Services*. Englewood Cliffs, N.J.: Prentice-Hall, 1983.

Benston, George, et al. *Safe and Sound Banking*. Cambridge, Mass.: MIT Press, 1986.

Bowden, Elbert V., and Holbert, Judith L. *Revolution in Banking*, 2d ed. Reston, Va.: Reston Publishing Co., 1984.

Burns, Arthur F. *The Ongoing Revolution in American Banking*. Washington, D.C.: American Enterprise Institute, 1988.

Crosse, Howard, and Hempel, George H. *Management Policies for Commercial Banks*. Englewood Cliffs, N.J.: Prentice-Hall, 1980.

England, Catherine, and Huertas, Thomas F. *The Financial Services Revolution*. Washington, D.C.: Cato Institute, 1988.

Golembe, Carter H., and Holland, David S. *Federal Regulation of Banking, 1986–1987*. Washington, D.C.: Golembe Associates, 1986.

Haraf, William S., and Kushmeider, Rose M., eds. *Restructuring Banking and Financial Services in America*. Washington, D.C.: American Enterprise Institute, 1988.

Hayes, Douglas A. *Bank Funds Management: Issues and Practices*. Ann Arbor: University of Michigan, Division of Research, Graduate School of Business Administration,1980.

Kane, Edward J. *The Gathering Crisis in Federal Deposit Insurance: Origins, Evolution, and Possible Reforms*. Cambridge, Mass.: MIT Press, 1985.

Kaufman, George G. *The U.S. Financial System: Money, Markets, and Institutions*. Englewood Cliffs, N.J.: Prentice-Hall, 1988.

Litan, Robert E. *What Should Banks Do?* Washington, D.C.: The Brookings Institute, 1987.

Prochnow, Herbert V. *Bank Credit*. New York: Harper & Row, 1981.

Sinkey, Joseph F. *Commercial Bank Financial Management in the Financial Service Industry*, 3d ed. New York: Macmillan, 1989.

———. *Problem and Failed Institutions in the Commercial Banking Industry*. Greenwich, Conn.: JAI Press, 1979.

Spong, Kenneth. *Banking Regulation: Its Purposes, Implementation, and Effects*. Kansas City, Mo.: Federal Reserve Bank of Kansas City, 1985.

Stigum, Marcia I., and Branch, Rene O. *Managing Bank Assets and Liabilities*. Homewood, Ill.: Dow Jones–Irwin, 1983.

INDEX

THE AUTHOR

BENJAMIN JOSEPH KLEBANER RECEIVED HIS
Ph.D. from Columbia University in 1952 after receiving a resident fellow-
ship in American economic history under a grant from the Social Science
Research Council. He taught at Rutgers University from 1951 to 1954 and
has been at his undergraduate alma mater, the City College of the City
University of New York, since 1954. He has taught banking courses for over
forty years, and the greater part of his research and writing has been in this
field. From 1975 to 1979 he served as associate editor of the *Journal of
Money, Credit, and Banking.* The present volume represents a thoroughgo-
ing revision, enlargement, and updating of *Commercial Banking in the
United States: A History* (1974).